Henry Parry Liddon

**Sermons to the people, preached chiefly in St. Paul's Cathedral**

Henry Parry Liddon

**Sermons to the people, preached chiefly in St. Paul's Cathedral**

ISBN/EAN: 9783337085858

Printed in Europe, USA, Canada, Australia, Japan

Cover: Foto ©Lupo / pixelio.de

More available books at **www.hansebooks.com**

# Sermons to the People

PREACHED CHIEFLY IN

ST. PAUL'S CATHEDRAL

BY

H. P. LIDDON, D.D.
CANON RESIDENTIARY OF ST. PAUL'S, AND IRELAND PROFESSOR AT OXFORD

WITH A PREFACE
BY THE AMERICAN EDITOR

NEW YORK
E. & J. B. YOUNG & CO.
COOPER UNION, FOURTH AVENUE
MDCCCLXXXI

# EDITOR'S PREFACE.

THE sermons contained in this American reprint are *verbatim* reports, taken down by persons specially trained for this purpose, and published originally in London. But considering the effect produced by the circulation of the sermons of the late F. W. Robertson, though printed from notes taken in many instances by untrained hands, it has been concluded that the present publication would be at least equally justified. No pains have been spared in the reprint: every line has been scrutinised; every quotation from the Bible has been verified; faults of punctuation and a few other obvious mistakes have been corrected: but the American editor has been truly surprised at the general accuracy of the reports. Any one acquainted with Dr. Liddon's style can substantiate this statement; and it is this fact alone that finally induced the editor to undertake the task proposed to him by the Messrs. Young & Co.

The accuracy of the reports being once assured, the publication in cheap and accessible form of sermons such as these carries with it its own justification. For not only do they contain much of the preacher's latest and best work, but they are unlike anything else which he has given to the world. They are not academic, like the "University Sermons" and "Bampton Lectures;" nor are they intended for a special occasion and a restricted audience, as were the Lent Lectures on "Some Elements of Religion." They are emphatically cathedral sermons: aimed at the multitudes that throng by thousands the great cathedral of the greatest city of the world. There is scarcely an element of modern civilisation, or a phase of modern thought, which they do not recognise. And in Dr. Liddon we have a combination of gifts peculiarly fitted for such a theatre. Starting out in life with the natural bent of an orator, he was bred according to the strict rule of England's greatest university. Then followed his experience as an instructor and guide of youth at Cuddesdon and at Oxford, with leisure for continuous study and accurate thinking. Here, too, he caught the impulse of the Tractarian movement, came in personal contact with its leaders, and under that influence began to preach at Christ Church and St. Mary's. A keen and distinguished audience gathered there, and that the preacher was fully alive to its exactions is proved by a remark made by one who knew Dr. Liddon at the time: "You never could find Liddon in those days, he was so busy over his sermons."

Such were the training and the atmosphere from which Canon Liddon passed to the more popular pulpit of St. Paul's Cathedral. He had had the discipline of an university education, and the privilege of companionship with saintly men, together with the ability and the will to avail himself of his opportunities; but back of all this was the original bent of the orator, ready to bring this acquired stock of spiritual and intellectual force to bear directly on the masses. Hence it is that in him preëminently we find accurate and patient thought in impassioned and popular form.

It is noteworthy, too, that Canon Liddon is peculiarly the spokesman of the Tractarian movement as developed in our day. By nature he is severe in his tastes and undemonstrative: sensitive, indeed, and impulsive, yet subdued by that "deep remorseful fear" of which the poet of the "Christian Year" makes so much. Hence by instinct he lays small stress on Ritual, and loves simplicity in the worship of God. But, on the other hand, he has what some of the original Tractarians had not,—a keen sense of the nature and the need of *the people*, and of the function of Ritual in teaching and impressing those whose souls are less quick and subtle than his own. And thus to-day in England men of all shades within the High Church school look to him, as to no one else, for counsel and guidance. They feel that he understands and sympathises with them all, but that he is strong where most are weak—that he can distinguish between the accidental and the essential, between that which is temporary and that which shall abide.

The sermons in this volume possess many features which make them models of what the Christian preacher of our day should say to our people. The richness and exactness of their exegesis, the clearness and compactness of their method, their sound dogmatic substance, their fine spirituality and yearning love for individual souls, are alike remarkable. But the sermons are particularly forcible in three respects :—

In the first place, like all true orators, Dr. Liddon's mind and heart are wont to move in a circle of great thoughts and generous themes. He is never petty, never ingenious. His speech is large and lofty. Only to look over the titles of these sermons reminds one of Goethe's memorable words: "The fashion of this world passeth away, and I would fain occupy myself only with the abiding."[1] And this is no less true of the preacher's handling

---

[1] "Die Gestalt dieser Welt vergeht; und ich möchte mich nur mit dem beschäftigen, was bleibende Verhältnisse sind." Quoted by M. Arnold, *London Quarterly Rev.*, Jan., 1878: Art. "A French Critic of Goethe."

of his themes, than of the themes themselves. His treatment of his subject is always broad. Compare him in this respect with Cardinal Newman. Both are men of genius and intense spirituality. But Newman seldom rises to great heights of eloquence, and seems purposely to keep a lower level. His power lies chiefly in his sweet familiarity of expression, in a nameless grace and nobility of style, in subtile intellectual insinuation, together with a marvellous command of Holy Scripture. Newman is the English Fénelon. But Liddon is like Bossuet. He lifts you to a plane where the range is wide and the air bracing; and his movement there, if often pathetic, sometimes even brusque, is always majestic. He does not merely persuade, he insists. He never insinuates, he overwhelms you with his thought.

Again Liddon, like Bossuet, always feels his audience. He never permits himself to evolve an idea merely for the idea's sake, or for his own private satisfaction; he strikes straight at the souls before him. If he sets out to meet an objection to Christian truth, it is not an objection of other times and peoples: it is a difficulty which you yourself have heard mentioned, which you yourself have experienced.[1] To the same purpose are his constant illustrations from current events. A sudden bereavement in the Royal Family, the wreck of a naval training-ship, the horrors of a recent war, the death of a great bishop, the foundation of a new college at Oxford, the latest book of a well-known writer—it is from sources such as these, matters which he knows to be uppermost in the thoughts of his hearers, that he draws the materials wherewith to enforce his text.[2] So too, if he makes a quotation, it is so telling and apposite as to justify itself immediately. He is not making a parade of his own learning; he is conscious of his audience.[3]

[1] E. g., pp. 102-105.  [2] See pp. 122-123; 150; 205; et alt.
[3] E. g., p. 14.

Lastly, Dr. Liddon impresses you with the fact that he is a real hater of sin and lover of righteousness. The Christian Creed is a reality to him. It is told of Carlyle, that when conversing with the new rector of his parish, he astonished him by remarking in his bold, blunt way: "It is my firm belief, that if these turbulent people could once be brought to know some one who really believed for himself the eternal veracities, and didn't merely tell them of some one else who in old time was *thought* to have believed them, they would all be reduced to speedy silence. It is much, no doubt, to have a decent ceremonial of worship, and an educated, polite sort of person to administer it. But the main want of the world, as I gather, just now, and of this parish especially, which is that part of the world with which I am altogether best acquainted, is to discover some one who really knows God otherwise than by hearsay, and can tell us what divine work is actually to be done here and now in London streets, and not of a totally different work which behooved to be done two thousand years ago in old Judea." [1] To listen to Liddon is to receive the impression that Carlyle longed for. His is the voice of a man of vital convictions. He bears a direct, an authoritative message. Jesus Christ is a veritable Person, Whom he loves and serves; the devil a veritable person, whom he hates. And if, through all his dread and detestation of sin, the preacher's tenderness to sinful souls still makes itself felt, nevertheless an infidel could never say of Liddon what Voltaire is reported to have remarked of Massillon: "You need not try to preach to me, for you are not really my enemy." [2]

Of the sermons included in this volume, the first twelve follow at intervals the course of the Christian Year and

---

[1] E. D. Mead, "Philosophy of Carlyle," p. 48.
[2] "Tu as beau me prêcher, tu n'es pas de mes ennemis." Quoted by Sainte-Beuve, "Causeries du Lundi," t. 9, p. 33: Edit. 1869.

treat of the leading verities of the Faith; the remainder are on various vital topics of the day. All but sermons X., XIII., XIX., XX., were delivered at the regular Sunday afternoon service in St. Paul's Cathedral, in the preacher's turn as Canon in Residence. Sermons X., XIX., were preached in the same place at the special Sunday evening service; Sermon XIII., on Sunday evening at Westminster Abbey. Sermon XX. was pronounced at St. James's, Piccadilly, in behalf of the schools of that parish.

NEW YORK, September 24, 1881.
    Ember Day.

# CONTENTS.

### SERMON I.
### Missionary Enthusiasm.

(Preached Sunday Afternoon, December 15, 1872.)

PAGE

"*I am come to send fire on the earth.*"—S. LUKE XII. 49 . 1

### SERMON II.
### Individual Responsibility.

(Preached Sunday Afternoon, December 9, 1877.)

"*So then every one of us shall give account of himself to God.*"
—ROMANS XIV. 12 . . . . . . 19

### SERMON III.
### Christ the Ideal Man.

(Preached Sunday Afternoon, December 6, 1874.)

"*The dayspring from on high hath visited us, to give light to them that sit in darkness and in the shadow of death, to guide our feet into the way of peace.*"—S. LUKE I. 78, 79 . 36

## SERMON IV.

### Christ the Authoritative Teacher.

(Preached Sunday Afternoon, December 13, 1874.)

"*The dayspring from on high hath visited us, to give light to them that sit in darkness and in the shadow of death, to guide our feet into the way of peace.*"—S. LUKE I. 78, 79 . 52

## SERMON V.

### Christ the Deliverer and Restorer.

(Preached Sunday Afternoon, December 20, 1874.)

"*The dayspring from on high hath visited us, to give light to them that sit in darkness and in the shadow of death, to guide our feet into the way of peace.*"—S. LUKE I. 78, 79 . 70

## SERMON VI.

### Christ the Giver of Grace.

(Preached Sunday Afternoon, December 27, 1874.)

"*The dayspring from on high hath visited us, to give light to them that sit in darkness and in the shadow of death, to guide our feet into the way of peace.*"—S. LUKE I. 78, 79 . 88

## SERMON VII.

### The Virgin's Son.

(Preached Sunday Afternoon, December 29, 1878.)

"*Now all this was done, that it might be fulfilled which was spoken of the Lord by the prophet, saying, Behold, a Virgin shall be with child, and shall bring forth a Son, and they shall call His name Emmanuel, which being interpreted is, God with us.*"—S. MATTHEW I. 22, 23 . . . 108

## SERMON VIII.

### The Blood of Christ.

(Preached Sunday Afternoon, April 7, 1878.)

"*For if the blood of bulls and of goats, and the ashes of an heifer sprinkling the unclean, sanctifieth to the purifying of the flesh: how much more shall the Blood of Christ, Who through the eternal Spirit offered Himself without spot to God, purge your conscience from dead works to serve the living God.*"—HEBREWS IX. 13, 14 . . . 125

## SERMON IX.

### The Solitude of Christ in Redemption.

(Preached Sunday Afternoon, April 14, 1878.)

"*O go not from me; for trouble is at hand, and there is none to help me.*"—PSALM XXII. 11: P. B. VERSION . . 139

## SERMON X.

### The Power of Christ's Resurrection.

(Preached Sunday Evening, March 28, 1869.)

"*That I may know Him, and the power of His resurrection.*
—PHILIPPIANS III. 10 . . . . . 154

## SERMON XI.

### The Inevitableness of Christ's Resurrection.

(Preached Sunday Afternoon, April 16, 1876.)

"*Whom God hath raised up, having loosed the pains of death: because it was not possible that He should be holden of it.*"
—ACTS II. 24 . . . . . . 178

## SERMON XII.

### The Valley of Dry Bones.

(Preached Sunday Afternoon, April 28, 1878.)

PAGE

"*And he said unto me, Son of man, can these bones live?
And I answered, O Lord God, Thou knowest.*"—EZEKIEL
XXXVII. 3 . . . . . . . 197


## SERMON XIII.

### The Adequacy of Present Opportunities.

(Preached Sunday Evening, June 18, 1876.)

"*And He said unto him, If they hear not Moses and the
prophets, neither will they be persuaded, though one rose
from the dead.*"—S. LUKE XVI. 31 . . . . 212


## SERMON XIV.

### Naaman's Expectations: A Representative Case.

(Preached Sunday Afternoon, August 30, 1874.)

"*But Naaman was wroth, and went away, and said, Behold,
I thought He will surely come out to me, and stand, and
call on the name of the Lord his God, and strike his hand
over the place, and recover the leper. Are not Abana and
Pharpar, rivers of Damascus, better than all the waters
of Israel? may I not wash in them, and be clean? So he
turned and went away in a rage.*"—2 KINGS V. 11, 12 . 230

## SERMON XV.

### The Call of Elisha.

(Preached Sunday Afternoon, August 11, 1872.)

"*So he departed thence, and found Elisha the son of Shaphat, who was ploughing with twelve yoke of oxen before him, and he with the twelfth: and Elijah passed by him, and cast his mantle upon him. And he left the oxen, and ran after Elijah, and said, Let me, I pray thee, kiss my father and my mother, and then I will follow thee. And he said unto him, Go back again: for what have I done to thee? And he returned back from him, and took a yoke of oxen, and slew them, and boiled their flesh with the instruments of the oxen, and gave unto the people, and they did eat. Then he arose, and went after Elijah, and ministered unto him.*"—1 KINGS XIX. 19-21 . . . . 246

## SERMON XVI.

### The Invisible World a Reality to Faith.

(Preached Sunday Afternoon, August 25, 1872.)

"*And Elisha prayed, and said, Lord, I pray thee, open his eyes that he may see. And the Lord opened the eyes of the young man; and he saw: and, behold, the mountain was full of horses and chariots of fire round about Elisha.*"— 2 KINGS VI. 17 . . . . . . 262

## SERMON XVII.

### Justification by Faith.

(Preached Sunday Afternoon, August 12, 1877.)

"*Wherefore the law was our schoolmaster to bring us unto Christ, that we might be justified by faith.*"—GALATIANS III. 24 . . . . . . . 278

## SERMON XVIII.

### The Relative Functions of the Spirit and the Understanding in Prayer.

(Preached Sunday Afternoon, August 19, 1877.)

PAGE

"*I will pray with the spirit, and I will pray with the understanding also.*"—1 COR. XIV. 15 . . . . 292

## SERMON XIX.

### Living Water.

(Preached Sunday Evening, March 19, 1871.)

"*Jesus answered and said unto her, Whosoever drinketh of this water shall thirst again: but whosoever drinketh of the water that I shall give him shall never thirst; but the water that I shall give him shall be in him a well of water springing up into everlasting life. The woman saith unto Him, Sir, give me this water, that I thirst not, neither come hither to draw.*"—JOHN IV. 13-15 . . . 308

## SERMON XX.

### Christian Education.

(Preached Sunday Afternoon, June 13, 1869.)

"*Other foundation can no man lay than that is laid, which is Jesus Christ.*"—1 COR. III. 11 . . . . 324

# SERMON I.

## MISSIONARY ENTHUSIASM.

LUKE xii. 49.

*"I am come to send fire on the earth."*

FRIDAY next, my brethren, has been appointed by the highest authorities in the Church of England to be observed as a day of special prayer to God. For some time past much anxiety has been felt on the score of our missions to the heathen, and particularly about the great duty of procuring missionaries to undertake the work. A great many speeches have been made on the subject; a great many articles have been written in newspapers and in reviews; colleges have been established, some of them quite recently, with a view to training and educating missionaries; and the great societies which undertake to organise and to stimulate work of this description have not been less active than in former years. Still it has been felt that these human agencies did not do, and somehow were not likely to do, what was wanted. The subject of missions to the heathen, notwithstanding its undeniable, its consummate importance, was felt to command at best but a languid interest even with persons who, generally speaking, were sufficiently alive to the claims of religious truth; and the efforts to make matters better only stood out in an uncomfortable kind of contrast with the evidences of their becoming worse. So at last we are going, as a Church, to ask God to help us. Of course all serious Christians make the success of Christian missions a matter of prayer from time to time, if not very frequently, yet regularly as a matter of course. Indeed, every time that we say, in the Lord's prayer, "Thy kingdom come," we do pray for all such missions among other things, if we know what we mean. Now, however, as a Church—as a united Church, let it be hoped—we are going next Friday with one heart, with one voice, to utter a great cry for help,—to ask God to do for us, in us, by us, that which of ourselves we cannot do. Much of course depends upon the earnestness, upon the unanimity, of the effort. Here, in St. Paul's, we hope to draw nigh to God in the early Communion at eight o'clock in the morning, and again at the half-past ten o'clock service; and, in addition to the usual morning and evening services, the special form which has been drawn up by authority for use in this diocese on this occasion will be used at two o'clock in the afternoon. The Bishop of London, as our chief pastor, will come to attend the morning service at half-past ten in this his cathedral church, to take the lead in the solemn intercessions offered by this diocese,—to address us from this pulpit, with the authority which belongs to his office and to his person, on the nature and duties of the occasion. Meanwhile it is in obedience to his printed instructions—it is in accordance, I venture to say, with the common sense of the case—that I proceed to draw attention to the subject this afternoon. For Friday next is not meant to be a day of many sermons: it should be a day of much prayer. If the effort is to be worthy of the idea which has been formed of it, God will be addressed on that day much more than man,—man only so far as may be necessary to stimulate him to turn his face upward in prayer to God.

But if this is to be the case, people must, so far as they can, have made arrangements beforehand,—arrangements, when possible, about laying out their time with a view to their taking part in this great spiritual work,—and, still more, arrangements of their thoughts, of their wishes, of their hopes, and of their fears, on the great subject in question, so that they may know what they mean to ask for more particularly, and how to ask it. What, then, is to be the main subject of our prayer to God on Friday next?

We are told that what missions want, beyond everything else, is men,—that missions are languishing, or even failing, for lack of missionaries. We have, then, to pray for the spread and strengthening of the missionary spirit in the Church—the spirit which produces missionaries, just as the military spirit in a country produces great soldiers, just as the æsthetic spirit of an age produces great artists.

Properly speaking, the Church of Christ is the one great missionary society. Over her gates we read, from age to age, the inscription which was traced by her great Founder in almost His parting words—" Go, make disciples of all the nations, baptising them in the name of the Father, and of the Son, and of the Holy Ghost."[1] If the Church of Christ could cease to be missionary, she would be utterly untrue to the plainest commands of her Lord. And the missionary spirit is not by any means only the spirit of actual missionaries; it is the spirit of all true Christians who have the faith at heart, who have their Lord's honor at heart. Every serious Christian is a missionary in intention and within the limits that his providential work makes possible, though he may never have looked upon the face of a heathen in his life, just as every serious Christian bears within his heart the spirit of the martyrs, though he

[1] Matt. xxviii. 19.

may never be called upon to witness his faith with his blood; for the wish to spread the knowledge of the love of Jesus Christ is, if I may so speak, a strong overmastering impulse in every man, in every woman, who really knows and loves Him. Although to do this among the heathen may and does require special aptitudes, and what is called a particular vocation from God the Holy Spirit, still I apprehend that, at some time or other in their lives, all true Christians hear within their hearts those thrilling words which we sing in the Benedictus, "Thou child shalt be called the prophet of the Highest: for thou shalt go before the Face of the Lord to prepare His ways; to give knowledge of salvation unto His people by the remission of their sins, through the tender mercy of our God; whereby the dayspring from on high hath visited us, to give light to them that sit in darkness and in the shadow of death, to guide our feet into the way of peace."[1] The absence of any kind of anxiety for the spread of the truth implies spiritual paralysis, if it does not imply actual spiritual death. The man who knows the happiness of peace with God through our Lord Jesus Christ cannot but desire that other men should share it; and this desire in its higher, its stronger, its more heroic forms, is one of the greatest gifts of God to His Church. It is that divine enthusiasm of which our Lord Jesus Christ spoke in the words, "I am come to send fire on the earth."

It is impossible to mistake the symbolical importance attributed to the element of fire in the Bible. God appeared to Moses in a flame of fire in a bush, and the Lawgiver refers to this afterward in words which are quoted by an apostle—"Our God is a consuming fire."[2] Fire is a symbol of God's essential Nature,—a symbol of the light and warmth of the uncreated Love. "God," says St.

[1] Lu. i. 76-79.   [2] Heb. xii. 29.

John, "is Love."¹ Love, that is to say, is not a quality which we can conceive as being apart from Him: it is His very Self. Especially does fire denote the third Person in the most holy Trinity, the eternal bond of love between the Father and the Son. And thus St. John the Baptist says that he himself baptises with water, but that One cometh after him Who shall baptise "with the Holy Ghost and with fire."² And thus on the Day of Pentecost, when the Holy Spirit descended on the apostles in the upper room, He chose out tongues of fire as a sensible token of His presence. And we may say with an ancient Christian father, that our Lord on Whom the Spirit rested in His fulness—our Lord Jesus Christ—is all fire because He is all love. His entire life, His words, His sufferings, His death, express a burning love for God and for man. This love, in the days of His flesh, radiated from Him on all who came in contact with Him; and so one of the disciples at Emmaus exclaimed, "Did not our hearts burn within us, while He talked with us by the way, and while He opened to us the Scriptures?"³ Jeremiah had felt a presentiment of this. "The word of prophecy",—he says with reference to what he said after his persecution by Pashur, the governour of the Temple—"The word of prophecy" (or, "of the Lord") "was in mine heart as a burning fire shut up in my bones, and I was weary with forbearing, and I could not stay."⁴ In substantially the same sense, although higher and deeper far, and while dropping the metaphor, St. Paul exclaims, "The love of Christ constraineth us; because we thus judge, that if One died for all, then were all dead: and that He died for all, that they which live should not henceforth live unto themselves, but unto Him that died for them, and rose again."⁵

¹ 1 John iv. 8.  ² Lu. iii. 16.  ³ Lu. xxiv. 32.
⁴ Jer. xx. 9.  ⁵ 2 Cor. v. 14.

This fire, then, which our Lord came to send was a divine enthusiasm inspired by His Spirit for the Glory of God, for the highest good of man,—an enthusiasm enwrapping like flame the faculties of soul and body, transfiguring weak and commonplace natures by the purifying and invigorating energy of a supernatural force. "I can do all things," said St. Paul, "through Christ Which strengtheneth me."[1] This enthusiasm has undoubtedly many other outlets, many other effects. The missionary spirit is one of its chief, its noblest manifestations—the spirit which burns to carry the name and kingdom of Christ wherever there are souls to be saved and blest.

What then let us ask, are the elements which go to make up the missionary spirit? Or, rather, what are the convictions by which the sacred flame is kept alive within the soul?

There are, I apprehend, three main elements, three ruling and inspiring convictions at the root of missionary enthusiasm.

Of these, the first is a deep sense of the certainty and importance of the truths of the gospel. The apostles were the first missionaries, and we see in their writings how deeply they felt both the importance and the certainty of their message. St. Paul speaks of "preaching among the Gentiles the unsearchable riches of Christ."[2] St. Paul prays that the Ephesians may have the eyes of their understanding so enlightened as to "know what is the hope of their calling, and what the riches of the glory of their inheritance in the saints."[3] St. Paul's language has sometimes been spoken of as hyperbolical and inflated, but only so because the great living facts which were so present to the apostle's soul are hidden from the soul of the speaker. If, my brethren, it be indeed true that the everlasting Son

---

[1] Phil. iv. 13.  [2] Eph. iii. 8.  [3] Eph. i. 18.

of God left the glory which He had with the Father before
the world was, and took our poor nature upon Him, and had
a human Mother, and lived on this earth for thirty-three
years, and then died in pain and shame to rise from death,
to rise from the grave in which He was laid, to return,
still robed in the nature in which He had died and risen,
to the glories of His heavenly home,—if this be a fact, it
is trivial to speak of it as "an important fact." It distances in point of importance everything else that has occurred in human history. What in the world are all the
triumphs, all the failures, all the humiliations, all the re-
coveries of which human history speaks, in comparison
with this? What heart have we to dwell on them when
we have really stood face to face in spirit with the Incarnation and the Passion of the Son of God? This is
what men like Xavier or Martin have felt; and this sense
of the overwhelming importance of the facts of Redemption has not, in the cases of these eminent missionaries,
been weakened by any suspicion whatever, created by a
sceptical atmosphere of thought around them, about the
truth of the facts. The apostles had no doubts about
the facts. "I know Whom I have believed,"[1] cries St.
Paul. "We have not followed cunningly devised fables,"[2]
protests St. Peter. "We were eyewitnesses of His majesty." "That which we have seen and heard," says St.
John, "declare we unto you; for the Life was manifested,
and we have seen It, and declare unto you that eternal
Life Which was with the Father, and was manifested unto
us."[3] In the mind of the apostles the truths of the Christian revelation centred, every one of them, in the living
Person of Christ, God and Man; and an utter devotion to
His Person, based on a profound conviction of the reality
in detail and as a whole of these truths, was at the root of

[1] 2 Tim. i. 12.     [2] 2 Pet. i. 16.     [3] 1 John, i. 1–3.

that spirit of enterprising charity which went forth to convert the world. In the heart of those first missionaries, as so constantly since, the crucified Son of God whispered daily, hourly, that He might keep alive within them the sacred flame,

> "Behold what I have borne for thee!
> What hast thou done for me?"

Now, this first element of the missionary spirit would seem to a certain extent to have suffered by coming in contact with certain sides of modern thought. It would be an injustice to say that the cultivated scepticism of our time treats the statements of the Christian creed as unimportant. Its very cultivation enables it to realise the overwhelming importance of these facts of the Incarnation and death of the eternal Son, supposing them to be true. But then it whispers, more or less distinctly, to too many a soul, "Are they true? Are they more than barely probable? May they not be explained in language which makes less demand upon our faith? May not the old language in which they were stated be emptied of its old meaning—of some of it, if not of all?" We have only to listen to the conversation which goes on around us, we have only to take up newspaper after newspaper which may be named—to observe, in short, the general current and direction of popular opinion,—to see how largely this counter-spirit is at work, how possible it is that we ourselves, deeply although unconsciously, are influenced by it. Now whatever else it may or may not do, it is certain that such a spirit does this: it is fatal not merely to missionary but to all great moral efforts; it eats out the core of those strong overmastering convictions which are the very leverage and strength of such efforts; it breaks up into a few feeble apprehensions—"views" as men call them—those mighty burning persuasions about truth and falsehood, about happiness and woe, which banish all fear and hesitation, which carry the soul imperiously forward into action or into suffering. This is, of course, only one of the many evils which the diseased spirit of doubt inflicts upon the generations which are its victims; but it is obvious that this single effect will account for its action in destroying missionary enthusiasm. Who would care to be a missionary—would care to be a preacher of any sort—on behalf of a very disputable probability which might be converted, on the questioning of some too inquisitive heathen, into an improbability in his master's mind? Who would go forth with his life in his hand to advocate a religion whose scriptures he believed to be penetrated with legend, whose creeds he was willing to mutilate or to disuse, whose evidences seemed to be more and more impaired by the assaults of intellectual enemies, whose great object was becoming to his apprehension less and less daily of a living reality—more and more only a transient creation of obsolete phases of thought? No, if a man would be a missionary, he must be a downright believer; and if we are to succeed next Friday in our supplications with God, we must pray, first of all, for a revival of that faith in God and in His message to man which can remove mountains—which can do all things in the conviction that Christ strengthens it. "Lord, increase our faith,"[1]—that is the first prayer that should be offered, if we are to carry our point.

And the second conviction which goes up to make missionary enthusiasm is a sense of the need which man has of revealed truth. The apostles were possessed by this element also of that sacred flame which Christ came to send upon the earth. The apostles did not invest contem-

[1] Lu. xvii. 5.

porary heathenism with that halo of false beauty which has been more or less fashionable in Christendom ever since the Renaissance. They saw in heathendom the kingdom of darkness: its material civilisation, its splendid literature, its vast organisations, civil and military, its social and political traditions, were nothing to them, or less than nothing. "We know," said St. John—"we know that we are of God, and the whole world lieth in wickedness."[1] "All that is in the world, the lust of the flesh, and the lust of the eyes, and the pride of life, is not of the Father, but is of the world. And the world passeth away, and the lust thereof."[2] The highest civilisation, so termed, was in St. Paul's eyes just as much in need of the gospel as the rudest types of savage life. He had as much to do for the cultivated heathens who listened to him on the Areopagus of Athens as for the wild heathens of the Mediterranean islands, who after their rude fashion showed him no little kindness when he was saved from his shipwreck; for he saw everywhere error and sin,—error which obscured the real Nature of God and the true destiny and the highest interest of man,—and sin which made man God's enemy, the antagonist of God's uncreated Nature as the perfect Being. The conviction that those who were not in Christ were lost—lost unless they could be brought to Him to be illuminated, to be gifted with a new nature, to be washed, to be sanctified, to be justified before the presence of the All-holy—this was the second element of conviction which urged the apostles onward through the world to convert it, —which urged them on even to martyrdom.

Now this second element of the missionary spirit is attacked on two sides by the modern spirit, that, first of all, in its more sceptical forms, exaggerates the elements of truth which are to be discovered in heathen religions. It

---

[1] 1 John v. 19.      [2] Ibid. ii. 16.

does not merely say, with St. Paul, that God speaks to man everywhere in some sense, through nature and conscience; it sees in each form of heathen belief another revelation pretty nearly as true, or rather not much more erroneous than the faith of the Christian Church. It would be easy to point to passages in recent writers which would illustrate this. The fact must be sufficiently notorious to those who pay attention to what is thought and said at the present day. Christianity is itself treated as one out of many world-religions, each of which, it is held, contains a great deal of truth,—each of which is said to contain a great deal of error. And when this is believed, it is clear that a mission from Christianity to Mahometans or Hindoos must look more or less like an impertinence; for one conglomerate of truth and error cannot, without immodesty, address another conglomerate of truth and error as if it had itself a monopoly of the revealed mind of God. And the heathen have after all, it is urged, a great deal of truth with them; and we Christians, who have our full share of error, have no right to attempt to interfere with those rival superstitions, so historical, so ancient, so respectable, so interesting.

The Christian sense of the need of revelation for those who have it not is also sapped by the modern depreciation of the real nature of sin. Too often sin is regarded only as a form of creaturely weakness—as a thing to be pitied, but not as a thing to be punished by a benevolent God; and so, just as a kind-hearted gentleman among ourselves forgives a rudeness whether it be apologised for or not, God will upon this hypothesis forgive adultery and lying and blasphemy and murder as a matter of good nature, and in virtue of that one attribute which it is convenient to recognise in Him—an easy-going benevolence. The only grave sins which He recognises are those which are hostile to the well-being of human society; but then these sins are punished by society in its self-defence, and that is enough. The idea of treating sins of intention and thought, sins of the intellect and the affections, sins of desire which never merge into visible action, as ruinous, is deemed a foolish morbid imagination which advancing cultivation must banish from the world. Heathen sin is veiled now-a-days beneath apologetic phrases which almost imply sympathy with it. It is not so serious after all. The hideous vices which disfigured the refined intellectual society of ancient Athens are spoken of gently as the product of a "different moral sentiment" from that which prevails in modern Europe. With this estimate of sin where is the need of a Redeemer Who should blot out its guilt—Who should destroy its power? What is the justification of the immense enthusiasm of the *bonâ fide* Christian for proclaiming the sinlessness of Christ as the Model of humanity, the power of the Blood of Christ as the Redeemer of humanity, the grace of the Spirit and of the Sacraments of Christ as the Restorer of humanity? Surely, if sin is so venial—if sin is almost interesting—man may very well do without the righteousness of Christ. Ah, if we are to succeed next Friday we must pray for a new and quickened and altogether higher sense of the need which man, lost in the entanglements of sin and error, has of a Redeemer to teach and to save him. No natural virtue, no quick aspiring intelligence, no splendid and glittering civilisation, no refined society, can bridge over the chasm which, apart from Christ, yawns between God and humanity. Our eyes, alas, are too often holden that we should not know the realities of the world of spirit half as well as we know the realities of the world of society and the world of matter. Good Lord, in Thy mercy open our eyes that we may see!

And the third conviction that goes to make up the missionary spirit is a belief in the capacity of every man for the highest good, for salvation through Christ. As God will have all men to be saved and to come to the knowledge of the truth, so every soul has that in it which, under the action of the divine Spirit, can receive the truth which saves. Intellectual dulness, want of imagination, want of what people have taken to calling lately "sweetness and light," want of moral fervor and quickness,—these are not barriers. Doubtless some minds, some natures—I would rather say some souls—present more points of contact with the gospel than do others. Some, I admit, present very few indeed. But no child of Adam is so constituted as to be incapable of receiving the truth which is necessary to his highest good; and the true missionary knows that if he can only get deep enough beneath the surface, beneath the crust of habit formed by sensuality, by indifference, by prejudice, he will at length find a home for truth,—he will at length find that which will respond to it in the secret spring of the soul. Nelson used to tell young midshipmen who were entering the navy that they ought to look forward, every one of them, as a matter of course, to commanding the channel fleet, or at least to commanding a line-of-battle ship. And this faith in general capacity for success is still more necessary in the Christian missionary. He looks upon every child of man as bearing within him capacities for the highest greatness—capacities which have only to be aroused and developed by the assured Grace of God.

Now, this faith in humanity—in what it may be made by Grace—is assailed in our day on the ground that character and circumstances are, after all, too imperious to be set aside,—that they, as a matter of fact, make us what we are,—that it is folly to think of overruling them by any doctrine or secret influence that can be brought to bear. And this is not a new idea. The learned physician Galen, who wrote in the third century of the Christian era, and who as a heathen was strongly prejudiced against the Church of Christ, remarks with reference to the education of children: "The cultivator can never succeed in making the thorn bear grapes, for the nature of the thorn is, from the first, incapable of such improvement." And then he goes on to say that if the vines which are capable of bearing such fruit be neglected, they will either produce bad fruit or none at all. Here Galen marks out what, in his opinion, could really be done with human nature—certainly, we must remark, within very narrow limits indeed —and what, in his opinion, it is folly to attempt. Tertullian, an eminent Christian writer of the period—in his treatise on the human soul, admits that the bad tree will bring forth no fruit if it be not grafted, and that the good tree will produce bad fruit unless it be cultivated. So much for nature. But then Tertullian proceeds, "And the stones will become the children of Abraham if they be formed to the faith of Abraham, and the generation of vipers will bring forth fruits meet for repentance if they expel the poison of malignity. For such," he says, "is the power of divine Grace, which, indeed, is more powerful than nature." The heathen Celsus probably expressed a general opinion among his friends when he said that it was literally impossible to improve a man who had grown old in vice before his conversion. Cyprian, who was afterward Bishop of Carthage and a martyr for Christ, had taken, he tells us, exactly the same view of the impossibility of changing natural habit. How he learnt the power of God's Grace he tells us in a most remarkable passage of one of his extant letters. "Receive," he says to his correspondent, "that which must be experienced before it can be understood. When I lay in the darkness, in the depths of the night, when I was tossed hither and thither by the billows of the world, and wandered about with an uncertain and fluctuating course, I deemed it a matter of extreme difficulty that any one could be born again—could lay aside what he was before, while his corporal nature remained what it was. How, said I, can there be so great a transformation as that a man should all at once lay aside what is innate from his very organisation, or through habit has become a second nature. How should a man learn frugality who has been accustomed to luxuries? How should he who has been clad in gold and purple condescend to simple attire? the man who has been surrounded with public honors take to privacy? or another exchange admiring troops of dependents for voluntary solitude? The allurements of sense, I said to myself, are surely very tenacious. Intemperance, pride, anger, ambition, lust—these must when once indulged, they must perforce, retain their hold. So I said to myself, for I was, in truth, entangled yet in the errors of my former life and did not believe that I could be freed from them; and so I complied with the vices that still cleaved to me, and in despair of amendment submitted to my evil inclinations as if they were a part of my nature. But when the stain of my former life had been washed out by the laver of regeneration, a pure and serene light was poured into my reconciled heart. When the second birth received from Heaven through the Spirit had changed me into a new man, things formerly doubtful were confirmed in a wonderful manner. What had been closed hitherto became open before my eyes; what had been dark was now illuminated; power was given to do what had seemed difficult; the impossible had become possible. I can now see that my former life, being of fleshly origin and spent in sin, was a life of earth. The life which the

Holy One has kindled in me is a life from God." This testimony has been re-echoed since by thousands and thousands of Christians; and, therefore, the barriers of habit enshrined within venerable traditions which the Christian missionary encounters to-day in China or in India, however serious they may be as practical obstacles, are not really insurmountable. By and by the gospel leaven will surely begin to ferment, and then these vast, ancient, and complicated societies will heave and break till they open a way to the influences of the Gospel, if not so swiftly, yet as surely, as do the uncultivated New Zealanders and Polynesians. To doubt this is to lose faith, if not in the gospel, at least in humanity—in the capacity of every being for coming to the highest truth, for coming to God in Christ. Such doubt is, alas, sufficiently widespread. We must pray against it, if we would aid to any purpose the cause of missions. If next Friday is to be a day of earnest prayer we must recollect, my brethren, that missionaries are a product of the missionary spirit, the product of a divine enthusiasm, spread throughout the Church, for the honour, for the name, for the kingdom of Christ. Let us pray that this enthusiasm be deepened and be extended among us, in us. Let us pray that we too, who stay at home, may sincerely share it. Let us pray against the causes, moral and intellectual, which impair its strength whether in ourselves or in others—our feeble faith, our want of unity. God, of course, knows what these causes are much better than we do. God will remedy them by a fresh gift of the Pentecostal fire, if He does not determine to afflict us as a Church with spiritual barrenness.

But if we are to pray in earnest, we must act as men who pray in earnest. We must take real interest in the subject-matter of our prayers, and make sacrifices for it.

We must give some time, some thought, some money, to the work of extending Christ's kingdom. If we cannot go out and help to extend it, we must put our desires and our enthusiasms into commission. The best way of doing this, as it appears to me, is for each person to interest himself or herself in a particular colonial diocese or parish,— to learn and read all that can be learnt and read about it, to get into communication, if possible, with the bishop or active laity or clergy; and thus to sympathise with the hopes and fears, the failures and successes, of those who in this particular spot are doing what they can for our Lord's glory and for the souls of men. This near, personal, individualising knowledge will be a stimulus to collect money, books, and other things that may be wanted, and to do what can be done to encourage any of our friends into whose hearts the Holy Spirit may have breathed the noble aspiration to become a missionary. Communications with any diocese can be carried on through the Society for the Propagation of the Gospel, or, if otherwise, through the Church Missionary Society. Whatever agency we employ, let us, in Christ's name, do something. An interest in missions, as distinct from merely belonging to a missionary society, is of the greatest moment to the success of this work. Enthusiasm for a mere organization which presents itself in the shape of meetings, a committee, a secretary, a balance-sheet, is well-nigh impossible. Organization, however perfect, is not fire. It was a flame which our Lord came to send upon the earth. It is in human souls struggling upward out of the darkness toward the truth—it is in human souls struggling at the cost of health and life to communicate that truth—that the real interest of missions must be sought and found; and when this is more generally the case among us, the work of our missionary societies themselves will be better appreciated as enabling us to maintain and to give expression to this essential part of our Christian duty.

Above all, let it not be thought that in praying or working for missions a man is neglecting either the cause of the Church at home or the interest of his own soul. Every earnest work has an effect far beyond its immediate range. "He that watereth shall be watered also himself."[1] Churches are generally living churches in the exact ratio of their missionary activity; and as men we cannot enter into the object of Friday next with any tolerable degree of certainty without wishing to be—without ourselves becoming—better men, more Christian, more earnest and consistent in our Christianity. No law is more certain in the spiritual world than this, that to give is to receive more abundantly than we can give,—that self-sacrifice for others, in the name of Him Who died for us all, inevitably carries with it the most genuine, the most lasting blessings for ourselves. If we have any real hand in passing on the fire which Christ came down to kindle in human hearts, depend upon it, that sacred flame, as it passes by us, will warm, will brighten us, proportionately.

[1] Prov. xi. 25.

# SERMON II.

## INDIVIDUAL RESPONSIBILITY.

ROMANS xiv. 12.

*"So then every one of us shall give account of himself to God."*

LAST Sunday we were considering this question: What is implied about the second coming of our Lord Jesus Christ, when the apostle compares it to the inroad of a thief in the night? It was only by the way that we touched on its main purpose, that is to say, the final judgment of men. And the Advent season, and the importance of the matter to each one of us, equally warrant us in returning to it to-day. Now all of us, I take it, must feel that, when St. Paul says that every man shall give account of himself to God, he makes one of the most solemn statements that are to be found even in his epistles. He is led into making it, as we should say, quite incidentally. He wants to lay down a principle which will check the rash judgments which were prevalent among Christians at Rome in his day respecting the common religious observances of their Christian neighbors. Some of the Roman Christians, it seems, were vegetarians; others ate anything that they fell in with. Some of them observed private family anniversaries; to others all days were pretty much alike. As yet the Church of Christ had not laid down any rule about these matters for Christians, and no individual

Christian, therefore, might challenge another's liberty, or judge another's conduct. "Why," asks the apostle, "dost thou judge thy brother? or why dost thou set at naught thy brother? for we shall all stand before the judgment-seat of Christ. For it is written, As I live, saith the Lord, every knee shall bow to Me, and every tongue shall confess to God. So then every one of us shall give account of himself to God."[1]

Here is a solemn truth which must, we think, have at once lifted the thoughts of the apostle's Roman readers above the little controversies in which they were engaged into a higher and serener atmosphere. Whatever food they ate or did not eat,—whatever days they did or did not privately observe,—one thing was certain: they would have to give an account of this particular act or omission, as of everything else in their whole lives. "Every one of us shall give account of himself to God."

Here, then, we have, first of all, a broad statement affecting every one of us human beings who are here present,—a statement as to something which every human being has to do. Every one of us has to give an account. When this account is to be given, where is it to be given, how is it to be given,—these are questions, certainly, of the highest interest; but for the moment we are looking hard only at the general fact—the accountability of man as man.

This is the aspect in which, for the time, man presents himself to the apostle. Man as man has a destiny before him of which one feature, at least, is certain,—that he has to give an account of himself. Certainly, human nature has many sides; and other qualities, or endowments, or prerogatives, have seemed to observers to be man's distinguishing characteristic: to one, the gift of reason, to

[1] Rom. xiv. 10-12.

another, the possession of free will, to a third, man's capacity for social progress, to a fourth, man's power of turning his thought back upon itself—in other words, his capacity for reflection. The apostle looks out upon human nature,—upon the many men and women whom he sees passing before him in the streets of some Asiatic or Greek town—and he says to himself, " These are beings who, each one of them, have to give an account. Much else about them is solemn, interesting, attractive, but this one thing is more serious than all else; they have, each one of them, before their destiny takes its final shape, to go through a scene of matchless importance in itself and in its issues. They have to make answer for themselves, to a Being who knows all about them. They are—and if they do not already know it they will find themselves to be—responsible."

Responsibility. It is one of those great words which, if they are dwelt on, shape the thoughts, the wills, the lives of men. There are not many such words in any language—words which have this high privilege of representing the deepest and most fundamental truth that can sway the soul of man. "Responsibility," however, is one such word, and "duty," is another. But, of the two words, "responsibility" is the more solemn and the more powerful. My duty is that which, as a man, as a Christian, I have to do. My responsibility recalls the account which I must render for what I do and what I leave undone. Duty looks to the present,—responsibility to the present and to the future. Duty may seem at first to represent the more disinterested of the two ideas. Responsibility, human nature being what it is, is the more practically vigorous. Duty is a word which men may use—I will not here discuss how reasonably or otherwise—who have no exact answer to give to the question why duty is duty at all, or virtue is right and vice is wrong, or industry, honesty, self-sacrifice are praiseworthy,—why sloth, deceit, self-indulgence, are blameworthy; but responsibility is a word which no man would use thinkingly who has not a great deal to say upon these topics. A man who does not look beyond the grave may talk in a vague, though yet in a sincere way, about his duty, using that word with respect to what he has to do in his present position, and, perhaps, in order to keep it. But no man talks of responsibility, in the true and wide sense of that term, who does not know and feel that "it is appointed unto all men once to die, but after this the judgment."[1] "England," we know, "expects every man to do his duty," here and now. St. Paul says, "Every one of us shall give account of himself to God." Not that a man need be a Christian in order to believe that he has to give an account of himself hereafter. The Mahometans, for instance, believe this as sincerely as we do; and, if this is one of the fragments of truth which they have borrowed from the Christian scriptures, it is probably retained by them because man's natural conscience bears such striking witness to its justice. It is impossible to believe in a moral Ruler of the world, and to believe that He has made His last—quite His last—reckoning with man on this side of the grave. There is too much of wronged innocence,—too much of unpunished wrong—to allow such a belief as this. The actual state of the world, if all ended here, would make belief in one perfectly good God all but impossible,—would force us, perhaps, to think either of a God who is Force and Intelligence, without being also Goodness, or else of two beings —one of them good and the other evil—not unequally matched in point of power, who have made the world of men the scene of their struggles for mastery, and that

[1] Heb. ix. 27.

with very varying results. Whenever men have risen to belief in a moral God, they have necessarily also believed in some sort of future account, on the ground that the area of operations afforded by human life in this earthly sphere is, it would seem, too confined to enable a perfectly holy Being satisfactorily to vindicate within its frontiers His essential attribute of justice.

And thus it is that we find the presentiment of judgment largely spread beyond the limits of the Church of God. Many of the better kind of heathen, from age to age, would have repeated thus far the creed of the apostle. "We men are responsible agents. Every one of us shall give account of himself hereafter." Nay, its philosopher, Seneca, did say not merely that such an account was to be expected in reason, but that the thought of it was a great help to virtuous action. Who of us does not recognise the solemnity with which a man's life is forthwith invested when some one trial, or danger, or suffering is inevitable —is known to be inevitable by himself and by those who are in his company? This is the secret of the interest, always and everywhere renewed, with which a soldier is regarded when he is setting out for a campaign. We must, of late, have read public or private accounts of the profound emotion with which the troops parting to take their share in the great struggle now raging in the East have been regarded by their countrymen; and the reason is that, however much the men who compose a regiment or a battalion may differ from each other in countenance, in antecedents, in bearing, in other claims to interest, this is certain about all and each of them—that they will have at no distant hour to encounter the shock of battle with all its tragic liabilities. That one clearly ascertained point of their impending destiny is the true secret of the interest with which they are regarded. And we must have been conscious of the same kind of feeling, if by any chance we have ever had to visit a person who is under sentence of death. Whatever he may have been, or whatever he may be, all else is dwarfed in our minds by the thought of the stern penalty which shortly awaits him at a fixed hour in a fixed place at the hand of the law. And yet, if we would look at things as they are, there is every reason for extending this special kind of interest to every single member of our race. Whatever else may be uncertain respecting the future of us—each and all of us who are here assembled in this cathedral—it is certain that one and all of us will die, and after death must give an account. Of all who ever lived on this earth,—of all whom we have seen in life, it may be only once, of all who will live till the end comes, of all of whom we have only heard the names, of those nearest and dearest to us, and of those most remote, whether in age, or station, or character, or occupation,—this one fact is equally true, and it invests every one of their lives with an equal solemnity, that they will give an account hereafter.

Every one of us, then, will give an account; every one of us is responsible. But responsible for what? What is it respecting which we have to give this account? The apostle answers by saying, "Every one of us shall give account of, or concerning, himself." What is the ground of this particular responsibility? Why is a man thus responsible for himself? Why shall we each one of us have to give an account of that which we do, and that which we leave undone; of that which we are, and of that which we are not, but might be, and should be; of that which we believe, and of that which we do not believe, but, it may be, which we could and should believe; of the motives which really sway us, of the passions which most powerfully affect us, and of the influences which we exert on those around us, and which they in turn exert upon us; of the drift and current of our lives as they lie beneath the eye which surveys them perfectly from first to last, without prejudice, without passion, searchingly, unerringly? The answer is because all this is for us, more or less directly, a matter of choice. Our acts, our omissions to act, our moral character, our moral deficiencies, our faith, our failure to believe, our ruling motives, our ruling passions, our relations, active and passive, toward the beings around us, the course of our existence, whether it be upward or downward, are all of them the result of choice—acts of choice carrying with them, more or less completely, the whole impetus of our being—acts of choice extending, it may be, over some scores of years. Millions upon millions of these acts of choice, determining in a particular direction the general movement of our wills, have made us what we are now—have determined what we do now, what we now omit to do, what we believe and what we reject now, what on the whole we are tending to, what we leave more and more behind us. Doubtless, this is not the whole account of the matter. Each of us starts with a natural outfit, which helps to a good choice, or which makes it difficult. Then, again, the opportunities of our several lives differ almost indefinitely, and, as we Christians believe, the Grace of Baptism and the assistance of the Holy Spirit given again and again in after life, though it does not act irresistibly and force a man up to heaven against his will, yet is a great force on the right side. But, allowing for all this, we are in the main, and we shall be still more when we come to die, what we have made ourselves.

And it is on this ground that we are responsible. Responsibility goes hand in hand with power—with power of choice. No man is responsible for the size of his body, or for the colour of his hair, or for the number of his brothers and sisters. These things are out of his power. His responsibility begins exactly where his power of choice begins. It varies with that power, and upon the use he makes of it will depend the kind of account which, sooner or later, he will have to give.

It will be most assuredly of ourselves that we shall have to give an account. It would not be difficult for many of us to give an account, more or less exhaustive, of other people. We spend our time in thinking them over, talking them over, discussing them. We know, it may be, some true things about them. We suspect a great deal which is not true, which is utterly false. To some of us, it may be, this discussion of others presents itself as at once an amusement and relief. It is an amusement, for it costs us nothing to dwell on their failings, and human nature, when we have no immediate stake in it, is always amusing. And it is a relief. To talk about others keeps us at the circumference of our life, far—very far—away from the centre. We dread being near the centre. We do not wish to be there with ourselves—within ourselves—alone with ourselves. There are wounds beneath the surface which we would not—which we dare not—probe. There are memories from which we fly, if we can manage it, to a something outside and beyond them. And yet, after all, it is of ourselves that we shall have to give an account. Others will come into that account only so far as they depend on us—so far as we may have injured, or wronged, or otherwise affected them. They may now take the place in thought which ought to be given to our own condition. A day will come when this will be impracticable. We shall be isolated—alone—before the eternal Judge; and, though amidst the countless multitudes, He will deal with each one of us as though we alone existed before Him—as though all the rays of His infinite wisdom and justice were concentrated on our particular case. It is, then, of ourselves that we must each one of us give account.

But to whom is this account to be given? "Every one of us," says the apostle, "shall give account of himself to God." It stands to reason, my brethren, that an account must be given, if given at all, to some person. Responsibility implies a person to whom the responsible man is responsible. There is no such thing as responsibility, except in the language of poetry and metaphor, to an idea—to an abstraction—to a sort of fancy in the air. A responsible man, I repeat it, is always responsible to some person—whether one or more persons—whether to a human or superhuman person. All human society is based on, and it is kept together by, this law of responsibility to persons. We all know that servants are responsible to their masters, and children to their parents and teachers, and soldiers to their commanding officers, and the clerks in a great business house to the partners, and those who are dependent on others to those on whom they depend. Not that responsibility to persons is confined only to the young, or the employed, or the subordinate, or the dependent; not that responsibility is found only at the base of society. On the contrary, the higher you mount the greater the responsibility, because, as we have already seen, responsibility implies power—power of choice—and varies with power, so that where there is most power there is most responsibility. In reality, masters are more responsible than servants, and parents than children, and officers than the soldiers whom they command, and the heads of a great firm than the clerks in their employment, and employers and superiors generally than those whom they employ and who depend on them.

But to whom do these highly placed people—more responsible because invested with more power—to whom do they owe their debt of responsibility? Well, in some cases we can still follow the subject upward from one superior to another, from one depositary of responsibility to a greater, till we reach the summit. But to whom is the highest of all—the king—the head of the government—responsible? In what are called absolute monarchies he is, practically, responsible only to God. And if you could be certain of always having for a monarch a man of great wisdom and of entire integrity of purpose, perhaps this would be the simplest, the most useful, the most beneficent form of government; but as you cannot be certain of this, or rather, to speak plainly, can only secure it very rarely indeed, it has happened that in most civilised countries government itself is made ultimately responsible to the common judgment of those whom it governs—responsible to the people. This has been the principle of the English constitution for nearly two centuries, and it illustrates the law on which society is based, that every man is responsible to some other man.

Responsibility, then, is the law of human society; and yet there are always certain members of society who seem to be, somehow, responsible to none. Wealthy people with no relations, and who, as they say, can do what they like with their money—idle people with no duties or engagements, who have, as they phrase it, "to kill time,"—clever writers, or speakers, with no clear sense of truth or duty, who think that they may write or say just what occurs to them without let or hindrance—if these men are really responsible to whom are they responsible? So far as this world is concerned, they seem at first sight to go through it without having to answer to anybody. If we could consider these cases in detail, we should, I think, find that the absence of any human person to whom responsibility is due is apparent only, and is not real. But be that as it may, most assuredly there is one Being to Whom all must give an account of themselves sooner or later—both those who have to give an account to their fellow men, and those who seem in this life to escape all real responsibility whatever. One such Being, I say, there is to Whom we all of us are responsible, the holy and eternal God. Our responsibility to Him rests on a strict basis of right. We answer to Him for the use we have or have not made of the powers and faculties which He has given us, and because they are His gifts. It is, as the Maker of all things, that He is the Judge of all men. The parable of the talents is the key to this aspect of human life. Whatever we possess comes from Him, and He expects it to be accounted for. All those persons to whom men are here responsible are shadows of His supreme authority—the parent, the teacher, the master, the magistrate, the monarch—nay, in its collective sense, the people. Behind each of these authorities, partial and transient, He stands—He, the real, the everlasting Judge of man—to Whom in the last resort all His responsible creatures must give in their account.

There is often something painfully artificial in the relation which in this life makes this man answerable for his conduct to that man—St. Paul, for instance, to Felix, or Seneca to Nero. The relation may have grown up out of a state of things now obsolete. It may be altogether at issue with the relative worth of the two men. But of this artificiality there is no trace whatever in the relation of responsibility in which every soul stands toward the eternal God. All are equally indebted to Him: all are equally dependent upon Him. His claims upon all, His rights over all, are equally absolute. And before Him, the Almighty and the All-holy, each and all of the children of men are but as vanity. "The children of men are deceitful upon the weights; they are altogether lighter than vanity itself." [1]

Every man must give an account of himself to God. And when we think of what God is, we see something of what this account perforce must be. It will not be measured out by us to Him, by or according to the standard of our fears, or our sensitiveness, or our bad memories, or our dulness of conscience, or our false and artificial views of truth and of duty. True, we shall give it, and yet He will receive or He will exact it in utter independence of us. He will read us off as being what we are—as being what already He knows us to be. All the veils which hide us from each other—which hide us from ourselves—will drop away before the glance of His eye. Even now there is no creature that is not manifest in His sight, for "all things are naked and open to the eyes of Him with Whom we have to do." [2] Even now what we owe each of us to God—what Grace He has given us—what dangers and sufferings He has spared us—He knows, and, as yet, He only knows; but when we come to give in our account we shall know too. A flood of light will be poured from His throne across the whole course of our separate lives, and into every crevice of our souls and characters. Whatever His verdict upon us may be, our conscience will have to affirm its justice. We shall see ourselves by His light as He sees us—as we perhaps have never seen ourselves before. We shall know what He meant us to be—what we might have been—what we are—as never before. All the illusions of our present life—all the fabrics of self-satisfaction built up by the kind words of friends—by the insincerities of flatterers—by all the atmosphere of twilight which encompasses our spiritual state here—all these will have rolled away. We shall stand out in the light before the Judge

[1] Ps. lxii. 9: P. B. Version.   [2] Heb. iv. 13.

—before ourselves. It may be that we have clung to some hope that we have lived on unobserved by Him—that we are beyond the eyesight of the Being of beings. It will be impossible to think this in the day of account. They say, "Tush, the Lord shall not see, neither shall the God of Jacob regard it. Take heed, ye unwise among the people: O ye fools, when will ye understand? He that planted the ear, shall He not hear? Or He that hath made the eye, shall He not see? Or He that nurtureth the heathen, it is He that teacheth man knowledge; shall not He punish?"[1] It has been said that the strongest of all the motives that can change a man's life, both within and without, for his lasting good, is the love of God. If we could love God quite sincerely for twenty-four hours, we should be other men, capable, spiritually speaking, almost of anything. But if this be so, the next motive in the order of efficiency is, beyond all doubt, the remembrance of the inevitable last account which we must each of us give before the judgment-seat of Christ. If we could only let that truth sink into our hearts and take possession of them—if, as we presently leave this cathedral, instead of saying to each other, "What did you think of the anthem?" or "What of the sermon?" we could be silent and make up our minds to live henceforth as men who will bear in their thoughts day by day the remembrance that they have to be judged by a holy God, we should find that that resolution would do three things for us:—

First of all, it would act as a check upon us. It may be that, until now, we have gone through life like grown-up school-boys, saying, doing, just what we like, with no thought beyond each act, each word. It may be that we pride ourselves on being untrammelled by creeds, by scruples,—on being, as we put it, "unconventional,"—on un-

[1] Ps. xciv. 7-10: P. B. Version.

derstanding life chiefly as freedom—freedom to think, to say, to do what we like without let or hindrance. So we bound along the path of earthly existence in our boisterous irrepressible spirits, as if along that path no mistakes could possibly be made by any high-spirited traveller—as if that path led in the end to no place in particular; or we bound along as if engaged in a continuous frolic—as if existence were an immense, inexhaustible joke from beginning to end. And thus we pass from boyhood to manhood, and from ripe manhood to its decline, as if we had eyes and ears and thought and imagination and sympathy ready for almost anything in the world except the one question, "What is to be the end of it?" And here it is that the thought of the future account does sometimes act as a sudden solemn check, not merely upon gross sin, but upon aimlessness, frivolity, lack of serious purpose in act and word. A voice comes to us in the dead of the night, or in some moment of enforced solitude, and it whispers, "This is all very well, but you have to give an account to God." So of old, said the preacher, the son of David, in Jerusalem:—"Truly the light is sweet, and a pleasant thing it is for the eyes to behold the sun: but if a man live many years, and rejoice in them all, yet let him remember the days of darkness. Rejoice, O young man, in thy youth; and let thy heart cheer thee in the days of thy youth, and walk in the ways of thy heart, and in the sight of thine eyes: but know that for all these things God will bring thee into judgment."[1] So said the beloved apostle in his island prison:—"I saw the dead, small and great, stand before God; and the books were opened: and another book was opened, which is the book of life: and the dead were judged out of those things which were written in the books, according to their works."[2] And if, when a man

[1] Eccles. xi. 7–9.     [2] Rev. xx. 12.

gets up in the morning, he would say to himself solemnly, "I shall have one day certainly to account for what I do, and say, and think this day," and if, ere he lays him down at night, he would say to himself solemnly, out aloud, if necessary, "I shall have to account before God for what I have done and said and thought, and failed to think and say and do this day," he would find, at the end of six months the truth of that saying of St. Augustine,—"Nothing has contributed more powerfully to wean me from all that held me down to earth than the thought, constantly dwelt on, of death and of the last account."

And this resolution to give thought to the last account would prove, secondly, a useful stimulus. If some men seem to regard life as a play-ground, others treat it as a sleeping-room. They use it with all its vast opportunities as a something that is only to be dozed away. They shrink from its demands on their exertions, from the repeated calls to do something for God's glory—something for the benefit of others—something for true self-improvement—as if these invitations were merely the importunate voice of an undeserving beggar, or the ravings of a fanatic. They are indolent at twenty. They say that when they are thirty they will be active men—men of prayer, men of work, men of resolution and sacrifice; but thirty comes and finds them, if I may say so, still in bed, with just those companions around them who assure them that they will be in time to make a fair use of life if they are up and doing at forty. The years soon pass, and forty is upon them, and they still are where and what they were. They are still alive to the necessity of some effort; but a man, so they say, is not old at forty, and, meanwhile, "yet a little sleep, a little slumber, a little folding of the hands to sleep."[1] And so they reach fifty or sixty, when youth

[1] Prov. vi. 10; xxiv. 33.

has fairly passed and habit has stiffened around them, and it is too late to rise. If anything can save them, surely it is the overwhelming thought of the account which they must give,—the account of all that they have received—strength, intellect, it may be, income, time, friends, God's grace, good thoughts and impulses, bright visions of usefulness and happiness, repeated discontent with self—only to be wasted,—only to be thrown aside as if they had never been received at all. "Awake, thou that sleepest, and arise from the dead, and Christ shall give thee light"[1]—the light of His wisdom, streaming from the words that are written in His gospel shining on thy soul,—the light of His love shining from the Cross on which He died for thee—the light of His justice as, to the anticipation of faith, He appears in the clouds of heaven coming to judge the quick and the dead. This may yet save thee ere it be too late.

And, lastly, a use of thinking much of the last account is that, like the old Jewish law, this thought is a schoolmaster to bring the soul to the feet of Jesus Christ; for the thought of that account does force us to think over our lives here, not once or twice but often, not superficially but with a determination, if possible, to see ourselves as we are. To think of ourselves thus, often, is to anticipate its result as far as we are concerned. It is to act on Paul's advice that, if we would judge ourselves, we should not be judged. And when we do this, what do we find but weakness, perverseness, determination to go wrong, indifference to God's leading,—all that can warrant the acknowledgment, "I know that in me (that is, in my flesh) dwelleth no good thing: for to will is present with me; but how to perform that which is good I find not?"[2] This is about the best that many of us can honestly say for ourselves;

[1] Eph. v. 14. [2] Rom. vii. 18.

and so we are driven to Jesus Christ our Lord for pardon and for strength, just as were the Jews and Gentiles in the first age of the Church. His Blood washes out the stains which else had forfeited acceptance at the last. With Him there is still plenteous redemption. His Spirit and His Sacraments convey the strength which make future obedience possible. We can do all things through Christ that strengtheneth us; and so, with His Cross before our eyes, with His gracious presence and blessing within our souls, we look forward to our account with trembling joy. It had been impossible—quite impossible—to stand before His throne unbefriended and alone; but He in His generous love has delivered us, if we will, from our strongest enemy, and has covered us already with His robe of righteousness.

# SERMON III.

## CHRIST THE IDEAL MAN.

### Luke i. 78, 79.

*"The dayspring from on high hath visited us, to give light to them that sit in darkness and in the shadow of death, to guide our feet into the way of peace."*

IT will be my endeavour, my brethren, to-day and on the three following Sundays, if God wills, to induce you to consider different sides of one single truth, namely, the immense blessing conferred on us men by our Lord Jesus Christ's first coming into this our world. Such a subject is sufficiently in harmony with the Church's mind and purpose during this present month, in which she begins by looking forward as if, for the moment, she were living over again the expectations and hopes of bygone centuries, and in which she ends by thankfully commemorating the advent.

Where there is so much to be said, we can only give our attention to a few salient points; but the time will not be lost if we endeavour to do what is really open to us with a simple desire to understand and to carry away as much positive truth as we can, and still more if we follow up this effort by a resolution to give some practical expression to our knowledge as quickly and as forcibly as may be.

Let me begin, then, by asking a simple question. What is the need felt by all or most human beings in their best moments? It will not do to reply that it is the need of being saved; because the fact, the nature, the need of salvation implies a great deal of faith and knowledge which may be altogether wanting. The answer is, the need of becoming better. Doubtless there are some who never feel this want. For my part I believe that they are comparatively few. In all lives there are times when a ray of sunlight falls from heaven into what is called in the text "the shadow of death," which generally overcasts them, and men yearn to be better than they are. Doubtless if you were to cross-question the men and women whom you meet in the street, they might say that, for the moment at any rate, to be quite frank, they wanted something much more earnestly than to be better. They are very poor, and they say that what they want is money, or at any rate the means of livelihood; or they are in bad health, and they say that amidst sleepless nights, and with a sense of weariness and weakness and uselessness, and the dull monotony of continuous pain, or, it may be, the sense or the apprehension that they are gradually breaking up, no blessing for the time seems to them so desirable as a restoration of health, if it could be had. Or they are in the midst of domestic trouble. Somebody or something has gone hopelessly wrong; or there is a great family quarrel in which every one is taking a side; and they say that that which is essential for them is peace and comfort in the home circle. These, however, are not universal wants; for all human beings, it is plain, are not in these particular circumstances; nor are they really—if the truth could be brought home to those whom it most nearly concerns—the chief wants of the men and women who are in these circumstances, although they look greater than any other wants because for the moment they press more closely upon the life than any others, just as a tree ten yards off looks taller and larger than a distant mountain.

It will be said, perhaps, that happiness is as universal a want as moral improvement, and a want much more generally felt. But then what is it that secures happiness? Nothing merely outward can do this. A man's happiness is not secured by his wealth or by his honours. These things bring troubles and annoyances all their own; and their presence or their absence no more touches the real springs of happiness than the color of a man's coat affects the circulation of his blood or the regularity of his breathing, or than the wind which plays upon the surface of the ocean troubles the depths below. Even such blessings as warm friends and an affectionate family, closely as they wind themselves around the heart, do not insure happiness, —first, because they are transient, and our happiness is always dashed by the apprehension of losing them; and next, because, in order to be made the most of, they must be relished by a certain moral appetite. The daintiest food is repulsive to a man who is hopelessly out of health. In short, happiness is essentially an inward thing. It cannot be inflicted; it cannot be conferred from without; and it consists, so far as we can see, first, in the repose of an open heart upon a really adequate and worthy object, and, secondly, in the due harmony of the several faculties of the soul. Until the heart is at rest, until the several powers of man's inward being are harmoniously adjusted, true happiness is impossible. But then, what is this repose of the heart, what is this internal harmony of the faculties, but the very fruit and evidence of our becoming better—of our increase in goodness? And thus we come back to this point: that, after all, the general desire to be happy is, when it is reasonably interpreted, a general desire to become better; although all true and noble hearts will feel that, if there were no such thing as happiness at all, goodness would still be worth almost any efforts on its own account.

Now, in order to become better we need, first of all, an ideal,—a true outline, present to our mind's eye—of what human goodness is. Do not let us think that this requirement is fanciful, and that we can, if we like, get on very well without it. All workmen, whatever they are doing, must know what they are going to try to do, or to come near, before they begin to work. This is, we know, the case in art. The painter tries to sketch out his idea in outline upon paper before he touches his canvas. The architect completes his drawings and his models before he begins to work at the foundations of his edifice. The poet tries to forecast, at least in his mind, the probable direction, the true limits of his song, of his argument, before he essays to submit his thought to all the restraints of rhyme and verse. Sometimes, indeed, an original idea may be discovered to be imperfect, and to require modification. A general, for instance, may find that circumstances oblige him to alter fundamentally the original plan of his campaign. But, speaking generally, the rule holds good that, in order to work well, we must have an ideal of work before us. We must, in other words, know at the outset what it is exactly that we mean to try to do. And this applies just as much to our becoming better as it does to other things. We must know what the precise improvement is to be, at which we are aiming. We must have a standard of true excellence before our eyes as a guide and as a stimulant.

Ah, there are persons who tell us that to confess thus our need of an ideal is to do a wrong to man's true dignity,—that it is essential to our position as "lords of the creation" that we should look up to nothing that is higher than ourselves. Certainly, if this be true, man pays very dear for his dignity as a lord of the creation; for if any one law of creaturely existence is certain, it is this, that improvement depends on struggling upward toward a higher existence than our own. Depend upon it, an ideal of some sort we must have: it is a necessity of our being. If it be not above us, it will certainly be beneath us. And since, in proportion to the consistency and to the force of a man's character, his desires and affections follow hard upon all the currents of his sincerest thought, it follows that when the ideal is below a man the whole character and being will inevitably sink, as it will inevitably rise when the ideal is above him. This is no new doctrine. Eighteen centuries ago our Lord said, "Where your treasure is, there will your heart be also."[1]

My brethren, if there be one variety of the human species of which I could almost despair, it is the boy or the young man who has no enthusiasm for any person or character or cause,—who is so buried in his self-complacency that he thinks it part of his excellence to admire nothing, or at least to profess that he admires nothing. There may be foolish enthusiasms, misdirected enthusiasms, enthusiasms which lead people into error, or which condemn them to disappointment; but to have no enthusiasm for anything that is beyond or higher than self—this means nothing less than moral ruin, because it is the forfeiture at the very outset of life of a prime condition of all real improvement. All of us, young and old, need an ideal. Probably there are some who hear me who can confirm the value of an ideal of goodness from their own experience. Early in life, it may be, while principles were unsettled, while affections were yet fresh, while habits were unformed, while the will and the character were still open to receive a de-

[1] Matt. vi. 21; Luke xii. 34.

cisive impulse in this direction or in that,—early in life, when that most fatal of all scepticisms, disbelief in any human disinterestedness, had not yet, like an early spring frost, settled down upon the soul to nip with relentless accuracy all its budding promise and beauty,—we passed, through God's loving providence, under the influence of some friend or relative to whom we could look up with sincere affection, with sincere respect. A great character, tender and yet strong, many-sided and yet capable of concentrated intensity, laid its blessed spell upon us. We had something to admire, something to believe in, something to attempt to imitate. It may well be that in that life which to us seemed so nearly perfect there were stains and flaws, as it lay out beneath the all-seeing Eye of the eternal Holiness; but as yet in those early days we had neither the experience of sanctity, nor yet the experience of sin, which enabled us to detect them. And so we were lifted for the time out of the reach of lower aims and attractions, out of the influence of perilous companionships, out of the dead level of our own miserable self-complacency; and this strong and beautiful life has left us with an influence which lasts. It has passed away now, perhaps many a year ago; but the effects remain. We have known the happiness, the advantage, the strength, of an ideal of human goodness.

Man needs, however, a perfect ideal,—an ideal that shall permanently defy criticism,—a sample of what human goodness is in its truth and completeness. We are sure— we men—that there is such a thing as this. How else, we ask, should there be so universal an aspiration toward that which would, upon this hypothesis, have no existence in fact? But if the question had been asked at any time or place, between the death of our first father and the birth of Jesus Christ, where such an ideal life could be found, what must have been the answer? Over the whole of the ancient world we trace the apostolic inscription, "All have sinned, and come short of the glory of God."[1] The great characters of pagan antiquity in literature are like the beautiful fragments of pagan art in our museums; they suggest perfection without reaching it. They are always, at the best, mutilated, even when there is in them nothing that is positively hideous or degrading. The best and the highest fail to satisfy the craving of the human conscience for some life that shall show what man was meant to be. Socrates has been named in our day as a sort of parallel to Jesus Christ, as a fearless apostle of truth in an age of unrealities and superstitions; but Socrates—not to dwell on graver blemishes— has so little of apostolic consistency that, after spending his life in exposing popular superstitions, he desires with his last breath that a cock may be sacrificed to Esculapius. And Cicero was undoubtedly one of the purest and noblest characters in the whole public life of ancient Rome,—a man who tried with great sincerity of purpose to wring perfection out of the philosophy which he had at hand; and yet Cicero's vanity is so egregious that at this distance of time it is almost impossible to read his letters and his speeches without a smile. And Seneca has still, as he always has had, his enthusiastic admirers. His writings, no doubt, represent one of the best efforts, if not the very best effort, of the pagan conscience, even if he did not get something from a higher source; but a subtle vein of pride runs through him and spoils everything. Seneca in practice is quite a different man from Seneca on paper. He is cowardly and avaricious. Nor is it otherwise with the saints of Israel. Israel had a divine, fixed rule of human life: it had no perfect living ideal. Israel's greatest and holiest, whether lawgiver, or prophet, or monarch, had each and

[1] Rom. iii. 23.

all a share of imperfection,—Noah, Abraham, Moses, Samuel, David, Elijah, Hezekiah. It seems unfilial, ungrateful, irreverent, to insist on the shortcomings of the saints; but then Scripture does record them. Each of them falls short. David especially—the man who loved God and goodness with an enthusiastic love—the man after God's own heart—David is so far from perfect that for us he is rather the model of penitence than of saintliness, of recovery than of perseverance. These great servants of God were, in fact, types of One greater than themselves,—of One Who would collect in His single Person their scattered excellences, while He rises above their characteristic failures—of One from Whom some rays of glory might seem to have fallen, by anticipation, upon these great forms among the ancient people, that the eyes of men might be trained to gaze on Him when at last He came.

It is our Lord, and our Lord alone, Who satisfies this human want of an ideal of goodness. He shows us what human goodness was meant to be. He offers us, in His life, the ideal life—the life of man at his best, in his perfection. This is the meaning, or one of the meanings, of that title by which, more frequently than by any other, He referred to Himself—"the Son of Man." No doubt the original purpose of His publicly adopting that name was to claim for Himself the great prophecy in which Daniel describes One like the Son of Man coming with the clouds of heaven to the Ancient of Days, and receiving dominion and glory and an imperishable kingdom, that all peoples and nations and languages should serve Him.[1] We have proof that this prophecy was, in our Lord's day, one of the most familiar to the Jewish people, and they understood it universally to refer to the expected Messiah; so that when our Lord spoke of Himself as the Son of

[1] Dan. vii. 13, 14.

Man, they understood Him to claim to be Messiah in the strongest language open to Him. Still the question why Messiah should be called by a title such as this remains; and to say that it was because He was to be truly human seems to be scarcely a sufficient answer, unless indeed we bear in mind that He was all along something more, so that His Humanity could not be taken for granted and is, from the point of view of revelation, something of a surprise, just as it would be always to describe a powerful monarch as poor, or a great general as a confirmed invalid. But a fuller and more satisfactory reason is to be found in the fact that our Lord is not merely human, but that He is the representative or ideal Man—the one Son of our race Who is not unworthy of its high origin, in Whom its original idea is perfectly realised. This is what St. Paul means by calling Him the second Adam,—the counterpart, that is, of the first father of our race, unlike the first Adam in this, that He is always true to the idea of a perfect humanity. And so He stands alone in history, the first of a new race of men, the faultless Pattern and Type of human goodness.

For in the ideal which His life presents to us, let us observe, first, the absence of any disturbing flaw. In the midst of a soiled and sinful world He alone is absolutely sinless. He too is tempted, as was Adam. Unlike Adam, He resists temptation. We shall seek in vain for any trace of evil in that perfect life—for any word, any action, any gesture or movement, which applies a will averted from good—which implies sin. Everywhere we see in Him simple and sustained elevation above the circumstances, above the opinions, of the world, above its pleasures, above its sorrows. "In vain," it has been said by no friendly writer, "in vain does the most keen-witted malice seek to trace selfishness in the motives of Jesus of Nazareth."

No lower inclinations of sin, no paltering with truth, no swerving from justice, no self-seeking, no covetousness, no ambition, can find a place in that Character of such lofty purity, of such stern veracity, of such considerate equity, of such unreserved self-sacrifice, of such disinterested love. Men have mistaken His anger against the buyers and sellers in the Temple for a mere outburst of vulgar earthly passion, forgetting what a just and holy zeal for God's honour, which they do not feel themselves, might make imperative in Him. Or they have excepted against His cursing the barren fig tree, not seeing that, for the Holy One, this material world is ever subservient to the moral, and that this act was designed to represent the impending condemnation of impenitent Israel. Or they have imagined that the choice of Judas betrayed a want of that higher insight into character which might be expected in a perfectly pure soul, here too mistaking merciful long-suffering for mere moral insensibility. Not that our Lord's sinlessness rests upon our inability to trace moral evil in His words and works. His forerunner, the Baptist, confesses it; His apostles insist upon it. For them He is, over and over again, the Lamb without blemish, immaculate, Who does no sin, in Whose mouth no guile is found. The judge who condemns Him washes his hands, to cleanse them, if it were possible, from the Blood of the Innocent. The centurion beneath the Cross, and Judas in his despair, insist equally with the holiest souls in aknowledging the stainless purity of Jesus. Nay, He Himself speaks always as a sinless Man. He calls men to repent without once implying that which must be an ever present thought to every one of His ministers, that He too is a sinner needing reconciliation and pardon in order to face the purity and the justice of God. He teaches men to pray "Forgive us our trespasses," but no prayer for the pardon of sin ever once passes His lips. He goes further; He challenges His contemporaries to convince Him of sin if they could. For any man whose character was not obviously spotless such a question would mean either consummate hypocrisy, or self-deceit pushed almost to the extremity of folly. In our Lord, it harmonises perfectly with everything else that we read about Him. The human conscience in all ages, like the conscience of His contemporaries, listens to that astounding question in reverent silence, and whispers to itself, " He, *He* has a right to ask it, for He—*He alone*—is without sin."

.And the ideal of goodness presented to us by our Lord is perfectly harmonious. We see in Him nothing of the narrowness or the one-sidedness which is traceable more or less in all merely great men. As a rule, we men can only appropriate one part of goodness at the cost of the rest. How often, for instance, are the best people that we meet with charitable, but indifferent to the claims of truth, or truth-loving, but careless about the requirements of charity. In our Lord there is no one predominating virtue which throws others into the shade. Every excellence is adjusted, balanced, illustrated, by other excellences. It is impossible to maintain, with any approach to a show of reason, that some one particular temperament shapes His acts and words: that He is cynical, or choleric, or melancholy, or phlegmatic. He is each of these: He is none of them. He combines the masculine with the feminine type of character. He combines the active instincts of life with the repose of contemplation. It is impossible to say that He surrenders Himself to any one especial duty to the prejudice of the rest. He obeys the law, but He proclaims man's freedom in obeying it. He rivals the sternest ascetics in not having where to lay His Head; yet He converses brightly with all the world, eats with publicans and sinners, attends a wedding banquet, sheds tears at a funeral. He is consumed, as He says, with zeal for God's honour; yet He is always calm. He rebukes the ill-considered fervour which would call down fire from heaven upon those who did not receive Him. He is ever contemplating, as none else could contemplate, the nothingness of all created things, the coming of that day which cometh as a thief in the night; and yet He sympathises with all that is tender and beautiful in nature and in life. He points to the birds; He lingers over the colours of the lilies; He calls from the homeliest incidents and features of country life the materials for those imperishable parables which, like flowers on the altar, by reason of their very simplicity, are so suggestive of divine and eternal truths. He is tender without false sentiment, benevolent without a trace of weakness, resolute without passion, without obstinacy. His condescension never degenerates into mere familiarity. His incomparable dignity never touches—it were blasphemy to think it—the confines of pride. His lofty freedom from the world's tyranny and prejudices never becomes contempt for man or any form of misanthropy. His implacable hostility to sin is always allied to the warmest love for sinners. Against evil in all its forms He brings not peace, but a sword; while on those who will He bestows a peace which the world cannot give. In His own words, He is as wise as the serpent, He is as harmless as the dove.[1] He is in His character, as by the terms of His mediatorial office, at once the Lamb led forth to sacrifice, and withal the Lion of the tribe of Judah.

Once more. The type of goodness presented to us in the life of Jesus is a strictly universal type. It is flavoured, so to speak, by no race or clime or sect. It is absolutely

[1] Matt. x. 16.

world-wide. Certainly the particular features of goodness are always the same; but a good Englishman, as we know, is in many ways figured with a different outline from a good Frenchman or German. National habits and modes of thought and action drape the eternal virtues in dissimilar guises; and, such is our finiteness, a very French type of goodness would not find many imitators here, just as a good Englishman would have to be studied by our neighbors across the channel before they would do him any sort of justice. Now, although our Lord was born in a province of the Roman empire marked by the very strongest peculiarity of race and thought, He does not exclusively belong to it. His character is just as intelligible to the Greeks or the Romans or the Germans, as to the Syrians or the Arabs. No Jewish sect could claim Him as its adherent; no Jewish teacher has left on Him a narrowing impress; no popular errors among the people of whom He was received any sanction at His hands. He will not hear of their superstitions about sabbath observance: He is Lord also of the sabbath. He will not sanction their cruel intolerance of the Samaritans: the Samaritans, both in His teaching and in fact, are objects of His special favour. They may judge hardly of the Galileans, whose blood Pilate had mingled with their sacrifices,—of the eighteen whom the tower of Siloam had crushed in its fall,—of the man who had been born blind; but He will not for a moment yield to their assumption that each form of bodily misfortune is the consequence of some secret sin. He has a wider and wiser philosophy of pain than that. Still less has any Roman or Greek or Indian thinker shaped Him into an intellectual mould. He rises above all the dividing lines of that or any previous or subsequent age. He speaks to the human soul in all countries and ages with the authority of One in Whom every soul finds, at last, its ideal representative. Although he wore the dress of a Jewish rabbi, and accommodated Himself to the usages of Jewish life, all His ordinary words and actions, although altogether suitable to His age and country, are yet also equally adapted to all people and all climes. And thus His character—let me repeat it—His character is correspondent to His world-wide claim, and in all quarters of the world men have recognized in Him an absolutely universal Type of human goodness. And if any have dared, of His grace, to say with His apostle, "Be ye followers of me," they have quickly added, "even as I also am of Christ."[1]

There is, indeed, one side of our Lord's bearing toward men—I mean His literally boundless claims upon their faith and their obedience—which would be fatal to the ideal which is presented to us, if it did not depend upon a fact, upon a necessity, of His Being as One higher than any of the sons of men. As it is, His self-assertion is only a part of His perfect veracity. He would not have been true to Himself,—He would not have been true to us—if He could have shrunk from claiming to be the Judge of the world, and already one with the everlasting Father in those distant times when as yet Abraham, the patriarch of Israel, had not been born. Into this momentous truth we must not enter farther to-day.

There are two very brief observations which I would make in conclusion.

My brethren, if our Lord is thus the pattern Man, the four holy gospels are, on this account, the most precious of all books in existence. They are the inner sanctuary of Scripture: they are its holy of holies. Certainly the eternal Spirit moves and breathes everywhere in the sacred volume, but His organs are very various. Else-

[1] 1 Cor. xi. 1.

where we are in presence of legislators, of historians, of prophets, of apostles: here we meet with, we listen to, the Master Himself, as one and the same Figure, so gracious and so awful, is reflected in four distinct yet ultimately harmonious types of teaching. Like those four mysterious beings whom Ezekiel and the Beloved Disciple successively beheld in vision, highest and nearest to the throne of the Uncreated, as representing the loftiest forms of created life, so the four Evangelists stand alone in the Book of God because they narrate the life of the perfect moral Being—the life of Jesus. Just as those rest not day and night, saying, "Holy, holy, holy," so these have but one aim—to show us simply and sufficiently their Lord and Master. In these incomparable pages there is nothing of what we should find in a human biography. No circumstances are dwelt on as illustrating His greatness. No attempts are made to draw attention to the beauties of His character. The writers evidently feel that, in such a Presence as that, comment or panegyric would be out of place,—that it would be irreverent. The narrative flows on in the very simplest and most unlaboured style, and we feel, as we read, that nothing else than a new Being is before us—One Whose words and acts reveal at once a matchless simplicity and an awful greatness. One work there is, the product of the highest uninspired Christian genius—the "Imitation of Christ" (whether by A'Kempis or by an unknown author I cannot say)—which, more than any other, has caught the spirit of the evangelists; but their sublimities, like jewels disguised among the pebbles on a sea-beach, are revealed now to all quick eyes and earnest hearts. The perfect Life they record is the first blessing of the Advent season. Let us remember it practically by studying them during the next three weeks

And lastly, if our Lord be thus the pattern or ideal Man, we men must love Him, not merely for what He has done for us, (of which more, please God, on another day,) but because He is what He is,—because He is fairer than the children of men while yet He is one of them. This love, I say, is no mystic reverie, no rare spiritual accomplishment; it is a moral necessity. For what is it that provokes human love? Always and everywhere beauty, whether beauty of form, or beauty of thought, or beauty of character. And as there is a coarse and a false beauty which commands the passion of degraded love, so should a true and pure beauty provoke the purest and strongest affection of a spiritual being. And therefore St. Paul says, "Grace be with all them that love our Lord Jesus Christ in sincerity."[1] Therefore St. Paul says, too, "If any man love not the Lord Jesus Christ, let him be Anathema Maran-atha."[2] The love of the one perfect Being is a true test or criterion of our actual state. We shall certainly love Him if we are looking upward,—if we are trying, however imperfectly, to improve, and have caught a sight of Him,—and it is the first condition of our becoming better. With this consummate Ideal of human perfection before our eyes, our whole nature will rise to a higher level with the upward movement of our hearts.

May the dayspring from on high visit our hearts indeed this Advent,—banish their darkness and their gloom by a revelation of His beauty,—and then, enwrapping us in His love, guide our feet, tenderly, strongly, swiftly, across all intervening obstacles into the way of eternal peace!

[1] Eph. vi. 24.      [2] 1 Cor. xvi. 22.

# SERMON IV.

## CHRIST THE AUTHORITATIVE TEACHER.

### LUKE i. 78, 79.

*"The dayspring from on high hath visited us, to give light to them that sit in darkness and in the shadow of death, to guide our feet into the way of peace."*

THE coming of our Lord Jesus Christ into this our world was considered last Sunday as settling for us men a primary and most important question, namely, What human life at its best was meant to be. For us Christians that can be no longer an open question. Our Lord Jesus Christ has offered us an Ideal of life which authoritatively closes it. The local and national drapery which, so to speak, encircles Him does not obscure the world-wide significance of His life and character. The accidents of His coming among us as a Jew eighteen centuries ago are easily translated into their equivalents at other times and places, and there remains an Ideal—the ideal of a Manhood which, by its perfection, disarms the most fastidious criticism, by its majesty awes irreverence itself into something at least like respect, by its tenderness takes millions of hearts age after age so altogether captive that they are constrained to lavish upon it the very best of their adoration and their love.

But side by side with man's anxiety to find the moral

ideal of his life, in view of which he may become better, is a wider anxiety, if possible, to understand if he can the secret and the object of his existence. While our moral instincts, making the most of that original sense of right and wrong which is a part of the outfit of every soul, are tracking their way toward an ideal life, our intelligence is at work all the while on a larger circle of ideas, and is constantly raising or encountering questions which cannot but present themselves. My brethren, there are times in the lives of most thoughtful men—of the most steadfast Christians—when those primary questions recur with a kind of awful freshness, starting up, as it were, out of the quiet routine life which we are leading, out of the very depths of the soul's being, and troubling us with their searching importunity,—" Whence am I? What am I? Whither am I going?" Man's real nature, his origin, his destiny—these are questions which cannot be treated as if they belonged to the mental department which many of us, perhaps, label "Notes and Queries." They are obviously questions of the very first importance—questions compared with which the literary and social and political trifles with which we amuse ourselves, during the greater part of our brief life here, dwindle away into their proper insignificance.

Do not let us, for the world, say, "These are merely speculative questions: we can do our duty very well while we leave them unanswered." They may, in themselves, belong to the speculative rather than to the practical sphere of truth, but they have immediate and important bearings upon practice. I need not spend time, my brethren, in pointing out to you that the whole idea of the meaning and solemnity of life and duty depends upon the answer which we give to these questions,—that to know that we are really imperishable beings, with an endless destiny of some sort before us, receiving from One above us this awful gift of life, and having to account most assuredly for the use we make of it, is, for serious persons, a most fruitful piece of knowledge, while denial or doubt of it is proportionately, in a moral sense, likely to be impoverishing and disastrous; for all such questions really run up into one,—Does any Being exist Who explains to each of us the mystery of His own existence—a Being to Whom we owe it that we are here at all,—Who upholds us in existence moment by moment,—Whom we are bound to serve now, and in Whom hereafter we may find our satisfaction and reward?

Now St. Paul tells us that in nature and conscience, taken together, man has materials at hand for learning that such a Being—that God—exists. And by God he means not a mere stupendous Force, nor yet merely an all-penetrating Intelligence, but over and above this—nay, especially—a Moral Being. "That," he says, "which may be known of God is manifest in the Gentile peoples; for God Himself hath showed it unto them, since from the creation of the world His invisible attributes may be clearly seen, being understood by the things that are made, even His eternal power and Godhead; so that," he concludes, "the Gentiles are without excuse,"[1] if they do not act upon this knowledge. And what nature teaches from without conscience echoes from within. "The Gentile nations," says St. Paul again, "having not the law that was once given to Israel, are a law unto themselves, since they show the work of the law" (that is, the conduct which God requires) "written in their hearts," just as for Israel it was written on the tables of stone, "their conscience also bearing witness to it."[2] And thus conscience within man, as nature without him, points to God even without a revelation.

[1] Rom. i. 19, 20.      [2] Ibid. ii. 14, 15.

The works of nature suggest an Author; the law of conscience implies a Lawgiver; and that the Lawgiver of conscience is also the Author of nature is, on the whole, apart from revelation, a presumption so intrinsically probable that man may be held responsible for presuming it, although its certainty is only attested by miracle, the weapon, so to call it, the weapon of revelation—the weapon by which revelation makes its way among human minds, one object of miracle being to show that the material world is under the control of the Lord of the moral world.

Here observe, my brethren, that St. Paul is speaking of what man may know by the aid of nature and conscience; but whether he will do so or not in a given age or country, depends upon whether he will or will not make the most of his resources. As a matter of fact he has, more frequently than not, closed his eyes to the natural light streaming around him. Unwilling to know more of the Lawgiver of a conscience which he disobeys, he has disregarded the teaching both of conscience and of nature; and hence the various idolatrous and polytheistic systems of the pagan world—the "lords many and gods many" to which St. Paul alludes. These systems, remark, do not represent man's gradual struggle upward from an utter darkness toward the recognition of one God; but, on the contrary, they represent different stages of his descent from a knowledge, more or less clear, of that primal truth downward toward fetichism. "When they knew God," says St. Paul, "they glorified Him not as God, neither were thankful; but became vain in their imaginations, and their foolish heart was darkened; and so they changed the glory of the incorruptible God into an image like unto corruptible man, and to birds, and four-footed beasts, and creeping things."[1] Indeed, if we wish to study this process of a

[1] Rom. i. 21–23.

gradual decomposition of faith, we need not look back to the pagan religions of the ancient world. The last number of some popular and brilliant review may possibly enough show us how, with a higher than any natural light flooding all intelligences that have eyes to see, men can at this day close their eyes to all spiritual truth whatever, and so bury themselves beneath the folds of matter that nature becomes to them, instead of the robe of beauty which everywhere speaks of the Monarch who wears it, only a thick veil that hides Him from the sight of His reasonable creatures.

But even where this is not the case—even where God is believed really to exist—the questions of our relations towards Him are still unsolved. Why did He place us here? Does He take notice of, does He care for, us? Shall we see or know anything really of Him by and by? Shall we exist in any practical sense after death? And to these questions even sincere theists only answer, "Perhaps." If we are to know anything certainly, God, Who sees the secret of our destiny, must Himself speak. "Behold, the darkness shall cover the earth, and gross darkness the people: but the Lord shall arise upon thee, and His glory shall be seen upon thee."[1] If there is a good God in existence Who has made us His creatures, such as we are, with these wants, with these capacities, with these aspirations, these hopes, these presentiments, these fears, then it is highly improbable, to say the least, that He should not show us something more of Himself and of His will than can be learnt from nature and from conscience. Nature has its dark patches of unintelligible ruin and pain. Conscience has its recurring moods of hesitation and bewilderment. A clearer, stronger, steadier light is needed to guide man along his difficult path to his future home. A clear

[1] Isai. lx. 2.

word of God—that is what is wanted; and it is unimaginable, for those who believe Him to be loving and wise, that He should allow His creatures, century after century, to grope after Him amid disappointment, when it would cost Him, they think, so little to speak. The sense of the great probability that God will speak meets, you observe, the evidence that He has done so nearly half way, and it is designed in His providence to do so.

And here it may be well to notice an old but by no means extinct objection to the very form and instrument of revelation as the word of God, spoken to man and uttered or written down by man as God's word. We are gravely told that for a spiritual Being like God to speak involves an anomaly, since speech—a movement in the air resulting from the vocal organs—implies an animal organism, so to say, behind it; and accordingly the phrase and idea of a word of God is said to be only one of the many ways of degrading the conception of Deity, for which the Christian revelation is held to be responsible. It is better to treat this anxiety for God's honour, wherever we find it, as sincere, though too often it shows itself only when some point of Christian doctrine is to be discredited. As God's justice and generosity are pleaded against His atoning love,—as His gifts of sacramental Grace are said to materialise the idea of His spiritual influence, so in like manner to suppose that He can speak is described as changing Him into the image of His animal creation. What, then, is this idea of the word of God, which the objection presupposes? It is, I reply, a purely physical idea of it. So much organic activity, so much atmospheric vibration, such and such an effect upon the nerves and the brain,—that is a word. It implies that by a word is meant only a regulated sound,—that sound is the essential thing in the word,—that apart from sound it does not exist;

whereas, in reality, sound is only the physical dress of the real word, whether it be the word of man or the word of God. The substance of the word, of which sound is the clothing, is thought—thought prepared for transmission from one thinking being to another. No doubt with us men, composite beings as we are, with our souls clothed in bodily forms, our ideas take a physical and outward dress too in order to be transmitted from one of us to another. But is no communication, then, possible between one disembodied spirit and another? And, if it is possible, is it to be supposed that such a communication passes in anything which we should recognise as an uttered language? And are we even sure that no beings communicate with us excepting through the organs of sense,—sure that the strange unaccountable thoughts, good and evil, which present themselves ever and anon to our intelligence are not infused into it by other beings, whether angels or evil spirits, or the spirits of the departed? In short, if by the expression "a word," be meant thought ready for transfer from mind to mind, whether through the medium of language or without it, who shall deny the power of any one spiritual existence to speak to another, to pour into another, by sympathetic contact, of the nature of which we can form only dim imaginings, a very tide of thought and feeling and resolve and passion—a vast power of spiritual good or evil,—to receive in return, in the case of created spirits, a reciprocal influence for evil or for good? And, if this be so, who in the world shall say that the one self-existing Spirit alone may not speak,—that while every creature has its appropriate language—its voice, as St. Paul puts it, whether articulate or not—God alone shall not communicate His will to created and independent minds,—that, while beneath His throne there is an incessant activity of intercommunication between beings of all orders of intelligence, He alone, the Maker of all, the Lord of all, is to be condemned to silence, to banishment, to isolation, in order, forsooth, to guard His dignity?

"No, no," it is said by another group of disputants, "we do not mean that. Of course the infinite Spirit can speak to other spirits if He chooses. We, for our part, believe that He has spoken, and that He still speaks, more or less, to all. Our objection to the Christian idea of revelation is that it is too limited,—that it confines to a few agents and to a single age a process which we maintain to be as ancient and as universal as humanity. God, we say, has always been revealing Himself; and Christianity can no more monopolise the privilege of being the one Revelation, than England can claim to be the one country upon which the sun shines."

Here, brethren, let us admit what must be cheerfully admitted, namely, that God has not left Himself without witness anywhere among men,—that, as we have already seen in nature and in conscience, He has provided means which, if they are made the most of, enable men to attain to a certain knowledge of Himself. If, enlarging the idea of revelation, you choose to call that primary lesson of nature and conscience "revelation," do as you please: only then let us understand each other. Of course, in that sense, all the false religions in the world, if not revelations, contain an element of revelation,—just enough to prevent them from decomposing at once,—just enough to prevent their forfeiting at once all claim on the affections and thoughts of men. But if by "revelation" we are to understand, as is usually understood, only such truths about the nature and the will of God as nature and conscience could not enable us to reach, then I say, advisedly, that revelation is a monopoly of Christianity and of that Jewish religion which Christianity presupposes and incorporates with itself; for revelation has two concurrent certificates of its reality. One is miracle, whereby the revealing God, the Lord of nature, steps, as it were, from behind the veil, and gives a sensible proof that He is in communication with the human agent who claims to be uttering His word; and the other is conscience, the seat of His original presence and legislation, now illuminated by a higher truth than heretofore, and recognising its illumination as being in substantial harmony with its best, first, earliest lessons. Thus our Lord appealed both to His works and to the inward light or eye in His hearers, when He urged His claims. Other claimants upon the hearts and thoughts of men have produced miracles, true or false, while conscience has been more or less drugged or perverted; or they have roused conscience into sympathy or morbid dissatisfaction without being able to show that any Being beyond the world of sense has sanctioned their appeal. The Gospel has combined the two—the best attested miracles with the most searching appeals to conscience; and the seed thus sown in honest and good hearts has brought forth its hundredfold, its sixty, its thirty.

Much, indeed, had been done within the limits of Israel to satisfy man's desire to know more about God and about himself than could be learnt from nature and from conscience. The history of Israel is, in reality, a history of successive revelations. First came the great lawgiver with his moral, religious, and civil institutes—with the divine law recorded independently of the memory and conscience of Israel, as we should say "objectively," upon tables of stone; and then a long line of teachers, rulers, leaders, saints, prophets, but especially of prophets, each adding a something to the sacred deposit,—each illuminating some more or less obscure portion of the will of God, completing the outline of some prediction, or reinforcing some moral truth, or rebuking some popular sin or error, or removing some fatal barrier between the heart of Israel and its unseen King. As we are told at the beginning of the Epistle to the Hebrews, God spoke His will in the old days in many fragments and in many modes. It is a wonderful procession, that, moving across the centuries—those organs of the revelation in ancient Israel—that long array of minds to which God whispered various portions of His will, each of whom, as an apostle says, "spake as he was moved by the Holy Ghost."[1] But it was a revelation which did not—could not—satisfy the needs of man. It was confined to a single race, whereas the existing want was as wide as humanity. Moreover, apart from its moral impotence, of which more, please God, next Sunday,—apart from this, although it taught all that Christianity teaches as to man's origin and his continuous dependence upon the strength of God, its disclosures as to the life beyond the grave,—as to the means of attaining the end of our existence—were partial and unsatisfying. It was, in fact, introductory to another and a fuller revelation as its proper explanation and climax,—a revelation which would radiate from—which would centre in—a single Person. "God, who in sundry parts, and in divers manners, spoke in time past unto the fathers by the prophets, hath in these last days spoken unto us by His Son."[2]

"His Son." Let us dwell on that prerogative name. It must mean at least a Being who shares the Father's Nature, yet is personally distinct—one Being Who, by right, stands towards the eternal Being in this unique relationship. But, lest we should think of some created and inferior nature, Scripture gives the Son another name. He is called "The Word;" that is the Thought or Reason, uttered or unuttered, of the everlasting Father. What is more inti-

[1] 2 Pet. i. 21.   [2] Heb. i. 1-2.

mately part of a man than his thought? What is more clearly distinct from him, while yet inheriting his nature, than his child? Thus Scripture teaches us the existence of One who is one with the Father, yet personally distinct from Him, His Peer and Companion from everlasting. "In the beginning," says St. John, "was the Word, and the Word was with God, and the word was God."[1] Our human nature is a poor attenuated likeness of the perfect uncreated Being. Fatherly affection among men is a shadow of the divine fatherhood in God. Filial dependence among men is a shadow of the eternal sonship within the Godhead. And in like manner, as the human soul has, as part of its outfit, thought, tending always from its nature to communicate itself through language, imperfect, hasty, transient, though it be, this thought also is an eternal shadow of Him—the personal Thought or Word of God, eternal as God is eternal, sharing His power, sharing His wisdom, sharing His goodness.

Well, my brethren, this is the first truth of the Creed of Christendom: the eternal Word or Son of God took flesh, and appeared in, and spoke through, Jesus of Nazareth. "The Word was made flesh, and dwelt among us, and we beheld His glory." Jesus was not a mere Man more highly illuminated by the divine Spirit than His predecessors had been. In the secret seat of His Being He was the personal Son or Word of God, clothed in a human Body and Soul which He had wrapped around Himself and made His own. And this it is which constitutes the specialty of His revelation. When Jesus spoke, it was the eternal Thought or Word of God Himself that spoke, not through the agency of another Being, but directly, although employing human organs and human speech, to those upon whom His words fell. "That which

[1] John i. 1.

was from the beginning," says the apostle, "that which we have seen with our eyes, which we have looked upon, which our hands have handled, of the Word of life (for the life was manifested, and we have seen it, and declare unto you that eternal Life which was with the Father and was manifested unto us;) that which we have seen and heard declare we unto you."[1]

What, you ask, is the certificate of all this? The answer is, again, miracle (that is, nature under certain aspects) and conscience. First, His resurrection. "He was declared," says St. Paul, "to be the Son of God with power, according to the Spirit of holiness, by His resurrection from the dead."[2] He had Himself appealed to this proof of the truth of what He said about Himself. If the Jews would destroy the temple of His Body, He would raise it again in three days. If they wanted a sign in His favour, the prophet Jonas would suggest one. The Son of Man would be buried, not in the whale's belly, but in the heart of the earth, and would then rise to life. And His resurrection is a matter of hard historical fact, only to be set aside by purely *à priori* assumptions of its impossibility; and as it covers, so to speak, all His other miracles, so its evidence is reinforced by the higher conscience of our Lord's contemporaries. "Never man spake like this man."[3] That was the feeling of those who listened to Him for a moment without prejudice. "The people were astonished at His doctrine: for He taught them as one having authority, and not as the scribes."[4] That is the evangelist's report of the impression which was produced by the Sermon on the Mount. They, the hearers, did not, indeed, know at the time the deepest cause of this profound astonishment; but our knowledge is illustrated by their experience. That which struck the people

[1] 1 John i. 1–3.  [2] Rom. i. 4.  [3] John vii. 46.  [4] Matt. vii. 28, 29.

was His possession of authority—a threefold authority as it might seem—the authority of certain knowledge, the authority of entire fearlessness, the authority of a disinterested love.

The authority of certain knowledge. The Scribes argued, conjectured, balanced this interpretation against that —this tradition against the other. They were often learned and laborious; but they dealt with religion only as antiquarians might deal with old ruins or manuscripts, so that when it reached the people the underlying elements of truth were overlaid with a mass of doubtful disputations, of which none could seize the precise value or drift. When, then, our Lord spoke with clear distinctness, as One Who saw spiritual truth—Who took the exact measure of the seen and the unseen—Who described without any ambiguities what He saw—the effect was so fresh and unlooked for as to create the astonishment which St. Matthew describes. Doubtless the prophets would have contrasted advantageously with the Scribes of our Lord's day in this respect; but there is an accent of authoritative certainty in our Lord, which no prophet ever assumes, when He corrects error, or when He unveils truth. "It hath been said by them of old time," He says again and again, and then He adds, "but *I* say unto you." His authority, He feels, supersedes all that has gone before. He knows it. Compare Him with His great apostle, St. Paul. St. Paul, no doubt, announces truth authoritatively too; but then St. Paul is a dialectician, who writes long argumentative letters to his converts—who preaches argumentative sermons in the Jewish synagogues. St. John more nearly resembles—but then it is because he more closely repeats—his Master. Jesus, with His "Verily, verily, I say unto you," is the Teacher of teachers—the most authoritative Teacher, pouring forth a flood of light upon all the great problems of human interest,—on the reality of the divine Providence, on the destiny of the human soul, on the secret miseries and certain cures of human life, on the means of access to the eternal Father; and He is conscious—always conscious—of His supreme place in the history of religion. As He says, "Blessed are the eyes which see the things that ye see: for I tell you, that many prophets and kings have desired to see those things which ye see, and have not seen them; and to hear those things which ye hear, and have not heard them,"[1] so He says also, "The queen of the south came from the uttermost parts of the earth to hear the wisdom of Solomon; and, behold, a Greater than Solomon is here."[2]

Observe in Him, too, the authority of entire fearlessness. In all ages this kind of authority among religious teachers has been comparatively rare. Many a man will occasionally say strong or paradoxical things, who is by no means continually fearless. If he fears not the world at large, or his declared opponents, he fears his friends, his supporters, his patrons. He fears them too much to risk their good will by telling them unpopular truth. To fear no man, high or low, educated or untaught, rich or poor,—to draw a clear line of distinction between love and honour, on the one hand, and fear, on the other,—to do justice to the element of truth which underlies all error, and yet to make no compromise for a moment with the substance of the error itself,—to offer no incense on any occasion to prejudice and to passion,—to refuse to suppress, or to enwrap in lifeless and unmeaning generalities, unpopular but certain truth,—to set aside if need be, the weight of custom and the influences of powerful personages or classes, while saying frankly, strongly, boldly, what is known to be true; and yet all the while to be considerate and

[1] Lu. x. 23, 24.   [2] Matt. xii. 42; Lu. xi. 31.

moderate—moderate with the self-restraint of conscious strength, and not from the feeble timidity which fears lest any one enunciation of absolute truth should give offence,—this, my brethren, God knows, is easier far for us to describe than to realise. The Scribes failed here. They were largely dependent on the people; and, like many ministers of truth elsewhere, they deferred largely to the superstitions and prejudices of their powerful patrons. Prophets, indeed, such as Elijah, as Isaiah, as Jeremiah, as Daniel, as—last, not least—the great Baptist, had nobly risen above this temptation. But then the first apostle yielded at Antioch to wrong-headed but affectionate followers, who would have brought back Jewish observances into the Christian Church. Here, as elsewhere, our Lord is above all. Look at the Sermon on the Mount, in which the most comfortable glosses upon the old awful law of Sinai are sternly exposed and set aside,—in which the exigency of its spirit, as distinct from the easy obedience to its literal requirements, is insisted on,—in which, as afterwards in those discourses reported by St. John, before the climax of the Passion, the great authority of the most powerful classes of Jerusalem is confronted with uncompromising resistance. Read the 24th chapter of St. Matthew; read the end of the 9th chapter of St. Mark; and say whether this language would have been spoken by a teacher who was balancing the claims of truth against the chances of success. Most human teachers wait till they are backed by numbers,—till their words are the echo of the multitude. Jesus enunciated truth as depending on its internal strength, harmony, necessity,—as a thing itself mightier than the errors, the prejudices, the passions, of the place or the hour,—as being no merely passing or local influence, like opinion, but unchanging and eternal and dear to God, and, whether in the triumphs of its representatives, or their failure—aye, their martyrdom—holding from God a charter of ultimate victory. With Him, we know, it could not have been otherwise; but with Him, as with the lowliest of His servants, it was an element in His great authority.

And observe in Him, lastly, the authority of His pure, His disinterested love. Here too, as a class, the Scribes were wanting. To them religious teaching was not a labour of love so much as a means of livelihood. They were more like lecturers on ancient religious literature, than envoys from, and exponents of, the heart of God. And this is much truer of the great teachers of the pagan world. A philosopher made the best he could of his clever guesses. He had nothing to do with love. He would have been ashamed of any exhibition of tenderness. He was supposed to be above the joys and sorrows of ordinary men. Even the great Jewish prophets, standing in some respects between the Law and the Gospel, were in this less like the Gospel than the Law. Hosea comes nearest to the yearnings for man's highest good which are so characteristic of our Lord; but Hosea cannot compare with the divine tenderness which sheds tears over Jerusalem, which welcomes and pardons the Magdalene. Especially do we miss in the prophets that tender love of individual souls which is so conspicuous in our Lord as a teacher. While His horizon of activity and aim is infinitely greater than theirs,—while He is gazing steadily upon a vast future of which they had only dim and imperfect presentiments, He devotes Himself, we may dare to say so, to a publican, to a Syrophenician stranger, to a Nicodemus, to a Samaritan woman, to a family at Bethany, as if for the time being there were none others in the world to engage His attention. Nowhere, perhaps, is this aspect of His teaching so prominent as in His last discourse in the upper room—the language, as that is, of the uncreated Love speaking directly to human hearts in words which, at the distance of eighteen centuries, retain this, the secret of their matchless authority.

It was with this accent of certainty, with this fearlessness, with this love, that our Lord Jesus Christ solemnly deposited His revelation in the souls of men. True, He did not state many formal propositions: He was mainly engaged in quickening consciences, rather than in instructing minds. But, in the fulness of His authority, in addition to the substantial truth which He Himself taught, He sanctioned the teaching of the by-gone centuries in Israel: He sanctioned the teaching of the apostles who should succeed Him. Looking backwards, He said, "Not one jot or one tittle shall pass from the law till all be fulfilled."[1] Looking forwards, He said, "When He, the Spirit of truth, is come, He will guide you into all truth."[2] And thus from prophets and from apostles having His sanction,—above all, from Himself, the Teacher of teachers,—we now know, or may know, all that is most important for us as men to know. As Tertullian said in his day, our little Christian children can answer the questions which are in debate among the philosophers. We know Who created this wonderful universe with all its mysteries of teeming life. We know Who placed us here, and why He placed us here, and how we may fulfil His high purposes respecting us. We know what is behind us, what is before us, what is above us—God our Creator, God our King and Ruler, God the last End of our being. We know, too, how marvellous is His love to have committed such knowledge to such puny intelligences as ours. We know something of the eternal harmony of His uncreated Life—of the mystery of a threefold existence within the divine Unity—of the unutterable condescension of Him

[1] Matt. v. 18.     [2] Jno. xvi. 13.

Who has brought us this knowledge, and of His Spirit Who continually recommends it to our inmost souls. We have before us, may I not say, in our possession, a body of fixed, unchanging truth, in its outward form like the opinions and philosophies which make up the staple of merely human thought, but, on a closer inspection, both in its substance, and in the authority on which it rests, utterly distinct from them. "The Daystar from on high hath visited us, to give light to them that sit in darkness and in the shadow of death, to guide our feet into the way of peace."

My brethren, if Jesus Christ, the eternal Word and Son of God, has indeed brought us from heaven this gift of revealed truth in its fulness, by His first coming, He has thereby imposed upon us—upon every soul among us—practical responsibilities. He does not force it upon our intelligences. We can elude its loving pressure if we will, by indifference as well as by ingenuity; but, plainly, it cannot leave us, in any case, as we should have been if it never had been given to us at all. In a Christian country like this, we have all of us more or less stood distinctly face to face with that truth. We have all of us had our opportunities—(when and what they have been God knows) —for becoming acquainted with it. "If," said our Lord, with mournful solemnity, to the men of His day—"If I had not come and spoken unto them, they had not had sin: but now they have no cloke for their sin."[1] Such knowledge is, or may be, an unspeakable blessing. Such knowledge may be also, for those who set it aside or make no use of it, the measure of an eternal loss. Which, dear brethren, which is it to be for you and for me? The time within which this question is to be answered cannot be long for any one of us. The issues which depend upon our decision are endless for us all.

[1] John xv. 22.

# SERMON V.

## CHRIST THE DELIVERER AND RESTORER.

### LUKE i. 78, 79.

*"The dayspring from on high hath visited us, to give light to them that sit in darkness and in the shadow of death, to guide our feet into the way of peace."*

IN considering our Lord, first as the Model, and then as the Enlightener, of mankind, we have been gradually making our way towards a third aspect of His work which His advent suggests: He is also our Deliverer from the guilt and consequences of sin. Had he only shown us what man was meant to be, He would have left us with the painful conviction that we are, one and all of us, in different ways, very unlike the intended model. Had He added to this a knowledge of our destiny beyond the grave, and pointed out its direct connection with our actual state during this present life, He would have heightened our misery without doing anything substantial to alleviate it. A revelation of moral beauty in a world of sinners, followed by a revelation, among other things, of the consequences of sin, would have been like the torchlight visit of a high-spirited and inquisitive traveller to the scene of a battle-field after night had separated the combatants. The ground is strewn with the disfigured bodies of the dying and the dead; the air is filled with the moans of despairing sufferers; but the traveller can only bring his torches to light up the scene in all its horrors for those who are still able to take the measure of their misery. He can only remind them, by his own bright appearance of the blessings they have too probably lost for ever. He is not a surgeon; he is not a hospital nurse; so he goes on his way, and night once more spreads its shroud over the scene of pain. But as such a traveller departs, he is followed—well, he is not followed by the *blessings* of the sufferers.

If our Lord's advent into the world could have recalled this description, he would have neglected the main source of human discomfort and apprehension, and, indeed, the cause of those other needs which have already been considered; for why has man ever lost the true ideal of his life? Why does he ever shiver in his inmost self at the possibilities which surround his destiny? The answer is that he is aware, more or less dimly, of the presence of a fatal flaw in his nature,—of a power which has entered into it, and put it out of harmony with itself, and with the true law of its action. The shadow of a great failure has fallen upon the human family; and so individual men, even before they begin to act for themselves, feel, like persons born out of wedlock, that they lie under a disadvantage at starting—a disadvantage which they have inherited. As was said by a clever wit of the inhabitants of modern Rome, some fifteen years ago, mankind in a natural state is born to an inheritance of ruins—ruins in the intelligence, which possesses fragments of truths that it once contemplated in their perfection; ruins in the affections, which, instead of rising up to heaven, constantly busied themselves in seeking their treasure beneath the soil of earth; ruins in the will, which has lost its original power and directness, and too often is the slave of the passions which it was meant to curb. This is what is called the doctrine—it might better be called the fact—of the Fall. If it is true that its results have been mischievously exaggerated in certain quarters of Christendom—if man has been represented as so utterly impotent as henceforth to be practically irresponsible—these exaggerations must not blind us to the truth which they distort.

The Fall of man is a fact which can be ascertained by observation. It is to be observed especially in man's difficulty in mastering what he knows to be good. The better pagans were fully alive to what they called the difficulty of virtue. It is to be observed in man's facility in lapsing into what he knows all the time to be evil; in his powerlessness, his indisposition, too, to rise out of himself heavenward; in his secret enmity to the thought of a perfectly holy God; in his natural dislike and suspicion of his brother man, apart from the ties of blood and the ties of self-interest; in the wild disorder of his own inner being; in the degradation of his soul—meant to command his body—to be its slave, I may say, its victim. "Behold I was shapen in wickedness, and in sin hath my mother conceived me."[1] That is the language, not merely of the psalmist, but of every child or man who attentively studies the facts of human nature. Predisposition to sin is as universal—it is almost as universal—as humanity; and though at times the fact may seem to be obscured by anomalous outbursts of generosity or courage, it is soon, too soon, reasserted. There was a depressing conviction of this truth in the ancient world, which expressed itself in a story that has often been quoted in illustration. Hercules—the representative hero of pagan fable—may reach what seems to be the climax of his glory as the conqueror of monsters and of tyrants, as the generous friend of the

[1] Ps. li. 5, P. B. Version.

weak and distressed; but, as he wraps around his frame the fatal garment which a woman has offered him, he finds himself a prey to the devouring flame, and the hands which were all-powerful against the tyrants are powerless to strip off the robe of Dejanira.

How has man succeeded to this inheritance of weakness and of sin? God—his instinct tells him, no less than revelation—did not make us as we are. He made our first parent a sinless being. He added to his stock of natural powers, instincts, aspirations, an endowment of grace which, while it did not force him to be loyal to God, made His loyalty easy. God wished to be served by a freely yielded service, and His gifts to Adam did not destroy Adam's liberty. Adam was free to try the experiment of evil, if he chose; and, with his eyes open, he tried it. We know the sequel. By that one act he entered upon a life under totally new conditions. Sin, which had before required an effort, henceforth became easy and natural; virtue, which had been natural, henceforth became difficult and unwelcome. And what he had thus become his children were to be. He left them his nature—his fallen nature—with all its traces of a splendid past, with all its actual and humiliating disabilities. He could not leave them what he had lost himself—the robe of righteousnss. That had been left within the gates of Eden. He could not,—if he transmitted his nature at all—he could not but leave them an entail of weakness and corruption, an inheritance of moral death. "By one man sin entered into the world, and death by sin."[1]

Now, this doctrine of the transmitted effects of the Fall is constantly urged against Christianity, as being a tenet inconsistent with the justice of God. At any rate, my brethren, we do not escape the difficulty which is here

[1] Rom. v. 12.

alleged by rejecting this particular doctrine, since the same feature of the Divine government meets us again and again elsewhere. Take the not unfrequent case of a parent who fatally impairs his constitution by habits of intemperance and debauchery, and then transmits to children and grandchildren a weakly type of existence, condemned by anticipation to an unusual share of disease and pain. The argument against original sin on the score of its alleged injustice would surely impeach the divine Creator for not having summarily prevented the debauched father from becoming a parent, for not having cut him off by death when it must have been foreseen that he would only add to the sum total of human misery. Or look at the moral disadvantages which are entailed upon children by irreligious or immoral parents. These children have no choice as to where they will be brought up, as to whether they will exist at all. These things are settled for them. Yet their first lessons are lessons in vice, lessons in blasphemy, lessons in dishonesty, lessons in all that will ensure for them a future of certain misery, unless some one interfere. Of such children, as you are aware, there are thousands upon thousands in this metropolis; and it may be urged, with just as much reason as before, that Almighty God's justice ought to prevent the existence of children placed in such circumstances as these. And yet there is the fact that He does nothing of the kind. Again, many a man is born into the world with good abilities, with ample means, with a desire to make himself as useful as he can to his fellow creatures, and yet his life has been from the first overshadowed by some one act of his father, against the social effects of which he struggles year after year in vain. "Why," men whisper to themselves, "why should the good God give so much, so rich with the promise of usefulness, and then allow all to be ruined by an entail of real or supposed dishonour?" Louis XVI., as everybody knows, went to the scaffold in consequence of the errors of a dynasty of which he was the most virtuous member. And we Englishmen of to-day pay taxes in order to defray the expenses of wars carried on by our grandfathers and great-grandfathers, but with the conduct of which we personally, I need not say, have had just as little to do as with the campaigns of Julius Cæsar.

In short, whether we look to man's physical nature, or to his moral and spiritual education, or to the structure of human society in families and in nations, we see everywhere the same law of the dependence of one generation of men upon another in the most vital respects. And accordingly the objection to original sin, which we are considering, is in reality little less than an impeachment of the general scheme of God's government of this human world. True, He does break through the fatal entail in conspicuous instances. The Jews of the captivity thought it hard that they should be suffering for the sins of bygone generations, and complained that the fathers had eaten sour grapes, and that the children's teeth were set on edge; and Ezekiel was told to assure them that in their instance every man would bear his own burden. The entail of punishment was there to end. But the rule still holds good as part of God's general government. God still deals with us as families, as nations, as parts of that vast organism which we name humanity, no less than as individual men. Clearly, as the Creator, if He likes He has the right to do this. Who shall dispute it? And observe, if he does so, this rule of His government tells both ways. It is the principle of the restoration of man, as it is the principle of his fall. As Adam's sin carries in its fatal consequences the natural family of man, so Christ, the

Restorer, acts and suffers on behalf of the whole redeemed family. God sees fallen man in our first parent; He sees restored man in our Second. And St. Paul balances the result, and exclaims, " Where sin abounded, grace did much more abound." [1] We must not, however, anticipate.

Let us observe, next, that, over and above this transmitted inheritance of a sinful disposition, there is the immeasurable mass of little sins of which all human beings are guilty,—of which every man and woman adds so much to the existing stock. We are so familiar with the name and with the fact of sin, it so clings to our whole life and thought and speech and action, that we think as little about it as of the weeds which grow in a country lane. But, for all that, it is not the less a serious matter.

Let us ask ourselves, before we go farther, what do we mean by sin? The question is a practical one for all of us. Do we mean by sin thoughts, or words, or acts, or habits, which fall short of being good? Do we mean merely imperfect goodness, so that the contrast between a thief and an honest man is only a contrast between the more perfect man and the less? This has been maintained by able men; but it is in contradiction to the common moral sense of the human race. Sin, all the world over, means something in opposition to good, not merely failure to attain good. Do we mean by sin a necessary step or stage in the development of a moral being, like those bodily diseases which, although painful and weakening at the time, are said to purify and strengthen the bodily constitution? This, too, has been maintained by a school of writers, but the common sense or judgment of men rejects it. When we name sin we mean not a factor in the progress of man or of society, but something which our sense of right condemns as that which ought not to be,

[1] Rom. v. 20.

whatever may or may not come of it. Do we mean, then, by sin merely brutalised human life, consisting in the sovereignty of the senses of man over his reason? Doubtless a good deal of sin takes this form; but there are spiritual sins with which the senses have nothing whatever to do, such as pride, envy, and the like. The form of sin is one thing; the common essence of all sins is another. The essence must be a something common to sins which take a sensual form and to sins which have nothing to do with the senses. Is this essence of sin, then, contradiction of received human opinion about goodness? The other day a clever off-hand writer said that the only satisfactory standard of conduct was obedience to the opinion or the law of one's country. According to this, sin would be contradiction of national opinion, or of national law. National opinion may, no doubt, support that moral truth which sin contradicts. It may proscribe theft or murder, and to commit murder or theft is assuredly to sin. But this national opinion varies at different times and in different countries. It permits many sinful things in England; it enjoins many sinful things, as Christians consider them, say, in China, or in India. A varying standard of right and wrong like this cannot possibly have that sacredness which makes offence against it sin; and this holds good of national human law just as well. Human law, indeed, wherever it is not opposed to the law of God, is sanctioned by God's authority as being law, and in that sense to break it, whatever it be, is to sin. But human law may, for instance, sanction the remarriage of divorced persons, in which case it sanctions that which our Lord Christ has expressly condemned; or it may bid Daniel fall down and worship the graven image which Nebuchadnezzar the king has set up, and, in that case, disobedience to law is so far from being sinful that obedience would be sinful. A higher than any human law has to be obeyed first. Although, therefore, a great many persons have no higher idea of right and wrong than that which is supplied by the law of their country and the opinion of their contemporaries, it is clear that these authorities give us a standard too uncertain, too self-contradictory, too equivocal, to enable us to describe all offence against it by so solemn a word as sin.

We are not losing our time, I trust, my brethren, in reviewing these misconceptions. They still enjoy, in different degrees, a certain vitality; and until we know what sin really is we have no adequate idea of our own misery, and therefore no adequate sense of what has been done for us in order to relieve it.

Once more, then, what do we mean by sin? We mean intentional contradiction, in thought, word, or act, of the perfectly holy will of God by the free will of His intelligent creatures. Why should contradiction of the will of God be of so grave a character as the word sin always implies? Because God's will, as to all matters of moral truth, expresses a necessity of His Nature. God is not good because He chooses to be good, as though it were open to Him to be something else. We may dare to say that, being God, He cannot help being good; He cannot help willing goodness. He would cease to be Himself could He be otherwise. We may see this if we reflect that the laws of goodness are just as eternal and necessary as the laws of mathematics. As it was always true that things equal to the same thing are equal to one another, so it was always true that veracity is good, and that falsehood is evil. Our minds refuse in either case to conceive a time or a set of circumstances when falsehood could have been good. In order to suppose it, their very texture and constitution must be destroyed, just as much as in order to suppose that there was a time when things that are equal to the same thing were equal to one another. But if the laws of goodness are as eternal as the laws of mathematics, then they must have existed thus eternally, independently of the eternal God, or as a part of His Nature. To suppose that they existed independently of God, is to suppose that He is not the alone Eternal—in other words, that He is not God. And therefore we are driven to conclude that, just as pure mathematical truth expresses facts of the divine Nature in ways which we shall possibly understand hereafter, so moral truths are parts of that Nature; and God prescribes truthfulness, justice, purity, and the like, not capriciously and as a matter of taste, but because He is what He is—what He cannot but be—the All-holy.

Now this enables us to see the real character of sin. It is a contradiction of what God wills respecting the conduct of us, His creatures—not of what He wills arbitrarily, as men have spoken, but of what He wills by virtue of His essential Nature as the necessarily holy Being. Sin contradicts God's Nature. Sin is in conflict with His existence. Sin, if it could be indefinitely exaggerated, would destroy God. And it is the dim perception of this awful truth which gives the word so much deeper a sense, in the customary speech of men, than is to be wrung out of those shallow explanations which were just now glanced at. The original biblical words for sin imply this without saying it. According to one, by sin man passes the line which separates good from evil. According to another, he falls from one state of existence down to a perfectly different state. According to a third, he misses—if he does not recover, he misses—the one true aim of his existence.

And this will enable us to see that sin cannot but have

consequences. It is not like a mood of thought and feeling, which arises in the mind and leaves no appreciable traces of its presence. It introduces a new state of things, which continues until it is reversed by some act as definite as the act which introduced it. Of these consequences some are within the soul and some are without it. Of those within the soul the gravest is the collapse of the higher spiritual life, which sin poisons. If the sinner is a Christian, he forfeits Grace, that "Grace wherein we stand,"[1] as St. Paul expresses it. If he is a heathen, he forfeits, partially or wholly, his hold on the natural moral truth which God has taught him. The symptoms may be more or less pronounced: there is no mistake as to their general character. The man's spiritual senses are benumbed, paralysed. He gradually sees no realities beyond the province of sense; he hears no voices that speak only to the conscience; he has no taste for the good things which God has prepared for the spiritual palate. His will is enchained. "Whosoever committeth sin is the slave of sin;"[2] but he cannot altogether, in his lowest moments, rid himself of a regret that he has done what he has. "A certain fearful looking for of judgment"[3] reappears from time to time in the secret recesses of his soul, and he is wretched. He is always liable to these recurring tortures, and there are times when the past masses itself against him, like breakers rolling one upon another towards a perishing wreck—when, as with Richard the Third, as Shakespeare has painted him on the eve of Bosworth Field, all the ghosts of past crimes present themselves before him with terrible vividness:—

> "My conscience hath a thousand several tongues,
> And every tongue brings in a several tale,
> And every tale condemns me for a villain.

[1] Rom. v. 2.     [2] John viii. 34.     [3] Heb. x. 27.

> All several sins, all used in each degree,
> Throng to the bar, crying all, Guilty, guilty!
> Methought, the souls of all that I had murder'd
> Came to my tent: and every one did threat
> To-morrow's vengeance on the head of Richard."

All these consequences of sin internal to the soul are correspondent to other consequences altogether independent of it. Whether the sinner remembers his sin or not, the infinite, all-surveying Mind cannot but—I will not say remember, but—know of it; for each sin is a spiritual fact, and no fact can be hidden from, or other than present to, the all-seeing Mind; and, noting it, He cannot but punish it. He would cease to be Himself if He could regard it with any approach to complacency or indulgence. Men sometimes use language as if sin were a sort of breach of the etiquette of the universe, rather than anything more serious, and as if God, like some good-natured earthly prince, might be trusted or expected to excuse that which could not really harm Him, and which only thwarted His personal inclinations. It is only when we see that moral truth is a necessity of God's Nature, that we understand the utter necessity which He is under of punishing that which contradicts it. Justice, in other words, is the reverse side of goodness. If God could indulge sin He would not be God.

And here let us note that no rules of conduct for the future, however excellent, and however valuable at other stages of man's life, will help us here. The Gentiles had such a rule in natural morality. As St. Paul shows, it only availed to condemn them as falling below and contradicting natural morality. The Jews had such a rule in the law of Sinai. As St. Paul shows, it only condemned them more emphatically, in proportion to its greater explicitness, as conspicuous breakers of that law which was their national boast. "By the law," says the apostle, "is the knowledge of sin."[1] "I had not known sin, but by the law."[2] That is the measure and the rule of conduct, even though it be divine. It does not—it cannot—do away with the guilt of a past transgression; it does not—it cannot—of itself confer any strength which will make future obedience easy. By itself it only illuminates the past. In proportion to its clearness and its authority it forces men to look beyond itself for real relief, and this is what St. Paul meant by that famous sentence of his, "The law is our schoolmaster, to bring us unto Christ;"[3] for the revelation of a moral God is a revelation not merely of justice, which belongs to the truthfulness of goodness, but also of mercy, which belongs to what I may call the active enterprise of goodness. If God hates sin, which He did not make, He loves the sinner, whom He did make. He hateth nothing that He has made. Degraded though he be, He never despises the work of His own hands. The sinner may be a rebellious child, but, after all, he is a child. His body and his soul are alike precious, notwithstanding his sin. They are masterpieces of wisdom and of love. God sees, beneath the ruins caused by sin, the buried remains of a past magnificence. He sees the outlines of a likeness which once was accurate, and which still is dear to a Father's eye; and thus the divine mercy yearns over the sinner, while the divine justice condemns him for the sin. And the Jews knew this truth as we know it. As we said in that magnificent psalm this morning, composed in the first bright days after the return from Babylon, "The Lord is full of compassion and mercy, longsuffering, and of great goodness. He will not alway be chiding; neither keepeth He His anger for ever. He hath not dealt with us after our sins; nor rewarded us

[1] Rom. iii. 20.   [2] Ibid. vii. 7.   [3] Gal. iii. 24.

according to our wickedness. For look how high the heaven is in comparison of the earth; so great is His mercy also toward them that fear Him. Look how wide also the east is from the west; so far hath He set our sins from us."[1]

But then the question is, How is this mercy to be a something different from mere indulgence? How is it to be true to those stern requirements of goodness which comprise hatred of evil? How is the song of the Church, as the psalmist has it, to be a song, not of mercy only, but of judgment too?

And here we reach the third aspect of our Lord's coming into this human world. He comes not merely to teach us how to live—not merely to lighten up the dark secrets of our existence and our destiny—but to take away our sins. He is a revelation alike of love and of justice, and of the true term of the reconciliation of love with justice in the councils of God. The old moral law still holds,—"The wages of sin is death."[2] But the new revelation is, "God so loved the world, that He gave His only begotten Son, that whosoever believeth in Him should not perish."[3] "He is," says His apostle, "the propitiation for our sins: and not for ours only, but also for the sins of the whole world."[4] And if it be asked, How can He possibly stand in this relationship towards man? we answer briefly as follows:—

In the first place, He is qualified for it as the sinless One, the one sample in all history of an entirely spotless manhood. "He did no sin, neither was guile found in His mouth."[5] One stain would have impaired His capacity for pleading for mercy on a world of sinners. He is "the Lamb of God"—the emblem of innocence, as well as the sacrificial victim—"Which taketh away the sin of the

---

[1] Ps. ciii. 8–12. P. B. Version.     [2] Rom. vi. 23.
[3] John iii. 16.     [4] 1 John ii. 2.     [5] 1 Pet. ii. 22.

world."[1] He is "made sin for us, Who knew no sin; that we might be made the righteousness of God in Him."[2]

And, secondly, He is qualified for this work as the Representative of man. When He came among us, "He took not on Himself," says the apostle, "the nature of angels, but He took on Him the seed of Abraham."[3] It was not a distinct personal man, it was human nature, which the personal Son of God wrapped around Himself, that He might be, not one among many, but the natural Representative of all. In a former sermon I have had occasion to dwell on the completeness of our Lord's representation of the race, considered as a model of true human life. We must now consider it as the basis of His atoning death. This principle of representation is universally admitted. Parents act for their children; governments act for the people; the elected everywhere act for the electors in all departments of human activity and life. There are certain conditions which, so to speak, make representation natural. Some men are elected to represent—others represent by virtue of their position, of their birth, of their age—such and such a number of their fellow-men. Jesus, as the one perfect sample of human kind, represents us all. The acts and words of His life were representative. His active obedience is, if we will, ours. Purified, restored, believing humanity—restored and purified because believing—acts and speaks in Jesus, and before the eternal Purity all the new generations of men are "accepted in the Beloved."[4] And, conversely, Jesus pays our debt to the justice of God. He bears our sins, as our natural Representative, "in His own Body on the tree;"[5] and, as a consequence, "there is no condemnation to them which are in Christ Jesus;"[6] for, "as in Adam," man's natural representative, "all die, even

---

[1] John i. 29.  [2] 2 Cor. v. 21.  [3] Heb. ii. 16.
[4] Eph. i. 6.  [5] 1 Pet. ii. 24.  [6] Rom. viii. 1.

so, in Christ," man's spiritual Representative, "shall all" who have a part in Him " be made alive."[1]

And thirdly, He was qualified for this work by offering Himself, voluntarily, to suffer. The notion of injustice as attaching to the Atonement proceeds upon the idea—the grave misapprehension—that Jesus was dragged against His will to Calvary, just as the sacrificial beasts of the old covenant were driven to the altar. He was offered because it was His own will. " Sacrifice and offering Thou wouldest not, but a body hast Thou prepared me. Then said I, Lo, I come to do Thy will, O God ! "[2] As He said just before His Passion, " No man taketh My life from Me, but I lay it down of Myself. I have power to lay it down, and I have power to take it again."[3] Surely, my brethren, there is all the difference in the world between a victim whose life is wrung out of him, and a soldier who freely devotes himself to death. He has a right to do this, I presume, for adequate reasons. Life is the noblest sacrifice which a mortal being can offer in the cause of truth and of goodness. There is something to be said about injustice when a slave is bidden risk his life for a cause with which he has no sympathy. We have not yet learned to think of injustice in connection, say, with the death of Regulus, or with the death of Bishop Patteson.

And, lastly and above all, He was qualified for this tremendous work, as more—infinitely more—than man. We can conceive a mere man becoming, by a rare Grace, the perfect model of humanity. We can conceive a mere man so filled with light from heaven as to teach his fellows the wisdom and the secrets of this and the other life. But we cannot conceive a mere man putting away the sin of a guilty world. Here, clearly, is some new power, communicating to the acts and sufferings of the sinless Representative of

[1] 1 Cor. xv. 22.  [2] Heb. x. 5, 7.  [3] John x. 18.

our race, Who thus freely offers Himself, a virtue that literally knows no bounds. Every human act is limited in its value. Every human pang, however instinct with moral motive, finds at last a sphere where its power throbs away into silence. The value of the death of Christ, extending itself in His intention, we know, to the whole human family, to all ages of the world, depends upon the fact that He is the eternal Son of God. And hence, every act and suffering of His is weighted, so to speak, with infinity. It has in it a force which is literally immeasurable. On the Cross, as in nature, we see the prodigality of the Divine love; and it was in His love and in His pity that He redeemed us. It is not hyperbolical to say, with St. Augustine, that one drop of the Redeemer's Blood might have redeemed a thousand worlds. But God does nothing by halves, and in His love, as in His justice, far beyond our poor notions of bargain and equivalence, there are depths that are past finding out.

Here, then, my brethren, on the eve of the Christmas festival, we see the end, as it were, in the beginning; we see the flower in the germ; we see the crowning significance of the Advent for a world of sinners. If for any of us his guilt has been put away—if we have been robed in white garments, and by God's mercy have not defiled them—if we can look up to the Face of our Father in heaven with filial confidence—if angels see in us their future fellow-citizens, and life is made bright to us by hope even more than by resignation, and death already has lost its sting, and the grave its ancient victory,—this is because the coming of our Lord into this human world is meant for our redemption—redemption from sin, redemption from death, redemption from fear. "Being justified by faith, we have peace with God through our Lord Jesus Christ."[1]

[1] Rom. v. 1.

We reach forth the hand of faith to receive a gift which flows through appointed channels, and which we never could have earned. He, in return, washes us from our sins in His own Blood, and robes us in His perfect righteousness. How He completes His work we will consider more at length, if it please Him, another Sunday. To-day let us reflect that to no one of us can such a gift as this be a matter of indifference.

If any are still sitting in moral darkness, in the shadow of an eternal death which already darkens life by anticipation, let them know that the birth of Christ means the visit of the Daystar from on high; it means the birth of the Redeemer. They may yet find at the Redeemer's hands, if they will, the fulness of pardon and of peace.

And let those who have washed their robes and made them white in the Blood of the Lamb remember that a redeemed life should be a long, practical preparation for taking part sincerely in the eternal song to the Lamb enthroned and glorified:—"Thou wast slain, and hast redeemed us to God by Thy Blood out of every kindred, and tongue, and people, and nation."[1]

[1] Rev. v. 9.

# SERMON VI.

## CHRIST, THE GIVER OF GRACE.

### LUKE i. 78, 79.

*"The dayspring from on high hath visited us, to give light to them that sit in darkness and in the shadow of death, to guide our feet into the way of peace."*

CHRISTMAS has come, my brethren. The echoes of the great festival are almost dying away, but we are still very far from exhausting the tremendous subject on which we entered in the early days of Advent. It is a subject which belongs to Christmas, as well as to Advent. If Advent is expectation, Christmas is enjoyment. If Christmas celebrates the birth of the Son of God, Advent persistently looks forward to it. We are not out of order, then, in still proceeding to consider a result of Christ's coming for which the earlier stages of this enquiry will, I trust, have prepared us. As our Model, He has taught us men what is the true ideal of our life. As our Instructor, He has taught us the most important secrets of our destiny. As our Redeemer, He has brought us out of the power of sin and death, and has made peace for us with God. But here a question occurs of painful urgency. He has destroyed for us for ever the guilty past; but will He help us in the future? Is His gospel, after all, like a hospital which cures its patients of some deadly disorder and then turns them out into streets and alleys which are hotbeds of infection and disease? Or has He provided for the future as well as for the past? Has He, besides curing us, furnished us with antidotes against the inroads of the old enemy? Is He really made to us, as His apostle says He is, Sanctification, as well as Redemption? Deliverance from evil, no doubt, is always a blessing; but if there be no provision against the recurrence of evil, or if this deliverance places the enfranchised man in a position which he is quite unable to fill, such deliverance is, at least, a very imperfect blessing. We see an illustration of this in the case of the negro populations which were emancipated at the close of the civil war in America, some years ago. Few Englishmen, I apprehend, would dispute the wrongfulness of the slave system, or the duty of emancipating slaves wherever the thing can be done; but, looking to recent events at New Orleans and elsewhere, it is equally impossible to deny that to confer the full rights of free citizenship upon a population which has none of the moral and social qualities that enable it to make use of them is to confer on such a population, though it be a just, yet certainly a very equivocal, blessing. And the question before us to-day is whether, to adapt the illustration to so solemn a subject, whether our Lord's work for us is open to this sort of criticism—whether He has not merely ennobled us with the gift of freedom, but furnished us with the means of doing justice to its high demands.

Now, reverting to one of the great truths with which we set out, let us remember that a first necessity of our moral nature is to become better, and that our Lord's undertaking is distinctly to make men better, or, as His apostle puts it, " to purify unto Himself a peculiar people, zealous of good works."[1] If, indeed, this were not the

[1] Titus ii. 14.

case—if the gospel really contented itself with making men comfortable, instead of aiming at making them good—then there would be a plain divorce between religion, on the one side, and conscience and morality, on the other,—a divorce which, in the long run, could not but be equally fatal to both. Now here we encounter the serious fact which was touched upon last Sunday; I mean the distressing weakness of poor human nature, when fairly thrown on its own resources. The sense of guilt, indeed, the dread of punishment, these are removed by our Lord's propitiatory work upon the Cross; but the collapse of strength remains, whether against the inroads of evil, or for purposes of energetic good. To man in his natural state, virtue is a difficulty; vice is the order of the day. Vice means movement with the stream of fallen human nature. Virtue means movement against the stream. Virtue—the very derivation of the word proves as much—virtue means always a serious effort such as becomes a man,—an act of force whereby man detaches himself from the tyranny of passion, from the tyranny of custom, from the tyranny of opinion, from the tyranny of surrounding circumstance, and makes head against them. My brethren, I put it to you whether this sense of the word is not justified in our day by what we may observe at either extreme of English society. Those who have read the recently published memoirs of the late Mr. Charles Greville will feel that the traditions of high life, as it is called, are too often hostile to anything that in any sense deserves the name of virtue; and those who know anything of the tyranny of vicious opinion in the dark haunts of London know that real virtue in many a man or woman among the poorer classes is a splendid triumph of force asserting itself against obstacles, against pressure of the most formidable kind, and at great risk and cost to those who practise it. Joseph in the house of Potiphar, Daniel at the court of Babylon, John the Baptist face to face with Herod and Herodias—these are reproduced in our age, in our country, in scenes of life around ourselves; and sometimes they triumph as of old; often, too often, they fail to resist threats, to resist seduction, to resolve that, come what may, the true shall be obeyed, the good shall be done, evil shall be put away. This is not easy when man is left to himself; it is—God knows—exceedingly difficult. That which makes virtue so difficult is that man in his fallen estate wants the heart for it. Vice, it has been well said, grows like thistles in a neglected garden. That garden is human nature ruined by Adam, and, as yet, unblest by Christ. Vice is at home in a garden like that. Vice does not need encouragement like virtue. Vice gets on very well without rewards for proficiency. We are told sometimes by great authorities—I do not say by great religious authorities—we are told that children are born good. "Look at that charming baby," they say; "look at his bursts of affection, at his sweet smile, at his innocent, his irrepressible joy, at his loveliness, his beauty; and tell me if it is possible, for one moment, to listen to these gloomy theologians who affirm that he is born in sin." Well, my brethren, in answer to that, I will only say, do not christen him; do not instruct him; leave him to the guiding impulses of his sweet nature, and just see what he will come to. He will be, a few years hence, selfish, tyrannical, greedy, cruel—first the terror of his nurse and of his mother, then the aversion of his companions and of his school-fellows, until at last, when grown up, he reaches the level possibly of an elegantly dressed and well-spoken savage—a savage, if he has the chance, in cruelty, and worse than any respectable savage, almost certainly, in debauchery. Society knows this quite well, even when its leaders sneer at the Christian doctrine of human nature; and accordingly, society —that is, the nation—tries to drill this charming, this sinless infant into something like an outward respectability by what it calls unsectarian or secular education. The child is to be whipped at regular intervals; he is to be taught reading, writing, arithmetic, geography, history; he is to be taught that he has duties as well as rights,—taught that he has superiors as well as equals and inferiors,—taught that work has its claims as well as enjoyment,—taught that he must give as well as take; and then he is turned out into the world of men, better—I admit it with all my heart—better, beyond all doubt, for this youthful drilling, so far as it goes—better, certainly, in a social and in an external sense; but his ruling motives are prudence and fear, and fear and prudence, depend upon it, are not equal in the long run to the requirements of virtue. They are too negative; they are too cold; they are too much engaged in habitual calculations to storm the breach when the moment arrives for doing so. They are reflecting that evil is attended with practical inconvenience, when they ought to be fired with a chivalrous passion for the beauty of goodness, and prepared to risk anything for her sake. However, it is plain that the effort which society has made to drill the boy shows this, that the raw material of human nature is not really, in the deliberate and practical judgment of society, so altogether admirable as a modern statesman is said to have pronounced it, and that there is room, or rather necessity, for the Christian doctrine of an inward influence, an inward force, in order to make man what he was meant to be.

Here the question will arise whether such a force is not to be found in the great motives of goodness which faith in the redemptive work of our Lord Jesus Christ so abundantly supplies. What can move a man, it may well be said, if the astonishing love of our God shown in the Incarnation and death of His only begotten Son does not move him? How are we ever to be led to act, except from conviction? How is the will to be aroused and sustained, except through the intelligence? And does not the work of Christ our Lord, when really apprehended by the understanding, provide adequate materials for firing, for invigorating, the human will?

Now, my brethren, nothing could be farther from my purpose than to depreciate, by any word I could say in this pulpit, the majestic power of Christian motive. St. Paul has consecrated this power in that passage which is so full of his characteristic intensity. "The love of Christ," he says, "constraineth us; because we thus judge, that if One died for all, then were all dead: and that He died for all, that they which live should not henceforth live unto themselves, but unto Him which died for them, and rose again."[1] Each act in our Lord's redemptive work, each labour of His life, each separate humiliation which He willingly underwent, each pang in the sacred Passion, constitutes for the believing Christian a separate motive which operates through the play of his intelligence and his affections with decisive force upon his will. If He, the Sinless One, acted thus, what must I do? If He, the Sinless one, bore this, and this, and this for me, what should I do, what should I bear, for Him? And yet, allowing all this, a motive by itself is not equal to what is wanted, in order to keep the will up to the level of the Christian life. It tells—to begin with—with very unequal force upon minds of different orders. It upheaves the will with a sudden activity, and then it dies away. The image upon the mind's eye becomes fainter, or more

[1] 2 Cor. v. 14, 15.

familiar, or less able to create an active enthusiasm. The tendency of a natural force, all the world over, is to spend itself. Let almost any one compare the force which the example and words of a parent have upon his daily life one month after the parent's death, one year after it, five years after it, twenty years after it, forty years after it. At each of these periods the old love and grief and reverence can be rekindled, but the difference between the first and the last period is that, in the first, the motive is always present and powerful, and, in the last, it is present only at rare intervals, and greatly weakened in its capacity for exciting and controlling the moral nature.

What is wanted, then, is something that will supplement this weakness of motive acting in a natural way. Certainly no properly Christian motive can operate at all apart from the presence of some higher influence; for—to begin with—it must be apprehended by faith, and faith, we know, is impossible without a special assistance from on high. "No man can say that Jesus is the Lord, but by the Holy Ghost."[1] But not merely the apprehension of the motive, but the giving it ample and lasting sway over the soul, is the work of a new influence, which redresses the defects of nature by reinforcing it from above; and thus we are taught in the General Thanksgiving to pray that God would give us a due sense of all His mercies, that we may show forth His praise not with our lips only, but in our lives. It might be thought at first—many of us, perhaps, have thought—that natural gratitude would do as much as this. As a matter of fact, we find that a new motive power, a distinct invigorating influence, is absolutely required.

Now, revealed religion undertakes to supply this influence; and it names this influence—it calls it "Grace."

[1] 1 Cor. xii. 3.

What do we mean by Grace? In the first instance, no doubt, the word means favour; and, as applied to man, the word need mean nothing more. You and I may well entertain favour towards a fellow man, and do nothing whatever practical for him. We get as far as the kindly feeling, and there we stop. We may be arrested by want of means, or by poverty of determination. Our feeling is just strong enough to exist as feeling; it is not strong enough to act. This, which is so familiar to us and which is part of the finiteness and imperfection of our being, is impossible with the everlasting God. The perfect Being cannot halt thus between a moral premise and its practical conclusion. If God entertains favour towards a creature, then by the same act He blesses; and, therefore, the grace of God means not a passing mood of feeling in the divine Being, but always a substantial gift. The characteristic of this gift, as implied by the word Grace, is that it is unmerited by the receiver. And since all that He gives in nature as well as in redemption is undeserved, the term grace is not unfrequently applied to our creation, preservation, and all the blessings of this life; and also, more frequently still, to outward aids which enable men to live for God, such as the knowledge of His will, the teaching of His Son, the preaching of His gospel, down to our time the examples of good men. The Pelagians, a set of people who did their best some fourteen centuries ago to get rid of this part of the divine revelation, applied the term Grace simply and altogether to these external blessings, but they refused to it its proper sense of an inward force acting on the soul. Grace, in the true, complete sense of the word, is an unseen influence which touches, controls, remoulds, the man within,—which inspires him with good thoughts, with pure desires, with strong resolutions. When the Bible speaks of God's turning the hearts of men, changing them, opening them, strengthening them, this language means God's unseen action upon the soul; and this action is exerted partly upon the understanding, darkened as it is by the Fall, and partly upon the will, weakened as it is by the Fall. We pray for one of these forms of Grace in the Collect for to-day (St. John's Day) when we ask God to cast the bright beams of His light upon His Church; and we pray for the other in the Collect for the last Sunday after Trinity, when we entreat Him to "stir up the wills of His faithful people, that they, plenteously bringing forth the fruit of good works, may by Him be plenteously rewarded."

Living, as we do, in an age which is pre-eminently devoted to the philosophy of experience, we may be disposed to look askance at such a conception as that of Grace. We do not see Grace; we cannot catch it and examine it through a microscope. We only note that there are effects which pre-suppose some such cause, and then revelation steps in and tells us that that is the cause. But is not this very like what has happened in more cases than one in the history of the physical sciences? Century after century apples fell from the trees and stones dropped from the hands of men, always downwards towards the ground, never upwards into the air; and yet no one thought of asking why this should be. In the first decade of the seventeenth century Kepler arrived at a clear idea of the law of gravity. He saw that the earth attracts a stone more than a stone attracts the earth; he saw that bodies move towards each other in the proportion of their masses. At the close of that century Newton published his "Principia," or the principle that all bodies attract each other with forces directly as their masses, and inversely as the squares of their distances. He was prepared to account for all the movements of the celestial bodies. The magnificent force or law of attraction, as we call it, was thus revealed to the human intelligence by this prince of science; but the force itself—the force *itself*—was just as invisible then as it had been in ages when its existence was unsuspected,—invisible in itself, visible through its effects. And in like manner our earliest fathers gazed upon the lightning, and listened to the thunder, with feelings of awe and apprehension. The subtle force which we know as electricity was unknown to, and unimagined by, them. We have been taught to take it captive, to make it a public—almost a domestic—servant, to bid it wait behind the desk for our orders in almost every post-office in the country, and then carry our thought with the speed of lightning, if we will, across the Atlantic. And yet we see the thing itself just as little as did the rudest of our forefathers. It does our work, but it remains inaccessible to our observation. Its effects—they tell us that it is there; but in vain do we attempt to bring it forth into the light of day, into the sphere which is open to the senses. And thus we are reminded of that force in the spiritual world which we shall presently consider.

First of all, men noted the effects of Grace; then they were informed of its reality, its source, its power. But in itself, and to the last, Grace remains invisible,—invisible like the electric fluid, or like the force of attraction; yet, assuredly, in the world of spirits at least as real, at least as energetic, a force as they.

Here, then, we see a fourth blessing dependent on the coming of our Lord Jesus Christ into this our human world. He reveals to us the nature, and He secures to us the gift, of supernatural Grace. That solemn blessing with which St. Paul closes his Second Epistle to the Corinthians, and which is repeated day by day at the close of our Morning and Evening Prayer, is no empty rhetorical courtesy. It describes an actual gift from Heaven: "The Grace of our Lord Jesus Christ be with you all." [1] Remark, it is not here, as we might have expected, the Grace of the Holy Spirit; it is the "*communion*" or "*fellowship*" of the Holy Spirit; it is the "Grace of *our Lord Jesus Christ.*" St. John, indeed, says expressly that "Grace and truth"—that is, the full gift of Grace and the complete revelation of truth—"came by Jesus Christ;" [2] and in the Christmas Collect, which we have been using to-day, the Church connects this gift with Christ's nativity. But Grace existed before His day. It was given here and there in a measure under the old covenant. The psalms of David are full of it. But Jesus Christ unveiled it in its completeness; He conferred it in its power. To Him we owe the full knowledge and use of this spiritual force which our fallen nature in its weakness so greatly needs, whether for right action or for intrepid resistance to evil. And from Him and His envoys we know Who is the immediate Administrator of this force, and what the force is meant pre-eminently to effect, and what are our own most assured points of contact with it. The immediate Minister of Grace is revealed as the holy and eternal Spirit. Whether as breathing on the individual intelligence or the individual will, or as filling, governing, and sanctifying the collective Church, or as transfiguring the Sacraments from dead forms into life-giving realities, the Holy Spirit is the Minister of Grace. All that is really good in the Christian or in the Christian Church, all that asserts truth, all that tends to unity, all that fosters charity, comes by Him. The regenerate soul and the whole spiritual society are alike His temple. The

[1] Rom. xvi. 24. [2] John i. 17.

prophecy of Joel is accomplished: God hath, in purpose, poured out His Spirit upon all flesh. The stream is widening year by year to embrace the nations. The awful, the blessed ministration of the Grace of God descended on the Day of Pentecost.

But then observe this: the gift of Grace is not the less originally due to our Lord Jesus Christ. The work of the Holy Spirit is sometimes most mistakenly represented as entirely separate from the work of Christ—so entirely separate that one dispensation is said to have ended at the Ascension, and another to have begun on Whitsunday. Now this misapprehension is due to a forgetfulness of our Lord's real relation to the coming of the Spirit. As from all eternity the Holy Spirit is revealed as proceeding from the Son as well as from the Father, so in time the Spirit is sent not merely by the Father, but by the Son. Until Christ had ascended, He tells us, the Spirit could not be sent. "If I go no not away, the Comforter will not come unto you; but if I depart, I will send Him unto you."[1] And just before departing, He bade His disciples tarry in the city of Jerusalem until they were "endued with power from on high."[2] It came—we know it came to those twelve poor unlettered men—the power of spiritual illumination, the power of enkindled affection, above all, the power of invincible will. But although the Spirit was the Minister, the Giver of the gift was Christ; and the gift was the new force of Grace in its unstinted fulness.

And secondly, we are taught how it is that Grace acts on us—what is the secret of its enabling power. Never acting apart from Christ, the Spirit unites us to, makes us partake in, His divine Humanity—in the glorified Human Nature of the ascended Son of God. This is why

[1] John xvi. 7.   [2] Luke xxiv. 49.

the Spirit is so constantly called in the New Testament the Spirit of Grace. His work is to unite us to Christ, to robe us in our Lord's perfect Nature—that new Nature whereby the Second Adam would repair, and more than repair, what the first had lost. The eternal Spirit does not act apart. He sets up in the Church and in the heart an inward Presence, but that Presence is the Presence not of Himself only, but of the Son of Man. How much does St. Paul make throughout his epistles of that one expression which covers so majestic a truth. The being *in* Christ, while securing for us inherence in the holy Body, is the Spirit's masterpiece. By one Spirit we are all baptised into that one Body. Again and again we are told in the apostolic writings that union with Christ's Manhood is the great blessing of the Christian life: that Christ lives, speaks, acts, in those who are really one with Him: that His life is incorporate with theirs, and theirs with His: that this is the work of His Spirit. So St. Paul of himself—" I live, yet not I, but Christ liveth in me." [1] So to the Colossians—" Christ is in you, the hope of glory." [2] So to the Ephesians, " We are members of His Body, of His Flesh, and of His Bones." [3] So to the Corinthians, " Know ye not that your bodies are the members of Christ ?" [4] When the Emperor Trajan visited Antioch, he summoned before him Ignatius, a disciple of the apostles, bishop of the infant church in that city. Ignatius went among Pagans, as among Christians, by the name of Theophorus, or " bearer of God," and this name, we are told, added to the hatred and suspicion with which he was regarded by the surrounding heathen. To the emperor's question whether he was a man who had led others to destruction and was inhabited by an evil spirit, Ignatius replied in the negative. To the emperor's

[1] Gal. ii. 20.   [2] Col. i. 27.   [3] Eph. v. 30.   [4] 1 Cor. vi. 15.

second question, why men called him Theophorus, he answered that it was because he bore within him the Christ, the Lord. To a third question, in which the emperor's surprise predominated, whether he really had within him the Man Who, years before, had been crucified under Pontius Pilate, Ignatius simply said, "Thou sayest it; it is written, 'I will dwell in them and walk in them.'" It was the sense of this inward Presence of the Lord Jesus, bestowed by His Spirit, which gave Ignatius, a feeble old man as it seemed to the eye of sense, the more than natural force that was required to endure all that followed.

And thirdly, we Christians are taught that the certificated points of contact (so to call them) with this stream of Grace administered by the Spirit, and consisting in union with the Manhood of our Lord, are the Christian Sacraments. No doubt the Holy Spirit acts elsewhere. He breathes in prayer; He illuminates Scripture; He bears in upon the soul thoughts and resolves, in the closet and by the wayside, which lead the soul up to God; and He acts upon us mysteriously in a hundred ways which we never suspect. "The wind bloweth where it listeth, and thou hearest the sound thereof, but canst not tell whence it cometh, and whither it goeth: so is every one that is born of the Spirit."[1] But His masterwork of uniting us poor fallen men to the one sinless Man, Who is one with God, is revealed as being effected in a special manner through the Christian Sacraments. And this is the real reason for that position of commanding importance which they occupy in the faith and life of serious Christians. "They are," says Bishop Jeremy Taylor, in his "Worthy Communicant"—mark the expression, my brethren, for it sets forth vividly a pregnant truth—"they are an ex-

[1] John iii. 8.

tension of the Incarnation."[1] They carry forward its power into Christian history; they pour a full tide of the very inmost life of Christ the Lord into the souls and bodies of Christians. "As many as have been baptised into Christ, have put on Christ."[2] "Except a man be born of water and of the Spirit, he cannot enter into the kingdom of God."[3] "Whoso eateth and drinketh unworthily, eateth and drinketh condemnation, not discerning the Lord's Body."[4] "The Bread which we break, is it not the communion of the Body of Christ? The Cup of blessing which we bless, is it not the communion of the Blood of Christ?"[5] "Except ye eat the Flesh of the Son of man, ye have no life in you."[6] Tricks, of course, may be played with this sacred language, so as to make it mean little or nothing, just as tricks are played with those great passages which teach the propitiatory virtue of our Lord's atoning death; and there are, of course, a great many well-intentioned and devout Christians who wish, with all their hearts, to serve our Lord, but are unable to understand fully this precious side of His revelation of His will. They think that they do Him a particular sort of honour by depreciating the value of His sacramental gifts. "Because," they say, "if we think too highly of the gifts, the chances are that we shall forget the Giver." It is, of course, possible to think more of the gift than of the Giver—of the natural gift of life, for instance, or health, or fortune, or means of usefulness, or happy years spent in a happy home, than of that good God to Whom we owe all these blessings. Many of us do this; but if we do, it is not rational to say, "Because I wish to think only of the Giver, I mean to insist on the

---

[1] Worthy Communicant, Chap. I. Sect. II. p. 23, Eden's Edit. 1854.
[2] Gal. iii. 27.   [4] 1 Cor. xi. 29.   [6] John vi. 53.
[3] John iii. 5.   [5] Ibid. x. 16.

worthlessness of His gift." It surely would be far better to say, " Because I value the gift so highly, I ought to be proportionately grateful to—I ought to be continually thinking of—the divine Giver." Our Lord, depend upon it, is not really honoured by our maintaining that Baptism is only a ceremony which gives a child a name and makes it a member of a religious society. He is not really honoured by our saying that the Holy Communion is only a means for recalling to the imagination of Christ's followers the memory of His death. If Baptism only gives a child a name, the name might just as well be given with much less ceremony; and if the Holy Communion only serves as a reminder of a past event in the life of an absent Christ, then a chapter in the Gospels, or a well executed engraving of the Crucifixion, might do much better than partaking of bread and wine in public. That the Sacraments should exist at all under such a system as the Gospel is, itself, a revelation of their real character. Unless they are, as the Prayer Book calls them, means of Grace, they have no real maintainable position whatever in the Christian system. For mark you, my brethren, the Gospel differs from the Law as a substance differs from a shadow, and Sacraments which are symbols and nothing but symbols are in no way better than the legal ordinances which preceded them, and therefore have no place in a system like that of the Gospel of Christ, where all is real. Those who see nothing in them beyond the symbolical would be logically right in dispensing with them altogether. They happily stop short of this through reverence to our Lord's express command. Yet His command to baptise all nations and to do what He did in the supper room to the end of time, of itself implies that the Sacraments are solemn realities—acts on His part towards us, and not mere instruments for raising our thoughts towards Him. And thus Hooker says, in his thoughtful way, that, "Christ and His Holy Spirit with all their blessed effects, though entering into the soul of man we are not able to apprehend or express how, do nothwithstanding give notice of the times when they use to make their access, because it pleaseth Almighty God to communicate by sensible means those blessings which are incomprehensible."[1]

It will be objected, perhaps, "Is there no danger of our treating them as charms which will operate anyhow? Is there no risk of a man thinking that it does not matter much what he is, or how he lives, if he only complies with certain sacramental prescriptions? Have we not lately heard of a materialism of the Altar which is said to be just as bad as the materialism of the lecture room? And is there not reason to fear that the natural tendency of men to rest in the external and visible, rather than in the spiritual and the unseen, may receive dangerous support and encouragement?" My brethren, let it be at once admitted that Sacraments are no more exempt than any other of God's gifts from abuse through the perverseness and wrong-headedness of men. No book has been so abused for directly mischievous and immoral purposes as the Bible; but that does not make the Bible forfeit its character of being the best of all books. No truth has been more sedulously pressed in the interests of an immoral antinomianism than the truth of Christ's atoning death; and yet that does not make it less certainly the truth which, as a consummate revelation of the tenderness of the Heart of God, has a pre-eminent power to chasten and to purify the heart of man. Granting, and we must grant it, that Sacraments have been abused to superstitions, to formal pur-

[1] Laws of Eccles. Pol. Bk. V. Ch. lvii. 4, vol. 2, p. 257. Keble's Edit. 1865.

poses—granting this, that they have been abused by those who, in using them, forget either their character, or their purpose, or their Giver—they are not on that account the less truly the chiefest blessings of the gospel of Christ. They are, indeed, moral and not physical causes. They do not always produce the same effect, as a fire always burns or gives light; and the reason is because they act upon a being who has the power of resisting their action, and who must welcome it by proper dispositions if it is to do him good. This, of course, cannot apply to the case of baptised infants, where the soul is as yet passive, and where Christ's Grace is correspondingly triumphant. It does apply to all Sacraments received by adults. More than this, Grace, once given, whether in Baptism or elsewhere, may most assuredly be lost by unfaithfulness. It is so far from being a licence to do wrong, that in doing wrong voluntarily a man immediately forfeits it. It is easy to misuse, it is less easy to over-estimate, these majestic acts of the invisible Christ, whereby, through the agency of His Spirit, He knits His redeemed to that Human Nature of His Which, to quote the words of Jackson, "by the inhabitation of Deity is made to us an inexhaustible Fountain of life."[1] This is the secret of that deepest of all joys which many a Christian soul knows here on earth, when kneeling before the Altar in the early morning, when as yet the world has claimed nothing of our renewed powers and we can give our freshest and our best to God, we know what it is to eat the Flesh of the Son of Man, and to drink His Blood,—" that our sinful bodies are made clean by His Body, and our souls washed through His most precious Blood."

And this communion with our Lord is the culminating blessing which He brought when He visited us from on

[1] Dr. Thos. Jackson, Works, Oxford Edit., vol. ix., p. 598.

high. His example, His instructions, His pardon, His reconciliation, lead on to this, which by uniting us with Him, the perfect moral Being, restores our fallen nature to more than its original glory and crowns His redemptive work. "We can do all things through Christ Which strengtheneth us;"[1] "We live, yet not we, but Christ liveth in us."[2] He inhabits, He all but supersedes, the life of His devoted servants, thinking in them, speaking by them, acting through them, so that their communion with Him is so complete as to make them outward organs of His invisible Life. These triumphs of His Grace differ in degree throughout the spiritual world to the end of time. "One star differeth from another star in glory."[3] But in all there is this: there is the presence of a new Force, of the Grace of communion with Christ's Humanity; and in varying degrees Christians are "strong in the Lord, and in the power of his might."[4]

Standing as we do to-day, this last Sunday in the year, close to one of those milestones which are placed along the road of life (there are not many of them to be passed by those of us who travel farthest)—those milestones which mark the lapse of our brief probation—we may well try to lay to heart the meaning of our Lord's coming to each one of ourselves. That heart-rending scene on the railway embankment at Shipton on Christmas eve, the details of which during the last three days have filled the papers and haunted the memory, shows us how thin may be the veil which separates any one of us, even during his most ordinary occupations, from the awful invisible world. It has been my effort to strengthen your conviction that one Being, and one only, can help us through the darkness, through the shadow of death—can guide our feet into the way of peace. Let each one ask himself, "Is He my

---

[1] Phil. iv. 13.   [2] Gal. ii. 20.   [3] 1 Cor. xv. 41.   [4] Eph. vi. 10.

Model, or do I place other ideals of life high above Him? Is He my Instructor, or do I prefer the language of human philosophies, of human teachers—it may be of human doubters? Is His atoning death my hope of acceptance, or am I imagining that I shall be fitted for the presence-chamber of the Holiest by my own natural excellence? Finally, is union with Him—closer and closer union through His Spirit and His sacramental Gifts—the practical object of my redeemed life? Or am I saying to myself that if my sins are pardoned His work is done, and that I need no longer be a pensioner upon His bounty?" Compared with these enquiries the questions which too often occupy us, immortal beings as we are, trembling on the brink of an existence at once irretrievably fixed and absolutely endless, are surely unimportant enough. May He, our divine Friend and Patron, Who is always tender, Who is always strong, deign in His mercy to lighten our darkness and so to defend us from the perils and dangers of this brief night, that His example, His instructions, His redemption, His gift of a new nature, may be the theme of our joy and praise to all eternity. To Him, with the Father, and the Holy Spirit, be ascribed all honour, power, might, majesty, and dominion, henceforth and for ever.

# SERMON VII.

## THE VIRGIN'S SON.

### MATTHEW i. 22, 23.

*"Now all this was done, that it may be fulfilled which was spoken of the Lord by the prophet, saying, Behold, a Virgin shall be with child, and shall bring forth a Son, and they shall call His name Emmanuel, which being interpreted is, God with us."*

MANY readers of the Bible must have been struck by the reason which St. Matthew here gives for the occurrences connected with the birth of Jesus Christ,—" All this was done, that it might be fulfilled which was spoken of the Lord by the prophet." We are perhaps tempted to whisper to ourselves that the event predicted is surely more important than the prediction, and that it would have seemed more natural to say that the prophecy existed for the sake of the event than the event for the sake of the prophecy, —more natural to say that Isaiah's utterance was meant to prepare the world for Jesus Christ than that the birth of Jesus Christ was designed to justify Isaiah by fulfilling his words. But, in truth, both the prophecy and its fulfilment were from God, and the independent and higher importance of the event does not really interfere with its being a certificate of the prophet's accuracy. There were other reasons, no doubt, for the birth of Jesus Christ of a Virgin Mother. But one reason for it was this, that it was already foretold, and on Divine authority. And it fell in with St. Matthew's formal plan throughout his gospel to insist upon this particular reason; for he here is writing for churches made up almost, if not quite, of converts from Judaism, and he is concerned at almost every step of his narrative to show that the life of Jesus in all its particulars corresponded to what the Jewish prophecy, as understood by the Jews themselves, had said about the coming Messiah. And so he begins at the beginning—with the birth of Christ; and he says that Jesus was born just as Isaiah had said that the Christ would be born, and, among other reasons, because Isaiah had said so. Those first Jewish Christians might feel wonder, even scandal, when first they heard of the embarrassment of St. Joseph, and of the angelic assurances, but they had only to open the roll of prophecy to find that the history had been accurately anticipated. "All this was done that it might be fulfilled which was spoken of the Lord by the prophet, saying, Behold a Virgin shall be with child, and shall bring forth a Son, and they shall call His name Emmanuel, which, being interpreted, is, God with us." In St. Matthew's eyes, then, Isaiah is almost as much the historian as he is the prophet of the Lord's nativity. But is it clear that when Isaiah uttered the words that are quoted, he meant to predict such an event as Matthew records? It has been suggested that this was not really Isaiah's meaning—that Isaiah had in view some other event at once nearer to his own times, and more ordinary and commonplace in its character than the birth of the Redeemer; and that St. Matthew accommodates the prophet's language, by a kind of gentle pressure, to the necessities of the supernatural which he is himself narrating. And the main reason which is urged for this view of Isaiah's meaning is that, if we look to the circumstances under which his prophecy was uttered, it is difficult to think that so distant an event as the birth of the Messiah would have at all served his purpose in giving a sign to Ahaz.

What, then, were the circumstances which led Isaiah to proclaim, "Behold, a Virgin shall conceive and bear a Son, and shall call His name Emmanuel."

Ahaz, the King of Judah, was besieged in his capital by the allied forces of Israel and Syria, under their kings, Pekah and Rezin. These kings were really leagued against the rising empire of Assyria, but they thought that they would best consolidate their own power in Western Palestine by deposing the reigning family of David from the throne of Jerusalem, and setting up a vassal monarch (the son of Tabeal, he is called,) on whose services they could reckon in the approaching struggle with Assyria. Isaiah was sent to encourage Ahaz and his son to make a stout resistance, and to assure them that, notwithstanding the project of the allied kings, God would be faithful to His covenant with the house of David. These associated kings, Isaiah said, need occasion Ahaz no sort of anxiety. They were like brands that were nearly burnt out. There was no divine force in Syria, there was no political future for Israel. Ahaz had only to trust God, and all would be well. Ahaz was silent—silent because he was suspicious and distrustful; and then Isaiah bade him ask for some token which might assure him of God's presence with and goodwill towards him. "Ask thee a sign of the Lord thy God; ask it either in the depth, or in the height above."[1] Had Ahaz then asked for a token of God's goodwill towards himself personally, or his immediate descendants, it would, no doubt, have been granted; but Ahaz was bent on an irreligious policy of his own. He thought that, by the aid of Syria, he would be able to do without God,

[1] Isai. vii. 11.

without the religion of his ancestors. He looked at God and His prophets as, in some sense, his personal enemies, who thwarted his plans; and he did not wish to commit himself, by asking for a sign, to a creed and to a system with which he hoped he had parted for ever. And yet Ahaz, standing before the prophet, could not refuse to say anything. He must accept or decline the invitation to ask for a sign. He declined to ask; and, as irreligious people often do in like circumstances, he pleaded a religious scruple as the reason for his refusal. The old law had warned Israel against tempting God by asking for new evidences or signs of sufficiently-attested truth; and Ahaz, who had freely resorted to the forbidden arts of necromancy, gravely pleads this entirely insincere reason to account for his resolve, "I will not ask, neither will I tempt the Lord."[1] And then it was that Isaiah spoke, not without righteous anger, to Ahaz and his son: "Hear ye now, O house of David. Is it a small thing for you to weary men, but will ye weary my God also? Therefore, the Lord Himself shall give you a sign."[2] A sign would be given; but Ahaz could now no longer determine its drift and character. A sign would be given which would show how God would be true to His promises to David; but it would not reassure the degenerate descendants of David as to their dynastic interests. The earthly throne of David might perish utterly; but the promise made to David of an unfailing empire would still be safe, though it would be fulfilled in a distant age, and by an unthought of agency. And just as Moses was assured that God had sent him by the sign of a future event—the complete deliverance from Egypt, which, at the time, must have seemed strictly impossible—so religious Jews of Isaiah's day (and it was for them that Isaiah was really now speaking)

---

[1] Isai. vii. 12.     [2] Ibid. vii. 13, 14.

were to be assured of the safety of the great religious interests entrusted to the house of David by a sign or predicted wonder without any parallel in history, but designed to convince them that God might punish the rebellious kings of Judah, and yet work out the promised salvation of Israel and the human race. "Behold," Isaiah cries, as he gazes across and into the centuries—as he gazes at a picture which passes as if present before his soul—"Behold *the* Virgin"—the language shows that he is speaking of one in particular—"Behold *the* Virgin is with child, and beareth a Son, and shall call His name Emmanuel."

It was, then, no part of Isaiah's plan to give a sign which should assure Ahaz of present deliverance. He had done that before in plain language; and, when he utters the prophecy quoted by St. Matthew, he has altogether other and higher objects before him, the nature of which must be determined, not by the real or supposed state of mind of Ahaz, but by the natural force of the prophet's words.

Here, then, let us consider the importance of the event to which Isaiah thus looks forward, and which the evangelist describes as fulfilled.

This importance is seen, first of all, in the strictly preternatural character of the occurrence itself. "Behold, a Virgin shall conceive and bear a Son." The foil to this prediction is the universal law by which our race is transmitted from age to age—that a child must have two human parents. St. Matthew is explicit in his account of the events which preceded our Lord's birth; but it has been contended that the word which Isaiah uses, and which is translated "virgin," may mean a young but married woman. If this were the meaning, it is difficult to see why there should be any allusion to the child's mother at all, since the predicted child would have been born like all other children, and would not be a sign in the sense of the prophet. But the original word for "virgin" is used of Rebecca before her marriage with Isaac, and of Miriam the maiden sister of the infant Moses; and, in the four other places in which it is found in the Old Testament, there is no reasonable ground for thinking that any but unmarried women are meant. I do not forget the names of scholars who, moved, as it would seem, by extraneous considerations, have disputed the accuracy of our present translation; but one fact in connection with it is instructive, and may throw a great deal of light upon the temper of recent criticism. When the first translation of the Hebrew Bible into Greek was made, some two centuries at the least before our Lord, in Alexandria, and nothing was supposed to be at stake, the Jewish translators rendered this word of Isaiah by "virgin;" but when, in the second century of our era, Aquila, a Jewish proselyte of Sinope, having his eye fixed upon the Christian appeal to Jewish prophecy, undertook a new translation of the Hebrew Scriptures into Greek, he rendered it by "a young woman." If the point could be decided by the natural force of language, without deference to the claims of Christianity, or without an eye to the possibility of the supernatural, then there would not be much room for doubt upon the subject.

The birth of Jesus Christ is not unfrequently discussed in our day as the birth of a great man, but without reference to the virginity of His Mother. Isaiah's prediction and St. Matthew's narrative are passed over as if they were not of much importance to an estimate of the event. My brethren, it is necessary to say plainly that the account in the Gospel is either true or false. If it is false, it ought to be repudiated by every honest man as a baseless superstition. If, as we Christians believe, it is true, then it is a very momentous truth. Then it implies a great deal more than is to be expressed by saying that the Son of the Virgin was a great or extraordinary man. It carries us beyond the limits of nature, of ordinary experience, into the preternatural. Doubtless, here and there in the heathen world, there were legends of sages and of poets who were born of virgins; but these legends are related to the history of our Saviour's birth as are false miracles to the true. As the counterfeit miracle implies the real miracle of which it is the counterfeit, so the idea of a virgin birth here and there discernible in Paganism points to a deep instinct of the human race, and to the high possibility that the absolute religion would satisfy it. Pagans though they were, men felt the oppression and degradation of their hereditary nature. They longed for some break in the tyrannical tradition of flesh and blood; they longed for the appearance of some being who should still belong to them, yet in a manner so exceptional as to be able to inaugurate a new era in the life of humanity. Revelation, surely, is not less trustworthy because it recognises an instinct which only needs men to do it justice and which is in accordance with moral truth; for here we touch upon a primary reason for our Lord's preternatural birth. If He was to raise us from our degradation, He must Himself be sinless—a sinless Example, a sinless Sacrifice. Our Lord Himself and His apostles abundantly insist upon this His sinlessness; but how was it to be secured if He was to become incorporate with a race steeped in a mighty tradition of evil? When, by his transgression, our first parent forfeited the robe of Grace with which God had clothed him in Paradise, he passed on to his descendants a nature fatally impoverished, and thereby biassed in a wrong direction, so that thenceforth throughout all generations evil was inherent in human nature; evil descended like a torrent, like a bad name, like a disease, from generation to generation;

and though here and there, as with Jeremiah or the Baptist, there was a special kind of sanctification before birth, yet the millions of mankind had ever to say with David, "Behold I was shapen in wickedness, and in sin hath my mother conceived me."[1] How, then, was this fatal entail to be cut off decisively—so cut off that all should understand it? The birth of a Virgin was the answer to that question. Her Son was still human, but in Him humanity had inherited none of that bad legacy which came down across the ages from the Fall; and, surely, such a High Priest became us sinners, Himself "holy, harmless, undefiled, separate from sinners."[2]

This indeed is not, as you will have felt, the whole account of the matter. The birth of Jesus Christ, as we Christians believe, marked the entrance into the sphere of sense and time of One Who had already existed from eternity. At His birth, St. Paul says, He was manifested in the flesh;[3] but whether He is in this passage called God, or not, according to the true reading, it is thus in any case implied that He existed before His manifestation. The Father sent forth His Son made of a woman, as St. Paul tells us in the epistle for to-day, but the Son existed before He was sent forth. The expression is evidently chosen to imply this; and this previous existence did not date from the creation, for "In the beginning was the Word, and the Word was with God, and the Word was God."[4] How was the entrance of such a Being into this our world so to be marked as to show that He did not originally owe existence to a human parent? We could not have dared to answer such a question as this beforehand. We can see how it is answered in our Lord's virgin birth. Was it not natural that nature should thus suspend her laws to welcome the approach, the blessing of her Maker.

[1] Ps. li. 5 : P. B. Version.   [2] Heb. vii. 26.   [3] 1 Tim. iii. 16.   [4] John i. 1.

The importance of our Lord's birth of a virgin Mother is further seen in the results of His appearance. At this distance of time we can plainly see that no other birth since the beginnings of history has involved such important consequences to the human race. We Christians have had nearly nineteen centuries in which to form comparisons and to arrive at conclusions. We have had time to take the measure of the great statesmen, soldiers, poets, teachers, who have been foremost among mankind. Who of them all has left behind him a work which can compare with that achieved by Jesus Christ? As the first Napoleon once asked, what was the empire of Alexander, or of Cæsar, or his own, at its best, when compared to that of Jesus Christ? Theirs were transient; Christ's is lasting. Theirs had soon reached a limit; Christ's is ever extending. Theirs were based on force; Christ's is based on convictions. Who, again, of the great men of letters has swayed the world like Jesus Christ? Doubtless, these men too have an empire. Who can dispute the influence at this hour of Plato, of Shakespeare, of Newton? But it is an influence which differs in kind from that of Jesus Christ. It interests the intellect, while He enchains the will. Nay, compare Him with the great teachers of false religions—with Sakya-Muni who preceded, or with Mahomet who followed him, in human history. I do not forget the statistics of Buddhism, or the undeniable activities of Islam, in certain portions of the Eastern world; but these religions—this is the broad fact before us—these religions are the religions of races with no real future. Christianity is still the creed of the nations which, year by year, are more and more controlling the destinies of the human race. And if it be urged that large portions of these very nations, Christian by profession, are now abjuring Christianity, it may be replied that such apostasy, partial it may be admitted now, is in the long run impossible. Man cannot dispense with religion; and when man has once come into contact with the highest type of religion, he has thereby exhausted the religious capacities of his nature. The absolute religion makes any after it impossible for free and sincere minds. The present efforts to replace Christianity by an imaginary religion of the future, distilled out of all the positive religions of the world, is doomed to a failure only less complete than the attempt to replace it by mere negations. There are not wanting signs of a rebound towards the faith. There are no signs whatever of a rising religious force capable of superseding it. Yes, all that is best, all that is most full of hope, in the civilised world dates from the birthday of Jesus Christ. Doubtless, we owe some good and precious things which rank high in the order of nature to the old pagan days. We owe philosophy to Greece. We owe law and well-ordered life to Rome. But the idea of progress which, however it may have been misapplied, is perhaps the most fertile and energetic in modern public life—this is the creation of the Christian Creed. It springs from those high hopes of the future, whether of individuals or of the race, which Christ has taught His disciples to entertain as a matter of loyalty to Himself. And the institutions which make life tolerable to the suffering classes, that is to say, to the great majority of human beings—such as hospitals—these date, one and all of them, from the appearance of Jesus Christ, and from the promulgation of those principles which He proclaimed to man with sovereign authority.

To take one point among many, the position of woman in Christian society is directly traceable not only or chiefly to our Lord's teaching, but to the circumstances of His birth. Before He came, woman, even in Israel, was little better than the slave of man. In the heathen world, as in

Eastern countries now, she was a slave to all intents and purposes. Here and there a woman of great force of character joined to hereditary advantages might emerge from this chronic oppression—might become a Deborah, or a Semiramis, or a Boadicea, or a Cleopatra, or a Zenobia—might control the world by controlling its rulers. But the lot of the great majority was a suffering and a degraded one. But when Christ took upon Him to deliver man, He did not abhor the Virgin's womb. In the greatest event in the whole course of human history the stronger sex had no part whatever. The incarnate Son was conceived of the Holy Ghost and was born of the Virgin Mary; and therefore, in and with Mary, woman rose to a position of consideration unknown before, in which nothing is forfeited that belongs to the true modesty and grace of her nature—by which a larger share of influence in shaping the destinies of the Christian races was secured to her in perpetuity. It was the Incarnation which created chivalry, and those better features which sweeten our modern life and which are due to chivalry; and they, as it seems to me, are no true friends to the real influence and to the real usefulness of woman who would substitute for the Christian idea of womanhood another in which woman is to compete with man in all the activities of his public life, and in the end to be relegated most assuredly to some such social fate as would inevitably follow upon an unsuccessful rivalry.

But these outward and visible results of the birth of Christ were far from being the most important. It is conceivable that such results as these might have been due to a religious genius of commanding influence, or to a man invested with miraculous powers, but still strictly, solely, a man. The birth of Jesus Christ meant more, much more, than this. It was the entrance of the Word made

Flesh into the scene of sense and time. It was the manifestation of the incarnate Son. Before the Incarnation there was a great gulf fixed between God and man. Man could think about God; he could pray to God; he could practise a certain measure of obedience to God's will; but, in his best moments, man was conscious of his utter separateness from God as the perfect moral Being. He was conscious of sin, and this consciousness meant nothing less than separation from the All-holy. The Incarnation of Jesus Christ was a bridge across the chasm which thus had parted earth and heaven. On the one hand, and from everlasting, Jesus Christ was of one substance with the Father, very and eternal God. On the other, he was made very Man, of the substance of the Virgin Mary, His Mother. As the collect says, He took man's nature upon Him. When He had already existed from eternity, He folded around Him, He made His own, a created Form, a human Body and a human Soul, to be for ever united to His eternal Godhead. Through this, His human Nature, He acts on God's behalf upon mankind. Through this, His human Nature, He pleads for man before the majesty of God; and thus there is "one Mediator between God and man, the Man Christ Jesus."[1] It is as Man that He mediates between the Creator and the creature, between sinners and the All-holy. But His Godhead secures to His mediation its commanding power. If He were not human, we at this moment should be unrepresented in Heaven, where He ever liveth to make intercession for us. If He were not divine, it would be impossible to say why His death upon the Cross should have infinite merit, or why the Body of Christ, which was given for us, should now in the Holy Sacrament preserve our bodies and our souls unto everlasting life. At one and the same moment

---

[1] 1 Tim. ii. 5.

He is, as Mediator, in the bosom of the Godhead and in the closest contact with the souls of His redeemed; and this is a result of His entrance in a created Form into our human world as the everlasting Son, yet, withal, as the Child of Mary. That this is the deepest meaning of Christmas and of the birth of Christ is implied in the name assigned in prophecy to the Virgin's Son—the sublime, the glorious name, Emmanuel. From the day of the nativity, God was seen to be with men not simply, as heretofore, as the Omnipresent, but under new and more intimate conditions. From the day of the nativity there was a change in the relations between earth and Heaven. To be one with Christ was to be one with God; and this union with God through Christ is the secret and basis of the new kingdom of souls which Christ has founded, and in which He reigns. Who shall describe the wealth of spiritual and moral power which dates from the appearance of the incarnate Son in this our human world as our Wisdom and Righteousness and Sanctification and Redemption? Here and there we see, as by glimpses through the clouds, some streaks of the glory of this, the invisible kingdom of souls; but only most assuredly in another life shall we understand at all approximately what it has meant—what it means—for millions of our race.

And here, though we are still, my brethren, in truth, but on the threshold of this tremendous subject, we must make two remarks in conclusion.

Observe the contrast between the real and the apparent importance of the birth of Christ. To human sense, what took place at Bethlehem may well have seemed at the time commonplace enough. An Infant was born under circumstances of hardship—was laid in a wayside stall. To those who do not look closely at what was passing, it might have occurred that a like event had happened scores of times before, and would often be repeated. Everybody then, depend upon it, did not hear the song of the angels, or mark the bearing of the virgin Mother or of her saintly spouse. The kingdom of God had entered into history, but, certainly, not with observation. Nay more; even among the worshippers of Christ the full meaning of His birth, as opening a new era in the history of the human race, was not at once by any means practically appreciated. For five centuries and a half Christians still reckoned the years by the names of the old Roman consuls, or by the era of Diocletian, just like the pagans around them. It was in the year 541 of the Christian era that Dionysius the Little, a pious and learned person at Rome, first ranged the history of mankind around the most important event in its whole course—the birthday of Jesus Christ. Christendom at once recognised the justice of this way of reckoning time; and the attempts to supersede it, such as that which was made in France during the First Revolution, have never had a serious chance of success. But how often do you and I use the phrase, "The year of our Lord," without reflecting that it proclaims the birth of Jesus Christ to be an event of such commanding importance that all else in human history, rightly understood, is merely relative to it—interesting only as it proceeds or follows, as it leads up to, or is derived from it. And yet, as I have said, five centuries and a half of the Christian ages passed before this was practically recognised. And so it has been ever since; so it is at this hour. Real importance is one thing; apparent importance is another. The events which move the world are not always those which men think about. The men who most deeply influence their fellows are not those of whom everybody is talking. The currents of thought and feeling which will shape the future are not those which are welcomed by the organs and interpreters of current opinion. When Christ appeared the palace of Cæsar seemed to be more important to the destinies of the world than the manger of Bethlehem. No, brethren, depend upon it, the apparent is not always, or even generally, the real.

And lastly, the importance of the birth of Jesus Christ must be recognised in many ways by the student of history, by the philosopher, by the divine; but there is one aspect of it which for you and me is more pressing than any other,—What is its practical meaning for us now and in the approaching future? Probably everyone in this cathedral has said to himself to-day, "This is the last Sunday in 1878." Yes, brethren; the hours of this year are quickly running out, and as those of us who have reached or who have passed middle life look back on it, we are tempted to say in the phrase of the Psalmist, "I went by, and lo, it was gone: I sought it, but its place could nowhere be found.[1] It seems now but as yesterday that we were standing here at the close of 1877. Yet since then how much has taken place—how much has there been to think about; and, after all, thought and occupation are the wings of time. Certainly it has been a year of anxieties, a year of struggles, a year of surprises, a year of achievements, a year in which, whether for good or for evil, the nations, as the phrase goes, have been "making history." This is not the hour to discuss it controversially. Probably those who come after us will be better able than we are to bring a large knowledge and a calm impartiality to the estimate of what this year has really been to our country, to the human race. But, as it passes, it leaves us Englishmen with a double burden on our hands,—widespread distress at home, which according to our means it should be our care to alleviate as we may, and

[1] Ps. xxxvii. 37: P. B. Version.

one war, perhaps two wars, in our dependencies abroad. All who think at all will find in these facts matter for sober and anxious thought—reasons, it may be, for some very serious misgivings. But, as the year passes, it sweeps away with it into the abyss of history—into the great company of the dead—many whom, in private or in public, we have known so well: the aged statesman, whose long life has been spent in the ardent struggles of political party; the great missionary bishop who will rank hereafter in a distant colony with our own Augustine; the divine in whom, now that he is gone, men have traced the spirit and the genius of a Butler; the earthly head of the largest of Christian Communions; and, not less, those whom we have mourned quite recently—the wife, the princess, who has shown us how high, even the highest, positions can be consecrated to God by works of charity and benevolence. Yes, they and many others, nearer it may be and dearer, some of them, to you and me, are now among the dead. And as the passing year sweeps them with its last hours from our sight, we seem— God grant that it may be so—we seem to catch a glimpse of those great realities which we too easily all of us forget. It is certain that many who prayed and listened in this cathedral on the last Sunday of 1877 have since passed into the presence of the eternal Judge. It is certain that many who pray and listen here this afternoon will have followed them before the last Sunday of 1879. Which of us it will be we know not; but, as we think steadily on the undeniable truth, surely some of the accustomed mists of our daily life must clear away, and we must see things more nearly as they are. In that world there will be no England, but only the souls of Englishmen. In that world there will be no distinctions of race, or rank, or wealth, or accomplishments, but only the great and the then efface-able distinction between the saved and the lost. Surely as from this vantage ground of passing time we look out into that coming world with its pleasing and terrific possibilities—with its glories, with its solemnities, with its nearness to each one of us—we must take heed that for each one of us the birth of the Redeemer shall mark— aye, ere this sacred week has gone—something more than a milestone on the road of life, something more than the occasion of a family gathering. There is one question, I repeat, which we should each of us lose no time whatever in answering, if it be not answered yet: "What is my relation to Him Who, for the love of me, was conceived of the Holy Ghost and born of the Virgin Mary, my present and most merciful Redeemer, my future Judge?"

# SERMON VIII.

## THE BLOOD OF CHRIST.

HEBREWS ix. 13, 14.

"*For if the blood of bulls and of goats, and the ashes of an heifer sprinkling the unclean, sanctifieth to the purifying of the flesh: how much more shall the Blood of Christ, Who through the eternal Spirit offered himself without spot to God, purge your conscience from dead works to serve the living God?*"

TO-DAY we pass the line which parts the first five weeks in Lent from that last fortnight which is especially devoted to contemplating the sufferings and death of our Lord Jesus Christ; and, accordingly, the Gospel tells us of the attempt of the Jews to stone Him in the temple —one of the first drops, as it has well been termed, of that storm which burst in all its fury upon Calvary; and the Epistle teaches us how to think about Him in the whole course of these His sufferings. He is not merely a good Man weighed down by so much pain of body and mind; He is the High Priest of the human race Who is offering a victim in expiation of human sin, and that victim Himself. He is the one real Sacrificer of Whom all the Jewish priests had for those long centuries been only shadows, and His sacrifice is the one offering which throughout all ages has power in Heaven. And so as He passes within the veil of the sanctuary above He is opening a way for us, if we will only follow, to an eternal home in the heart of God. "Christ being come a High Priest of good things to come, by His own Blood entered in once into the holy place, having obtained eternal redemption for us."[1]

Now that which must strike all careful readers of the Bible, in those passages which refer to the sufferings and death of our Lord Jesus Christ, is the stress which is laid upon His Blood. A long course of violent treatment, ending in such a death as that of crucifixion, must involve, as we know from the nature of the case, the shedding of the blood of the sufferer; but our modern feeling would probably have led us to treat this as an accidental or subordinate feature of the event. If we had had with our present human feelings to write those books which are the title-deeds of Christendom, we should either not refer to it, or we should pass lightly and quickly over it. We should throw it into the background of our description. We should give the outline; we should let the details be taken for granted; we should trust to the imagination of our readers to fill up the blank; we should shrink from stimulating their sensibilities to pain—from harrowing their feelings by anything beyond. Does it not seem, my brethren, as if we carried into our modern life that rule of the old Greek tragedians, that nothing violent or horrible—nothing that shocks or gives pain—if possible, should meet the eye of the beholder? If a deed of violence takes place in our streets or in our homes, do we not, as quickly as may be, remove all traces of it? Has it not been urged as a reason for continuing to put criminals to death by hanging, instead of adopting some more rapid and certain mode of destroying life, that it is desirable to spare the bystanders the sight of blood? Now, I do not say that this modern feeling is mere unhealthy sentimentalism. On the contrary, it may

[1] Heb. ix. 11, 12.

very well arise from that honourable sympathy with, and respect for, human nature which draws a veil gladly over its miseries and its wounds. But the New Testament in its treatment of the Passion of Christ is, as we cannot but observe, strangely and strongly in contrast with any such feeling. The four evangelists who differ so much in their accounts of our Lord's birth and public ministry seem to meet at last around the foot of the Cross, and to agree, if not in relating the same incidents, yet certainly in the minuteness of the detail of their narratives. In the shortest of the gospels when we reach the Passion, the occurrences of a single day take up a space which had been assigned to years. From the Last Supper to the burial in the grave of Joseph of Arimathea, we have a very complete account of what took place almost from hour to hour. Each incident that added to the pain or the shame, each bitter word, each insulting act, each outrage upon justice or upon mercy, of which the divine Sufferer was a victim, is carefully recorded. But especially the agony and bloody sweat, the public scourging, the crowning with the thorns, the nailing to the wood of the Cross, the opening the Side with a spear, are described by the evangelists—incidents, each one of them, be it observed, which must have involved the shedding of Christ's Blood. And in the writings of the apostles to their converts more is said of the Blood of Christ than of anything else connected with His death—more even than of the Cross. As we read them we might almost think that the shedding of His Blood was not so much an accompaniment of His death as its main object and purpose. Thus St. Paul tells the Romans that Christ is set forth to be a propitiation through faith in His Blood.[1] He tells them that they are justified by the Blood of Christ.[2] He writes to the Ephesians that

[1] Rom. iii. 25. [2] Ibid. v. 9.

they have redemption through Christ's Blood;[1] to the Colossians, that our Lord has made peace through the Blood of His Cross;[2] to the Corinthians,[3] that the Holy Sacrament is so solemn a rite because it is the communion of the Blood of Christ. Thus St. Peter[4] contrasts the slaves, whose freedom from captivity was purchased with such corruptible things as silver and gold, with the case of Christians redeemed from death by the precious Blood of Christ, as of a lamb without blemish and immaculate. Thus St. John[5] exclaims that the Blood of Jesus Christ, the Son of God, cleanseth Christians from all sin; and in the Epistle to the Hebrews[6] this Blood is referred to as the blood of the covenant, wherewith Christians are sanctified—as the blood of the everlasting covenant—as the blood of sprinkling which pleads with God for mercy, and so is contrasted with the blood of Abel which cries for vengeance. And in the last book of the New Testament the Beloved Disciple at the very outset gives thanks and praise to Him that has "washed us from our sins in His own Blood."[7] And the blessed in heaven sing that He has redeemed them to God by His Blood;[8] and the saints are there because they have washed their robes and made them white in the Blood of the Lamb;[9] and they have overcome their foe, not in their own might, but by the Blood of the Lamb;[10] and He whose Name is called the Word of God, and Who rides in the vision on a white horse, and on Whose Head are many crowns, is clothed in a vesture dipped in Blood.[11]

Much more might be said on the subject, but enough has already been said to show that in the New Testament the Blood of Christ is treated as no mere accident of His

---

[1] Eph. i. 7.
[2] Col. i. 20.
[3] 1 Cor. x. 16.
[4] 1 Pet. i. 18, 19.
[5] 1 Jno. i. 7.
[6] Heb. x. 29; xiii. 20; xii. 24.
[7] Rev. i. 5.
[8] Ibid. v. 9.
[9] Ibid. vii. 14.
[10] Ibid. xii. 11.
[11] Ibid. xix. 3.

death, but as a very important feature of it—nay, as having a substantive value of whatever kind which is all its own; and the question is: How are we to account for the prominence which is thus assigned to it?

This question is sometimes answered by saying that the language of the apostles about the Blood of Christ is, after all, merely the language of metaphor and symbol. The apostles, we are told, found in the Old Testament a stock of poetic illustration and imagery ready to their hands, and, although it had reference to the ideas and usages of a dying system, they employed them freely for their own purposes, much as a cultivated gentleman in a past generation used to quote the Greek and Latin poets in Parliament or in society, by way of decorating new ideas with the phrases of a literature that had passed away. This is what has been urged by some modern writers; but it must be at once said that any such account of the apostolic language about the preciousness and power of the Blood of Jesus Christ is unworthy at once of the seriousness of the men, and of the seriousness of the subject. Unworthy of the seriousness of the men; for, after all, the apostles and apostolic writers were not mere retailers of splendid phrases. They were teachers of a truth which they believed to have come from Heaven, and for which they were prepared to die. And unworthy of the seriousness of the subject, too; for surely the deepest truths that can move the wills and hearts of men are not fit subjects for mere antiquarian or literary display. They would be better avoided altogether, if they are not set forth in the most glorious and plainest language which those who profess to teach them can command. If the apostles used the language of the Old Testament about the Jewish sacrifices in order to describe their own living faith in the atoning work of Jesus Christ, this was because in the belief of the apostles a real relation already existed between the two things. The Jewish sacrifices were predestined types and shadows of the sacrificed Son of God. In the passage before us the Day of Atonement and its characteristic rites are present to the mind of the sacred writer, and of those rites the sprinkling of the blood of the victim was a prominent feature. But then the question still remains, Why should this sprinkling of blood have been a prominent feature on the Jewish Day of Atonement? Why should it have been allowed to colour so largely the thought and the words of the apostle? Why, in a word, should the Blood of the Redeemer rather than His pierced Hands, rather than His bruised or mangled Body, rather than His Face with its radiance—its divine radiance, scarcely shining through the tears and the shame—be dwelt on in the apostolic writings as the chosen symbol of His Passion and His death?

Certainly, my brethren, in all the languages of the world, blood is the proof—the warrant—of affection and of sacrifice. To shed blood voluntarily for another is to give the best that man can give. It is to give a sensible proof of—it is to give almost a bodily form to—love. This, our profound human instinct, is common to all ages, to all civilisations, to all religions. The blood of the soldier who dies for duty,—the blood of the martyr who dies for truth,—the blood of the man who dies that another may live—blood like this is an embodiment of the highest moral powers in human life. And these powers most assuredly were, all of them, represented in the Blood that flowed from the Wounds of Christ on Calvary.

And yet in saying this we have not altogether accounted for the apostolic sayings about the Blood of Christ. That Blood involves something more than any of these moral triumphs, something more than all of them taken together.

Observe, then, the peculiar and deep significance which

is ascribed to blood in the earliest books of the Bible,—the five books of Moses. There we are taught that between the blood, whether of man or of animal, and the life-principle, or soul, there is a certain and intimate connection. In those first laws which were given to Noah after the flood, man was authorised to eat the flesh, but not the blood, of the animals around him. Why was this? Because the blood is the life or soul of the animal. "Flesh with the life thereof, which is the blood thereof, shall ye not eat."[1] The laws of Moses himself go farther. The man, whether Israelite or stranger, who eats any manner of blood is to be put to death, and the reason is repeated. The soul of the flesh, that is of the nature living in the flesh, is in the blood.[2] This is why the blood of the sacrificed animals is shed by way of atonement for sin. The blood atones—this is the exact sense of the original language—by means of the soul that is in it. Once more. In the fifth book of Moses permission is given to the Israelites to kill and eat the sacrificial animals for common food, just as freely as the roebuck or the hart which were not used for sacrifice; but again there follows the caution,—"Only be sure that thou eat not the blood," and the reason for the caution—"The blood is the life; and thou mayest not eat the life with the flesh. Thou shalt not eat of it; thou shalt pour it upon the earth like water."[3] This thrice-repeated precept not to touch animal blood has passed away together with much else of the ancient ceremonial law. True, it was enforced by prophets, who insisted little or not at all on the ceremonial precepts of the Mosaic code. True, it was enforced for a while even by apostles as binding on the first converts from heathendom. It was adhered to, not indeed by any means universally, but with much tenacity, in the primitive Christian Church.

[1] Gen. ix. 4.   [2] Lev. xvii. 10, 11.   [3] Deut. xii. 23, 24.

But it has gone the way of the ceremonial system of which it really formed a part, and it was only fulfilled to disappear. And yet the reason of the precept remains as a matter of lasting interest,—the reason, namely, that blood is the element of our animal existence which is most closely associated with the principle of life. My brethren, what life is in itself, whether in the tree or in the animal,— whether in a man or in an angel,—who of us shall say? Life is a mystery ever close to us, yet ever eluding our inquisitive research. We track it only in its symptoms— only piecemeal. We associate intelligence with the brain. We trace the unspoken language of the soul in the movements or in the motionlessness of the countenance, in the expression of the eye, in the gesture of the hand,—even in the gait or the sway of the body. But of this we find little in Scripture, which, without at all denying the relation of the soul to other parts of our bodily frame, does unquestionably, so far as the soul is the principle of life, of feeling, and of growth, associate it with the blood. And the question may be fairly asked, whether this scriptural doctrine of the intimate relation of the soul or life-power to the blood is borne out by independent inquiry. It is obvious first of all, I take it, that the strength of the body depends on the quantity of the blood,—that with the loss of blood, feeling, power of movement—all the bodily activities—are lost also. The blood, then, is the basis or support of bodily life. But it is more. It is also the material from which the body and its various secretions arise. It is the substance out of which the animal life in all its forms is actually developed. Whether the various kinds of material which make up the human body are contained in the blood in a state of actual diversity, or whether they exist, indeed, only in potency, and are drawn out of it by the functional powers of the bodily organs—

this may be a matter of controversy; but it is agreed by high authorities on such subjects that they do thus preexist in the blood, which is thus the principle, not merely of bodily life, but of bodily growth and formation.

This, then, is what is assumed when Holy Scripture speaks of the blood as the life or soul of a man or animal. But, as an acute Jewish writer has well observed, the soul in question is only the sensitive soul which man possesses in common with animals. It is not the thinking, intelligent, self-conscious being; it is not the spirit which proceeds immediately from God, and which is encased in the sensitive soul as the apple of an eye is in the eye. The spirit of man is only so far resident in the blood as it is already resident in the sensitive soul which is in the blood. The existence of the spirit of man is strictly independent of any element of his bodily life, and, as we know, it will survive it.

But in Christ our Lord there was something more than body and soul and spirit. In Him dwelt all the fulness of the Godhead. As man differs from the animals in possessing an undying spirit, as well as, and together with, a sensitive soul or life, so in Christ our Redeemer were joined by an intimate—by an indissoluble—union, not merely a human Soul and Spirit, but also, above these, that Divine Nature Which was begotten of the Father before all worlds. Nay rather, it was this His eternal Person Which owned all else in Him,—in Which all else centred,—to Which all else attached itself. When He, Who had already existed from all eternity, vouchsafed to enter into the sphere of time, He wrapped around Him in its completeness, but without its stains, that human nature which He then made His own. He took it upon Him, not as a garment which He might lay aside, but as that which, from the moment of His Incarnation and for ever, was to form part of His Being. And therefore the Blood which flowed in His veins and which He shed at His circumcision and in His mental agony, not less than in His scourging and on the Cross, was the Blood, not merely of the Son of Mary, but of the infinite and eternal Being thus condescendingly united to a created form. It is an apostle who bids the pastors of the church of Ephesus, "feed the Church of God, which He hath purchased with His own Blood."[1]

This, then, is what is meant in the text when it contrasts the atoning power of the Blood of Christ with that of the blood of bulls and goats. The blood of the sacrificed animals had a certain value, because, as we have seen, it was so intimately connected with the life or sensitive soul of the animal. It did, as the apostle puts it, and by divine appointment, sanctify to the purifying of the flesh. By the flesh is here meant the natural, outward, earthly life of man, especially all that bore in the way of outward conduct and condition upon his membership in the commonwealth of Israel. The sacrifices on the Day of Atonement, and especially the sprinkling of the blood of the red heifer towards the tabernacle, did signify the substitution of life for life, and were at any rate accepted as establishing the outward religious position of those for whom they were offered. That they could do more was impossible. The nature of things was opposed to it. It was not possible, says the apostle, that the blood of bulls and goats should put away sin. The blood of these animals could not operate in the proper sphere of spiritual natures. But then it foreshadowed nothing less than the Blood of Christ. It was His Blood Who, "through His eternal spiritual Being" (it is not the Holy Ghost who is here meant, but the divine Nature of the incarnate Christ) "offered Himself without spot to God." The eternal spiritual Nature of Christ vivi-

[1] Acts xx. 28.

fying the Blood of Christ is contrasted in the apostle's thought with the perishing life of the sacrificed animal resident in the blood of the animal; and so the value of the sacrifices, and so the power of the blood to cleanse or to save, varies with the dignity of the life which each represents: in the one case that of the creature not even endowed with immortality or reason, in the other that of the Infinite and Eternal Being Who, for us men and for our salvation, had come down from heaven.

"How much more shall the Blood of Christ." At length we see what it is that the sacred writer really means. He says in effect to his readers, "You have no doubt that under the Jewish dispensation the sacrifices on the Day of Atonement, the blood of the slain goat and red heifer, could restore the sinful Israelite to his place and his privileges in the sacred nation. It did 'sanctify to the purifying of the flesh.' But here is the Blood not of a sacrificial animal, not of a mere man, not merely of the very best of men, but of One Who was God manifest in the flesh. Who shall calculate the effects of His self-sacrifice? Who shall limit the powers of His voluntary death? Who shall say what His Blood may or may not achieve on earth or elsewhere? Plainly we are here in the presence of an agency which altogether distances and rebukes the speculations of reason. We can but listen for some voice which shall speak to us with a divine authority, and from beyond the veil. We can but be sure of this, that the Blood of the eternal Christ must infinitely transcend in its efficacy that which was shed upon the temple altars. It must be equal—more than equal—to redress the woes, to efface the transgressions, of a guilty world." This, indeed, is what the argument invites: the absolutely limitless power of the Precious Blood. But the sacred writer puts, as it were, a strong restraint upon himself, and he contents himself economically with pointing to one single result: "How much more shall the Blood of Christ cleanse your conscience from dead works to serve the living God."

"Dead works;" works that are—not good, in that their motive is good, or bad, in that their motive is bad, but—dead in that they have no sort of motive at all,—in that they are merely outward and mechanical affairs of propriety, routine, form, to which the spirit and the heart contribute nothing. Dead works! To how much of our lives, ay, of the higher and the religious side of our lives, may not this vivid and stern expression most justly be applied? How many acts in the day are gone through without intention, without deliberation, without any effort to consecrate them to the Author of our being, without any reflex effect upon the faith and love of the doer. How many prayers and words and deeds are of this soulless character; and, if so, how are they wrapping our spirits round with bandages of insincere habit, on which already the avenging angels may have traced the motto, "Thou hast a name that thou livest, and art dead."[1]

The Blood of Christ delivers us from much else, but especially from these dead works; for just as the blood of the slain animal means the life of the animal, so the Blood of Christ crucified means the Life of Christ, His Life Who is the eternal Truth and the eternal Charity. And thus, when a Christian man feels its redemptive touch within him, he has a motive, varying indeed in its strength, but always powerful; for being, at least, genuine, he means his deeds, his words, his prayers. He knows that life is a solemn thing,—that it has tremendous issues. He measures these issues day by day by the value of the redeeming Blood. If Christ has shed His Blood, then life must be well worth living, well worth saving. A new en-

[1] Rev. iii. 1.

ergy is thrown into everything; a new interest lights up every surrounding circumstance. The little incidents of life, its great opportunities, its trials, its failures, its successes, the characters, the dispositions of friends, the public events of the times, the details of the home, are looked at with eyes that see in them nothing whatever that is indifferent. And when all is meant for God's glory, though there may and must be—ay, to the very end—much of weakness and inconsistency, the conscience is practically purged from dead works to serve the living God.

"The Blood of Christ." It was shed on Calvary eighteen centuries ago, but it flows on throughout all time. It belongs now not to the physical, but to the supersensuous world. It washes souls, not bodies. It is sprinkled not on altars, but on consciences. But, although invisible, it is not for that the less real and energetic. It is the secret power of all that purifies—of all that invigorates—souls in Christendom. Do we believe in one Baptism for the remission of sins? It is because to the eye of faith the Blood of Christ tinges the water of the font. Do we believe that God has "given power and commandment to His Ministers to declare and pronounce to His people, being penitent, the Absolution and Remission of their sins?"[1] It is because the Blood of Christ, applied to the conscience by the Holy Spirit, makes this declaration a solemn reality. Do we find in the Bible more than an ancient literature—in Christian instruction more than a mental exercise—in the life of thought about the unseen and the future more than food for speculation? This is because we know that the deepest of all questions is that which touches our individual moral state before God, and that therefore, as sinners, we are above all things interested in the fountain opened for sin and for uncleanness in the Blood of Christ. Do

---

[1] Declaration of Absolution at Morning and Evening Prayer in P.B.

we look to our successive Communions for the strengthening and refreshing of our souls during the days of our pilgrimage? This is because the Blood of our Lord Jesus Christ, Which was shed for us, can preserve our bodies and souls unto everlasting life. Does even a single prayer offered in sincerity of purpose avail to save a despairing soul? This is because we have "boldness to enter into the holiest by the Blood of Jesus."[1]

"The Blood of Christ." Who of us does not need to be sprinkled with it? Christians as we are, what are our lives, our habits, our thoughts, the course of our existence, as these lie spread out before the eyes of the all-seeing Being? The works from which we need to be purged are, it may be, not merely soulless or dead, but actively evil. The prayer which befits us kneeling before our crucified Master, is not merely "Purge my conscience from dead works to serve the living God,"[2] but "Wash me throughly from my wickedness, and cleanse me from my sin."[3] Let one or both of these prayers, dear brethren, be ours during these ensuing solemn days. If they are offered earnestly they will not be unheard. The eternal Spirit is here to sprinkle with the Precious Blood all souls that seek purification or pardon, and the promise made to Israel in Egypt still holds good—still may be claimed in a far higher sense by the Israel of God, whether in life or in death:—"When I see the Blood, I will pass over, and the plague shall not be upon you."[4]

[1] Heb. x. 19.
[2] Ibid. ix. 14.
[3] Ps. li. 2: P. B. Version.
[4] Ex. xii. 13.

# SERMON IX.

## THE SOLITUDE OF CHRIST IN REDEMPTION.

PSALM xxii. 11 : P. B. Version.

"*O go not from me; for trouble is hard at hand, and there is none to help me.*"

THIS is one of the cries of the ideal or superhuman Sufferer, of Whose agonies, both of mind and body, we have so complete a picture in this 22nd psalm. Many attempts from time to time have been made to explain this psalm by some of the circumstances in the life of David, or in the life of Hezekiah, or of other persons in Jewish history, who have combined eminent piety with great misfortunes; but these attempts one and all have been unsuccessful. The psalm describes a kind and a degree of suffering of which we have no records in the Old Testament, and to which, most assuredly, nothing in the known life of David at all corresponds. Yet, there is no doubt whatever, as the best scholars agree, that the psalm is from David's own hand; and the question is, how David could ever have brought himself to write as though he were himself feeling and thinking as he here describes. The answer is, that the picture of a great Sufferer presented itself to David's soul—took possession of it—took such an entire possession of it that, as in the highest natural poetry may also sometimes happen, the writer forgot himself and lost himself utterly in the subject which possessed him. The words were David's words, but the thoughts, the hopes, the fears, the anguish, the exultation—these were of another and a higher than David. David was but a copyist. David was writing down, for the good of the times to come, what in his illuminated spirit he saw with his eyes and heard with his ears. His picture of an ideal Sufferer was laid up among the sacred books of Israel; but many a century had to pass before men could know what it meant and to Whom it referred. When Jesus our divine Lord hung dying upon the Cross, He interpreted this psalm of Himself by using its very first verse as the fourth of those seven last words which He uttered. Those solemn words "Eloi, Eloi, lama sabacthani?"—"My God, my God, why hast thou forsaken me?"[1]—as uttered by the Redeemer in the darkest hour of His sufferings, give the key to all that follows. Henceforth we Christians read this psalm as if repeated throughout by Jesus on the Cross, or at least by Jesus in His Passion. As His dying eye surveys the multitude of human beings in whom an unreasoning hate of truth and goodness had for the time quelled all other thoughts and emotions—in whom the wild beast that is latent in our human nature had asserted, for the moment, his sway with a frightful power—Jesus might say, "Many oxen are come about Me; fat bulls of Bashan close Me in on every side. They gape upon Me with their mouths, as it were a ramping and a roaring lion. Many dogs are come about Me, and the council of the wicked layeth siege against Me." And as He glances down on His mangled Body, at His pierced Hands and Feet, and as He feels the parching thirst, the inward collapse, the exhaustion of approaching death, He murmurs, "I am poured out like water, all My Bones are out of joint; My

[1] Mark xv. 34.

Heart also in the midst of My Body is even like melting wax. My strength is dried up like a potsherd, and My tongue cleaveth to my gums, and Thou shalt bring Me to the dust of death. They pierced My Hands and My Feet. I may tell all My Bones." And as He listens to the taunts which fall upon His ear, and as He watches the doings of the men who crowd eagerly around the foot of the Cross on which He hangs, He complains, "They that see Me laugh Me to scorn; they shoot out their lips, and shake their heads, saying, He trusted in God that He would deliver Him; let Him deliver Him, if He will have Him. They stand staring and looking upon Me. They part My garments among them, and cast lots upon My vesture." And as He strains the eye of His human Soul to gaze into futurity—to pierce the veil that parts the agony and desolation of the moment from the triumph and the peace that await Him beyond—He cries, "The Lord hath not despised nor abhorred the low estate of the poor; He hath not hid His Face from him; but when he called unto Him He heard him. My praise is of Thee in the great congregation. The ends of the world shall remember themselves, and be turned unto the Lord. My seed shall serve Him: they shall be counted unto the Lord for a generation."[1] The psalm is throughout written—we might almost say written to order—to describe, as from within, the sufferings of our divine Lord upon the Cross. Nowhere else in the Old Testament does the Holy Spirit more vividly testify beforehand the sufferings of Christ and the glory that should follow.

In this psalm there is one feature of our Lord's sufferings upon which particular stress is laid: I mean His desolation, or solitude. It is the key-note of the psalm, the very first words of which complain, "My God, why hast

---

[1] Ps. xxii. 12-31: P. B. Version.

Thou forsaken Me?" It finds expression again and again; nowhere perhaps, more pathetically than in the cry, "O go not from Me; for trouble is hard at hand, and there is none to help Me." Some centuries, my brethren, after David, a Figure passed before the soul of the greatest of the prophets,[1] Which shadowed out this aspect of a superhuman suffering, but from another point of view. It was the form of One coming as from Edom,—coming along the wonted road of Israel's deliverance,—coming with garments dyed in the vintage of Bozrah, emblems of a struggle which meant wounds and blood,—glorious in His apparel—His moral apparel of righteousness and mercy—and travelling in the greatness of His strength. And when the seer gazed intently at this Figure and asked who He was, the reply came, "I that speak in righteousness, mighty to save." And when a further question was ventured—"Why art Thou red in thine apparel, and Thy garments like him that treadeth in the winefat?" it was answered, as though this were of the very essence of the conflict, "I have trodden the winepress alone, and of the people there was none with Me." Yes in His sufferings Jesus was alone,—alone in spirit, though encompassed by a multitude. In His Passion He experienced a threefold solitude: the solitude of greatness, the solitude of sorrow, and the solitude of death.

The loneliness of the great is one of the ironies of human life. The great are lonely because they are great—because, had they peers and companions, they would cease to be what they are, at least in relation to those around them. This holds good of greatness in all its forms, whether greatness of station, or greatness of genius, or greatness of character. Take the word "great" in its most popular, but least warrantable, sense. What is the

[1] Isai. lxiii. 1-3.

case with the great in station? The solitude of the throne —it is proverbial. Not that the monarch is without companions. From the nature of the case, the monarch can command companions as can no other person in the realm. No court in the world is wanting in deferential ministers of the royal will, whose business it is to furnish companionship to royalty, whose hourly effort it is to carry out the wishes of the sovereign, and to thwart or to screen from his sight all that may traverse a passing inclination. But companionship such as this is perfectly compatible with solitude. That free, buoyant intercourse of mind with mind, of heart with heart—that entire reciprocity of sympathy which knows no limits save those which are imposed by truth and charity—is banned by the exacting etiquette of a court, is hardly, if at all, possible for the occupant of a throne. "The divinity which doth hedge a king" has its drawbacks, and it is costly. A monarch is always more or less of a solitary; alone in his joys, alone in his sorrows. Reverence and envy conspire to deprive him of his ordinary share in the hearts of men around him. And this solitude of the throne, let us never forget it, is one reason for the claim of its occupants upon the charity and the prayers of the Christian Church. This, our tribute of the best sympathy, is one means of redressing the privations and of lessening the dangers of a great position occupied for the public good.

Then again there is the greatness of genius. Even when genius unbends—when it is popular and fruitful—even when it ministers to the enjoyment and the instruction of millions, it is by its instinct solitary; it lives alone. The mountain peaks which are the crowning beauty of a vast and fertile plain, purchase their prerogative elevation at a great cost. They are cold, bleak, inaccessible. Genius lives in distant realms of thought. Genius lives amidst flashes and aspirations which do not exist for others. In the presence of these it is alone. We may be sure that a man like Shakespeare was familiar with much that he never thought of communicating to the quiet, sensible, excellent, commonplace people among whom for the most part he passed his days. In his highest and deepest thought, from the nature of the case, being such as his God had made him, he was a solitary.

And then there is greatness of character. This is the most legitimate use of the word. True greatness might seem at first sight to be very far from solitary—to be, on the contrary, unselfish, beneficent, communicative. Undoubtedly such greatness draws to itself human hearts; it wins human interests. And yet how often are there features in a really noble character which, when they become plain to us the mass of mankind, repel rather than attract. The unswerving adherence to known truth, the resolute sacrifice of immediate advantage to the claims of principle, the flashes of severity which radiate from the purest and from the highest love—these are not popular qualities. History is full of examples of men whose benevolence and kindness and activity have at first won general applause and admiration, but who have been deserted, hated, denounced, perhaps even put to death, when the real character of their greatness was discovered. Such a man was Savonarola. His story has been made familiar to Englishmen—we may well and gratefully remember it in this place—by the pen of Dean Milman. Savonarola, amid imperfections which are inseparable from our human weakness, was one of the greatest religious teachers that the world has seen. He aimed—as all sincerely great minds must aim—at carrying Christian principles into the public and social life of man. He held that politics might be no less Christian than personal conduct. The people which had welcomed his teaching with passionate enthusiasm assisted at his cruel and ignominious death. Savonarola was too great even for Florence. And there have been few ages in the world's history when this lesson has not repeated itself,—when integrity of character and elevation of aim have not experienced the alternate vicissitudes of popular favour and popular dislike or violence. Our own age and country are not exceptions to the rule.

Now our Lord in His Passion was great in these various ways. He was indeed, as it seemed to the eye of sense, a worm and no man, a very scorn of men and the outcast of the people; and yet, as He said before Pilate, He was a King, and He felt as no other can ever have felt, the isolation of royalty. His mental eye took in vaster horizons than were ever suspected to exist by any around Him. He had meat to eat that they knew not of.[1] In this, as in so many other ways, He lived in a sphere of thought which was for them impossible. And, above all, in character He was not merely courageous, true, disinterested, loving, and all these in a degree which distanced the highest excellence around Him; He was also that which no other in human form had been before, or has been since: He was sinless. And thus, as He went forth to die, He was in a moral and an intellectual and a social solitude,—a solitude created by the very prerogatives of His Being. His elevation above His fellows itself cut Him off from that sympathy which equals can most effectually give. And hence one motive of the prayer of His human Soul in the psalm, "O go not from Me, for trouble is hard at hand, and there is none to help Me."

There is the solitude of greatness, my brethren, but there is also the solitude of sorrow. Certainly sorrow is a link of human fellowship. Sooner or later all men suffer. "Man is born unto trouble, as the sparks fly upward."[2]

[1] Jno. iv. 32.     [2] Job v. 7.

No condition of life, no variety of temperament, can purchase exemption from the universal law of suffering. To some it comes as the chastening which is necessary to perfection; to others it comes as the penalty which is due to sin; but, sooner or later, in whatever sense, it comes to all. And yet, though suffering is thus universal, no two human beings suffer exactly alike. There is the same individuality in the pain which each man suffers that there is in his thought, in his character, in his countenance. No two men, since the world began, among the millions of sufferers, have repeated exactly the same experience. And this is why human sympathy, even at its best, is never quite perfect. No one merely human being can put himself exactly, by that act of the moral imagination which we call sympathy, in all the circumstances of another human being. Each sufferer, whether of bodily or of mental pain, pursues a separate path, encounters peculiar difficulties— shares a common burden, but is alone in his sorrow.

> "Each in his hidden sphere of joy or woe
> Our hermit spirits dwell, and range apart."[1]

And especially was Jesus our Lord solitary in His awful sorrow. We may well believe that the delicate sensibilities of His bodily frame rendered Him liable to physical tortures such as ruder natures can never know. But we know this, that the mode of His death was exceptionally painful, and yet His bodily sufferings were less terrible, so it might seem, than the sufferings of His Mind. His Agony in the garden was of a character which distances altogether human woe. Our Lord advisedly laid Himself open to the dreadful visitation. He embraced it as by a deliberate act. He began to be sorrowful and very heavy. He took upon Him the burden and the misery of human

---

[1] Keble's "Christian Year:" 24th Sunday after Trinity, 2nd Stanza.

sin—the sins of all the centuries that had preceded and that would follow Him—that He might take it to the Cross and expiate it in death. As the Apostle says, "He bare our sins in His own Body on the tree."[1] But the touch of this burden, which to you and me is so familiar, was agony to Him. It drew from Him the Bloody Sweat which fell from His Forehead on the turf of Gethsemane hours before they crowned Him with the thorns or nailed Him to the Cross. Ah, brethren, we endeavour to enter into the solitary sorrows of the Soul of Jesus, but they are beyond us. We may at some time in our lives have found ourselves in a family circle when a heavy blow had just fallen on it. We may have noted the efforts of the younger children to understand the gloom and the misery of the elders. The elders know what has happened. They know that all that upon which the family depends for daily bread is irretrievably lost; or they know that some loved one—a father, a mother, an eldest child—has just been taken away, it may be by a sudden, by a terrible, catastrophe. They have no heart to speak. Or they know, worst of all, that some misery worse than death—some crushing burden of shame and sorrow—has fallen upon the family through the misconduct of one of its members. And so they sit silent in their grief. And the young children gaze wistfully up into their faces, as if trying to make out what is so strange—what is so beyond them,—as if wishing to sympathize with what is to them an incomprehensible woe. They are doing their best—those children. They are concerned at beholding those sorrowing faces. They note those subdued tones, those quiet movements, those hushed sighs—it may be, that darkened room. But, alas! they are trying to understand what they cannot understand. They are touching but the fringes of a

[1] 1 Pet. ii 24.

sorrow that is altogether above them. And so, brethren, it is with all of us in the presence of the sorrows of Jesus Christ expiating the sins of a guilty world. Before Him we are indeed, the best of us, but children—happy indeed if we share their simple and free sympathies, but certainly, like them, unable to do more than watch with tender and reverent awe a mighty burden of misery which we can not hope to comprehend. All that we can do is to lay to heart the words which sound everywhere in believing souls around Gethsemane and Calvary: "Is it nothing to you, all ye that pass by? behold, and see if there be any sorrow like unto My sorrow?"[1]

And, lastly, there is the solitude of death. Death, whenever it comes to any man, must be an act in which no other man can share. Even if I die at the same moment with another, I can not sympathise with him in the act of dying. We have no solid reason to presume that each of us would even be conscious of what is happening to the other. Death strips from a man all that connects him with that which is without him. It is an act in which his consciousness is, from the nature of the case, thrown back into itself and absorbed in that which is happening to itself. A dying man may be distracted up to the moment, but not in the moment, of death. Warm-hearted friends may press around him. Well remembered faces and objects may pass before his failing eyes. At one deathbed the prayers of childhood—at another (so it has been) soft strains of familiar music—may fall upon his ear. But when the soul, by a wrench which no experience can possibly anticipate, breaks away from the bodily organism with which since its creation it has been so intimately linked, it enters upon a lonely path, which may indeed be brightened by the voices and the

[1] Lam. i. 12.

smiles of angels, but into which no human sympathy can follow. Few things, my brethren, are so tragic as the sharp contrast between the crowd that may surround a dying man, and the necessary solitude of the soul in death. When the cholera, many years ago, struck its victims in a crowded drawing-room abroad, the world was hushed with a passing awe. And the same contrast may be under more accustomed circumstances. What, for instance, can be more pathetic than the deathbed of the French statesman who played so great a part under the Republic and the First Empire, and who lived down into the boyhood of those among us who are yet in middle life? Talleyrand passed the last forty-eight hours of his life sitting at the side of his bed—he could not bear to lie down—leaning forward on two servants who were relieved, we are told, every two hours. In that posture he received, on the morning of the day on which he died, King Louis Phillippe and his Queen; and he never for a moment, we are told, forgot what was due to the etiquette of the court. He received his visitors with the distinction and the attentions to which they were accustomed. Outside his room, in the antechamber, all that was distinguished in the society of Paris was gathered together. Talleyrand's death was viewed as a political and social event of the first importance. Politicians, old and young—even grey-headed statesmen—crowded the hearth, and talked with animation, while young men and young women exchanged bright compliments with each other, which formed a painful contrast with the deep groans of the dying man in the adjoining room. Talleyrand, who was first a bishop and then an apostate from Christianity, made some sort of reconciliation with Heaven, and God only knows its value. But no sooner had the long agony terminated in death, than, to use the words of the narrative, it might have been supposed that a flight of rooks was leaving the mansion, such was the eagerness with which each visitor rushed away to be the first to tell the news in the particular circle of which he or she was the chosen oracle. The corpse of Talleyrand lying alone in those deserted chambers was a visible emblem of the solitude of the soul in the act of death.

Nor can we refer to such a subject to-day without reminding ourselves that it is only three days since death has claimed as his own a man whom the Church of England will always honour with affectionate reverence. It is for those who had the happiness of knowing him intimately to say, as no doubt they will say, what Bishop Selwyn was in his private life and conversation—what were the thoughts, what the enthusiasms, that gave impulse and shape to such a splendid life. We who have reverenced him from afar can merely note that his was a figure of apostolic proportions,—that he was one of that comparatively small band of men who reproduce, in our age of clouded faith and of soul enervation, the manners, the virtues, and the force by which long centuries ago the Christian Church was planted on the ruins of heathendom. Surely, many of us have accompanied him with the reverent sympathy of our prayers in his last hours of pain and weakness; nor can we doubt that for him the solitude of death has been brightened by all that our gracious Master has in store for those who by their works and their lives turn many to embrace His righteousness and become the disciples of His truth.

In the death of our Lord himself it might be supposed that this sense of solitude would be escaped. Living in hourly communion with the Father, surrounded by hosts of angel guardians, how, we may ask, could He taste of the solitude of death? Was not His Human Nature so united to His Divinity that, even in death, the union was not forfeited? And how is this reconcilable with the supposition that He experienced the loneliness of dying as we men experience it? The answer is that our Lord by a deliberate act became obedient unto death. Whatever might have been the law of His Being as a sinless Man united to a higher Nature, He did not, if I may dare so to say, claim its privileges, but laid Himself open without reserve or stint to all the ills to which our flesh is heir without at all escaping its lowest and its last humiliations. He selected as the mode of dying that which conspicuously involved most pain and shame; and He would not, most assuredly, defeat His purpose by sparing Himself that accompaniment of death which causes so much apprehension to us sinful men—its solitariness. He might have prayed His Father for twelve legions of angels, but He would be alone. He might have enjoyed unceasingly the joy, at least, of those who always behold the Face of the Father in Heaven. He willed to share the misery of the souls who cry in their last moments—some, we may be sure, every day that passes—"My God, my God, why hast thou forsaken me?" He submitted Himself to all those elements of our nature which sterner characters affect to scorn,—to its sense of dependence, to its craving for sympathy, to its consciousness of weakness. "O go not from me, for trouble is hard at hand, and there is none to help me," is the natural language of the feeblest sufferer in the poorest and most wretched lodging in London; but it was the language also of our divine Saviour, contemplating, with a true human apprehension the loneliness of approaching death. Yes, when as on this day He rode in triumph towards the Holy City, surrounded by a great multitude who cried, "Hosanna"—who spread the branches of the palms and the garments which they wore along the path of His advance—even at this moment of His seeming triumph

He was really alone. He knew what was before Him. The surging multitude around Him was for Him as if it was not. We may see men in Cheapside, in the middle of the day,—when it is difficult to force a passage along the footway from this cathedral to the Bank—we may see men in whose faces some unconcealed care, some absorbing passion, proclaims their virtual solitude amid the crowd. "Never less alone than when most alone," is the motto of the soul as it gazes upward towards the heavens. "Never more alone than when least alone," is the motto of the soul, when, under a great stress of pain or doubt, it looks downwards to the earth. The crowds which sang "Hosanna," as Christ entered Jerusalem, and the crowds which cried " Crucify him," as He passed along the Way of Sorrows, touched but the surface of His awful solitude as He rode on—as He walked on—to die.

Surely, my brethren, this solitude of our Saviour in His sufferings is full of great comfort for us. It shows to us, first, that at the moment of death, and before it, the best Christians may experience a desolation of spirit which is no real test of their true condition before God. Many of the best men in the Christian church have done so, and it has been supposed by those who do not reflect sufficiently upon the teaching of the Passion that this desolation of the soul must needs imply its rejection by the good God. No conclusion can be less warranted. The confident assumptions of a deathbed which follows upon a life of disloyalty to known truth and known duty, may be—I do not say that they always are — God forbid — they may be only physical illusions; but the anguish of a saintly soul which fears on the threshold of eternity that God has left it to itself is, surely, a token of its conformity to the divine Saviour.

And, secondly, we see in the solitude of Jesus crucified

a warrant of His constant sympathy with the dying. In that "He Himself hath suffered being tempted, He is able to succour them that are tempted."[1] Nothing that we may experience in His gracious providence—no anguish of soul —no weariness or torture of body—has been unexplored by Him Who overcame all the sharpness of death, before He opened the Kingdom of Heaven to the great company of the faithful.

May He take pity upon us, as sinful and erring yet believing children, and suffer us not at our last hour for any pains of death to fall from Him. May He look upon us with the eyes of His mercy, and give us comfort and sure confidence in Him, and defend us from the dangers of the Enemy, and so bring us safely to our Eternal Home, for His own infinite merits.

[1] Heb. ii. 18.

# SERMON X.

## THE POWER OF THE RESURRECTION.

PHILIPPIANS iii. 10.

*" That I may know Him, and the power of His resurrection."*

"THE Lord is risen indeed, and hath appeared unto Simon"; that was the whisper, the exclamation which passed from mouth to mouth among the astonished disciples on the morning of the first Easter Day—that He Who had been crucified and laid in the grave had actually burst the bonds of death and was again abroad, visibly moving in the world of living men. What was the astonishment, and joy, and triumph of those first followers! First one and then another, and then groups of friends, and then large bodies of men were admitted to see this Conqueror of the grave, to listen to Him, to speak with Him, to satisfy themselves by hearing, and sight, and touch, that the day of Calvary had not for them really closed in a night of unrelieved darkness,—that a brighter morning had begun to dawn upon the earth.

"That I may know Him, and the power of His resurrection"—that was the aspiration of the apostle of the Gentiles some thirty years later, breathed forth from his prison in Rome. In St. Paul's mind there was not a shadow of a doubt as to the fact of the Resurrection. It was, when he wrote these words, some twenty-five years or so nearer to him in point of time than the battle of Waterloo is to us Englishmen of to-day, and he had been pondering over it, if we except some two years at most, during the whole of the intervening interval. He had heard all about it from a large circle of witnesses whom he could implicitly trust, and his unquestioning belief in it is the necessary key to the chief efforts and enthusiasms of his later life. But he had not yet done with it simply because he was certain of its historical truth. He would fain grasp more and more perfectly what he calls its power, and hence the aspiration: "That I may know Him, and the power of His resurrection."

Now what is the meaning of this word "power?" There is no room for mistake, I submit, as to its general import. By the power of a fact we mean the bearing, the consequences, as distinct from the existence, of the fact: we mean the inferences which may be drawn from it, or the influence it will naturally exert. Apart from its power, a mere fact, looked at in its barren isolation, is an uninteresting thing; and in truth there are no facts altogether without some kind of power in God's universe. That so many thousand human beings have assembled to worship our Lord and God beneath the dome of this Cathedral Church this Easter night, is a statistical fact which, if it were ascertained, would have no particular interest if it were not that, linked to that fact, is the idea of its vast, its complex, its (for all but one Being) unascertainable power. So many intelligences enlightened by the truth of Christ, so many hearts warmed by the love of Christ, so many wills braced by the grace of Christ, so many souls brought face to face with truth yet without spiritual benefit, and therefore most assuredly not without spiritual loss,—this is the power of the fact before us, not the less certain because its precise measure cannot be taken, not the less interesting assuredly because its import reaches far beyond the present moment—far beyond the confines of time to the distant horizon of eternity. And St. Paul's meaning in the text is that, so far as he may, he would in respect of a far more momentous fact measure at least some departments of its power, make some progress in discoveries which as man he could never hope to exhaust.

"The power of the Resurrection." Let us endeavour with the apostle to consider it this evening in some very few of its several elements, and with a view, if it may be, to a practical effect upon our hearts and lives.

"The power of the Resurrection," then, is to be seen first of all in Christian thought. The Resurrection is the fundamental fact which satisfies a Christian of the absolute truth of the religion of Jesus Christ. When after their Master's ascension into heaven the apostles went forth to convert the world to His gospel, what was the most prominent topic in their sermons? Every child who has read the Acts of the Apostles will at once answer, "The Resurrection of Jesus Christ." It was, as you have just now heard in the second lesson, the burden of the first sermon that apostle ever preached—St. Peter's on the day of Pentecost. David had foretold how Christ should rise: Jesus Who came to be the Christ, had risen just as David had foretold. "Whereof," says the apostle, speaking for himself and for his brethren, "we all are witnesses."[1] This is the substance of the explanation which the same apostle made to the crowd of people who had witnessed the healing of the lame man at the Beautiful Gate of the Temple. It was not the voice of the apostle, it was the Name of Jesus, which had made the lame man whole; and this was because, though Jesus had lately been crucified,

[1] Acts ii. 32.

yet He had also risen from the dead. The apostles were there to witness it. This was deliberately repeated by St. Peter before the court which afterwards sat to try the apostle; and the Sadducees, who mainly composed the court, are expressly said to have been particularly irritated because the apostles preached through Jesus the resurrection from the dead. And when, after their imprisonment and deliverance, the apostles were again brought before the Sanhedrim, the answer was still as ever the same: "We ought to obey God rather than men. The God of our fathers raised up Jesus, Whom ye slew and hanged on a tree. We are His witnesses of these things."[1] And the private instructions of the apostles corresponded with their public teaching. The main point in St. Peter's private address to the household of Cornelius is this: "Him Whom they slew and hanged on a tree, God up-raised the third day, and shewed Him openly, even to us who did eat and drink with Him after he rose from the dead."[2] Indeed, when the historian of the Acts wishes to describe the substance of that very earliest form of Christian preaching, he states simply this, that "with great power gave the apostles witness of the resurrection of the Lord Jesus."[3] Nor was it otherwise in the missionary teaching of that other great apostle, who is to the latter part of the history of the Acts what St. Peter is to the earlier. St. Paul had not seen the risen Lord on earth, although at and after his conversion he had evidence that Jesus was living and ruling both on earth and in heaven. Still he relies on the witness to the resurrection almost in the very words of Peter. Preaching in the Jewish synagogue at the Pisidian Antioch,[4] he first observes that the Jews had, without intending it, fulfilled the prophecies in pleading that Jesus should be slain; and then he adds that God had raised

[1] Acts v. 29, 30, 32.   [2] Ibid. x. 39-41.   [3] Ibid. iv. 33.   [4] Ibid. xiii. 14-41.

Jesus from the dead; that Jesus was actually seen many days of those which came up with Him from Galilee to Jerusalem, who were still, when St. Paul was preaching, His witnesses to the people; and finally, that it was by thus raising up Jesus that God had substantially fulfilled the great promises to the fathers of Israel. And again, preaching to a crowd of more or less educated pagans from the steps of the Areopagus in Athens,[1] St. Paul insists that God's dealings with men in times past and His mercies to them now all point on to a coming judgment, and that God has shewn Who was to be the Judge by raising Him from the dead. The Resurrection was so prominent in St. Paul's teaching in Athens that the heathen audience actually supposed that the word was another name for a new divinity. And, to omit other illustrations which crowd upon me, the climax of St. Paul's defence before Agrippa[2] is, that it was only the natural, the inevitable end of the Jewish prophecies that Christ should suffer and that He should be the first that should rise from the dead. And so St. Paul summarises his teaching to the Corinthians: "I delivered unto you, first of all, that which I also received, how that Christ died for our sins according to the scriptures; and that He was buried, and that He rose again the third day according to the scriptures."[3]

Now here, first of all, it is abundantly clear that the apostles felt certain of their facts. They did not merely whisper that Jesus was risen in the assemblies of the faithful as a topic of private comfort for Christian souls; they carried the bold assertion of the Resurrection to the foot of tribunals which were filled by their keen, bitter, and contemptuous enemies, and challenged those enemies to gainsay it if they could; and if, after the fashion of

---

[1] Acts xvii. 22–31.   [2] Ibid. xxvi. 22–23.   [3] 1 Cor. xv. 3.

modern times, those ruling Sadducees had appointed a scientific commission to investigate the matter, nobody would have been better pleased than the apostles themselves. They had nothing to lose, they had everything to gain by the most searching and thorough enquiry. It has been said of political revolutions that they are not to be made with rosewater, and it is certainly true of great religious changes that if you do not effect them, as Mahomet did his, by material force, you must have some strictly impregnable facts at your disposal. And if the apostles had believed the Resurrection to be only probable and not really certain—if they had felt the ground of hard fact on which they stood to be giving way ever so little under their feet—they never could have braced themselves to defy all the intellect, the learning, the world's wealth, the social and political power, the undisguised hostility and vengeance, which at the very outset of their work they saw in all its serried ranks marshalled against them. They must have flinched from the encounter unless they had been sure of their main, of their sustaining, fact. We may be very certain that they looked hard at it again and again, as was natural to men who felt that they had staked their all upon its certainty; and as they looked at it, first in their own memories and next in the memories of those around them, all only testified to its irresistible reality. It was a fact about which they felt and knew that there was no room for mistake or collusion. They had done what the experimentalist philosophers of our day are for ever bidding us do—they had trusted their senses; they had for themselves seen the risen Jesus, listened to Him, touched Him, eaten with Him; they had seen Him again and again under circumstances the most various; they had questioned their impressions in moments of doubt; they had been reassured; they had seen Him in the city, seen

Him at the lake side, seen Him in Jerusalem, in Galilee, and again at Jerusalem. Five hundred persons had seen Him at once, of whom more than one-half were still living thirty years after the event. If one person might be entranced, or hallucinated, or mistaken, all these could not be so simultaneously. If collusion was possible between two or three, surely it was impossible in a multitude. "We have not followed," one of them said in after years, "cunningly devised fables." [1] "We cannot," they said, only a few years after the event, "but speak the things which we have seen and heard." [2] They trusted their senses sufficiently to believe in One Who revealed to them a world higher and greater than this world of sense; and in this certainty they could say with the Psalmist, "Thou hast set my feet upon a rock, and established my goings. Thou hast put a new song in my mouth, even praise unto our God." [3]

Certainly since then many have been the endeavours to prove them wrong. Men have even talked of a conspiracy to deceive the world, alien to the character and beyond the capacity of a company of Jewish peasants. Men have hinted that Jesus did not really die, in spite of the verdict which modern medical science has passed upon the history of the crucifixion. Men have suggested that the apostles confused the spiritual resurrection of an idea with the bodily resurrection of its Author, forgetting that a confusion which may be possible in the metaphysicised brain of a modern would have been impossible in that of a Jew nineteen centuries ago, for the simple reason that its very materials did not exist. Men have hinted that after all it was an hallucination, a delusion, half physical, half mental,—a suggestion of fancy and affection combined,—a vision which partial disciples saw in a trance, having their

[1] 2 Pet. i. 16.    [2] Acts iv. 20.    [3] Ps. xl. 2-3.

eyes open,—a product in the first instance of the over-excited, almost diseased brain of a Magdalen,—which generated this belief in the Resurrection of Christ; although, as we have seen, an *ignis fatuus* like this, made up of poetry, sentiment, fable—made up of everything but hard evidence of truth—would never have supplied the moral momentum with which the apostles breasted a hostile world. Then again, they insist on the discrepancies between the gospel accounts of the resurrection, while in reality, upon a careful examination, such discrepancies will be found only to correspond to such difference of statement as are natural to writers describing the same event from different points of view, or following distinct yet equally praiseworthy sources of information. It is impossible for these writers to lay their finger upon that which alone would serve their purpose—one case of absolute and necessary contradiction between the narratives. And then the ground has been shifted, and it is argued that whatever evidence may be producible in a particular instance, the Resurrection cannot be true for anterior reasons. It does not become the Creator, they think, to innovate in this way upon the usual rules of His work, and thus to substitute what they call caprice for the reign of law. But how can you be certain that a miracle is caprice—that it is anything more than the deliberate and fore-ordained suspension of a lower law by the intervention of a higher law—in the case before us, of the lower and temporary law of death by the higher and eternal law of life? How can you be clear that thus to intervene does not become God, if He be a moral Governor of this world, and if there are vast moral reasons for His intervening in it? Ah, if you say, "He cannot thus intervene," I understand you. You mean that having created a universe made up of matter, regulated by force, He has actually abdicated in favour of the work of His hands,—that the real matter-of-fact disposer of life and death is a power, or a series of powers, which you name Nature, and that the Author of Nature has been dismissed with even an exaggerated tribute of respect to a very, very distant Heaven, where He is well out of the way of your theories and your apprehensions. But you are surely too sensible to suppose that still to give to this impotent abstraction, which you have banished beyond the precincts of all practical life, the sacred Name of God really bridges over the chasm between us. If there be a God in the sense of Scripture, in the sense of the human heart, at least He can do what He wills with His own; and if there be not, it is better not to perplex the discussion by a fruitless equivocation. But then, you have never yet observed a miracle like the Resurrection within the range of your personal experience. So it was with these ancient Greeks, described by Herodotus, who were told by some African travellers that they had reached a point where at noon-day their shadows turned the wrong way. While listening to their statement, even the "Father of History" himself was entirely incredulous; but every child now knows that those travellers must simply have crossed the equator. Whether you can explain the fact or not, at least in the name of truth respect it—respect it until you can disprove it. Equatorial Africa was inaccessible to all but the most adventurous of ancient explorers, but the real evidence of the actual, literal Resurrection of the Lord Jesus Christ is not out of the reach of any one intelligent man; and I say that the Resurrection is a fact attested by the most various and converging evidence, defying up to this very moment all the action of the critical solvents which unbelief has applied and does apply to it—a fact let me add, reigning in the thought of every thinking Christian as a vast evidential power.

Now the apostles felt that for the purpose of propagating the religion of Jesus Christ the certain fact of His Resurrection from the grave was of the greatest possible practical value. Jewish prophecy, as the Jews themselves understood it, pointed to a Messiah Who would die and Who would rise. Our Lord had been asked for a sign which might convince His countrymen that His mission was from God; and although he disliked the temper which put the question, He pointed to the prophet Jonah. Jonah sojourning in and delivered from the belly of the sea fish, would correspond to His own burial and resurrection from the grave. More emphatically and explicitly still at the outset of His last journey to Jerusalem He foretold His death and His resurrection, and thus His whole credit was staked upon this issue; and when in the event He did rise from the dead, His resurrection was not merely a thing intrinsically wonderful, it was the fulfilment of a condition to which any one who came to be Messiah was bound down by prophecy, and to which Jesus Himself was bound by personal assurances which He had volunteered both to His disciples and to the world.

Now in order to do justice to the evidential power of the Resurrection which the apostles felt themselves and communicated to others with such astonishing results, let us, my brethren, think of some one holy and venerable friend, better far than the best that you or I have ever known in life. Let us suppose that he could address us in this way: "I am shortly going to die, but after I am dead and you have closed my eyes, and laid me in my coffin, and carried me to my grave, I shall on a given day burst upwards from the tomb and appear among you—not for a moment, then to vanish, but again and again to talk, and walk, and hold with you all the endearing converse of bygone years. And if up to this moment I have ever told you anything that you have thought hard or strange about truth and duty, about the character of God, about the nature, the destiny of the soul,—nay, if I have gone beyond this, and have spoken of myself and of my relationship to God and to mankind, and of my coming empire over the souls of men in unborn ages—the warrant, the justification of all this will be plain to you when I do really rise out of my grave. You will be satisfied then, if not before, that I am entitled to speak to you as I have spoken to you." Well, my brethren, I will not even attempt to say how we should receive a prediction of this kind. I will only say this, that it would require the most spotless of lives, the most penetrating of spiritual intelligences in the speaker, ay, and a great deal besides this, to make us even patient under it, patient enough to wait for its verification. But let us suppose that it is verified; that our friend does die; that there is no room whatever for mistake as to the fact of his death; that he is duly buried; and then, when all seems over and in our thoughts as in reality the tomb has closed over his body, he actually bursts up from his grave, introduces himself to us one by one as we can bear to see him, and becomes to us all and much more than all that he was in past years before he leaves us again for good. Now this was actually what did happen to the apostles. This experience was the force, the tremendous force, which made a few peasants and teachers, selected from the lower and middle classes of an out-of-the-way province, equal to nothing less than the moral and intellectual conquest of the world. For the apostles the Resurrection warranted the truth of Christ's mission, the truth of Christianity. All that Christ had said, all that He had promised and foretold, was raised by the Resurrection to the high level of undisputed certainty. With this tremendous evidential power impelling and sustaining them they went forward, they could not but go forward, to win first the attention and then the faith of men in the truth which the Resurrection attested. What became of them personally it mattered not. If they succeeded, it would be in the strength of the risen Jesus; if they failed, the mighty risen One could not but succeed. There it was ever before them— the imperious, the invigorating fact that He had burst up from His grave as He said He would; and it only remained for them, as it remains for us at this hour, to do justice to the evidential power of the Resurrection.

There is a disposition abroad now-a-days to treat doubts of the truth of the Christian religion as anything but a misfortune, as an interesting form of intellectual vigour; and accordingly a popular poet [1] assures us that

> "There lives more faith in honest doubt,
> Believe me, than in half the creeds."

Now if that means that an earnest doubter, who has lost his way among the difficulties of controversy, may possibly have a keener sense of the unseen which he seeks but has not found than the careless adherent of a creed, who has never seriously thought either of its meaning or its grounds, then the words may pass muster; but if their true drift is to compare the average doubter with the average believer, or still more the earnest doubter with the earnest believer, and then to imply that there is a balance of the moral qualities of faith on the side of doubt, it is simply a duty from this chair of truth to meet the poet with a flat contradiction. To be tender towards doubters is one thing, to glorify and canonise doubt is another. If faith is, as spiritually speaking it is, health, then doubt is beyond all question disease; for doubt is the solvent which persistently breaks up faith and destroys it,

[1] A. Tennyson, "In Memoriam," cant. xcv.

and unless you would enter the ward of a fever or consumptive hospital and airily congratulate the patients who lie there on their weariness and their pain, do not be guilty of the heartlessness, the folly of treating doubts of the truth of Christianity as a matter of congratulation to those who entertain them. Surely it were better, if only they would allow it, to surround them as you would surround the sick and the suffering, with all the care of an active charity; and then, if the root of the doubt be not moral—if they have not reasons for wishing that Christianity should be untrue—guide the doubter's steps to the empty grave of Jesus Christ on Easter morning. There beyond all question he plants his foot firmly on the rock of history; there beyond all question, too, he stands face to face with the traces of a well-attested and stupendous miracle.

> "Reason and Faith at once set out
> To search the Saviour's tomb;
> Faith faster runs, but waits without,
> As fearing to presume,
> Till Reason enter in and trace
> Christ's relics round the holy place." [1]

After all what is this but to ask a man to put himself simply into the position of the apostles of Christ when the power of the Resurrection in all its evidential force dawned upon them? Certainly if on that sacred ground, and in view of that evidence, the Resurrection could be denied, we may not disguise the consequence. The Resurrection is not merely the great certificate of Christianity; it is the main part, it is the very heart of its substance. The apostles do not countenance the notion that you can throw the Resurrection of Christ into the background or deny it outright, and still be a Christian—that you can make an

[1] Keble's "Christian Year," S. Thomas' Day, 3d stanza.

extract of so many of the precepts, of so much of the history of Christ, and pronounce that extract to be the really important and vital element of the religion, and then throw all that requires belief in the Supernatural forthwith to the winds. Such a Christianity as this could have been no Christianity at all in the judgment of St. Paul. St. Paul maintains that the Resurrection of Christ is so bound up with Christianity that to deny it is not simply to cut its most important incident right out of the heart of the Christian creed, but that it is to part with Christianity as a whole. "If Christ be not risen, then is our preaching vain, and your faith is also vain."[1] "If Christ be not raised, your faith is vain; ye are yet in your sins. Then, they also which are fallen asleep in Christ are perished."[2] Deny the Resurrection and Christianity collapses altogether, as certainly as does an arch when the keystone is removed; and in place of the Conqueror of death, and the Redeemer of souls, there remains only a Jewish rabbi, whose story has been curiously encrusted with legends, and some of whose sayings may still be thought to be entitled to attention. But admit the Resurrection and you admit the Creed; you admit a fact which, if you are a thinking man, must govern, colour, impregnate your whole thought, must make faith intellectually easy and doubt unlikely. For the Resurrection guarantees the absolute truth of Christ's teaching and mission. It converts His death into a transient preliminary of an eternal triumph. It leads on to the Ascension and the perpetual intercession in Heaven. It is the warrant that He will come to judgment. To admit His Resurrection and to be perpetually braying about the results of His mission, ever explaining away His miracles, or grudging their due authority to His apostles, or questioning the

[1] 1 Cor. xv. 14.   [2] Ibid. xv. 17, 18.

power of prayer, and the reality of Providence, or undervaluing the Sacraments which Christ ordained for the life of man, or denying the truth of those Old Testament Scriptures to which He set the seal of His personal witness—this is to be guilty of mental inconsistency as well as of religious hardihood; it is to have granted the greater, and then to raise a difficulty about granting the less. The only question for a believing Christian is, What is and what is not warranted immediately, and by a necessary inference, by His authority, Who was "declared to be the Son of God with power, according to the Spirit of holiness, by the Resurrection from the dead."[1] When that question is once settled, controversy ought to be absolutely at an end; it ought to be ended by the evidential power of Christ's resurrection.

But it is in the conduct, in the moral and spiritual life of the Christian that the power of the Resurrection may chiefly be felt. This was the main scope of the apostle's prayer. He had no doubt whatever about the truth of the Gospel; but to know Christ risen in his heart and will —this was a field in which boundless improvement was possible even for a St. Paul, a region in which on this side the grave perfect satisfaction was unattainable. What are the necessary conditions of an effective moral power, of a power which shall stimulate and control feeling, resolution, action? There are, I apprehend, two main conditions which must be satisfied by any such power, which are satisfied, and that amply, by the resurrection of our Saviour. For human life looked at on its practical side is made up of two things, action and suffering. We are all of us doing something, even when we are reduced to the degradation of killing time; we all of us have our something, perhaps much, to suffer before we come to die.

[1] Rom. i. 4.

And what is the first necessity of every agent and every sufferer but an end,—some end to look forward to, some end to be compassed by action, or to be reached by endurance? And when endurance is over, what is the second necessity but an assurance of assistance and support—of assistance in efforts to which our strength is unequal, of support under trials by which our weakness must be crushed? And Christian life corresponds to human life in this, that it too, and in an eminent degree, is made up of action and of suffering. A Christian acts and a Christian suffers, not because he cannot help doing so, but with his heart and in virtue of a principle. He transfigures the necessities of ordinary human life into opportunities for acts of virtue. But then, if he attempts more he also needs more than natural men, a more definite and higher aim, a more present and sustaining aid. For a Christian is, in his way, a soldier, an artist, a statesman; although in the first instance and pre-eminently his battlefield, his canvas, his political arena, are bounded by the precincts and history of his own soul and life. And what is a general who has no plan of campaign embodying the hope of ultimate victory, or who cannot place any dependence whatever upon his troops? What is an artist who has no ideal before his mind's eye which he proposes to realize in stone or in canvas, and who is utterly unable to command the materials which would enable him to do so if he had one? What is the statesman who can conceive or shape no possible future for his country, or who, at least, has not at his disposal the influence or the skill which could enable him to secure it? These illustrations what do they suggest but pictures of demoralisation, impotence, failure, collapse? Depend upon it, that if you would be each within himself the true soldier, the true artist, the true statesman, if you would beat down and imprison the brute that is latent in you, if you would trace upon the inner sanctuaries of thought and feeling and motive the moral beauties of a noble and unselfish life, if you would carry out in the humblest of conditions, or in the greatest, works of benevolence, works of real utility and of substantial good, then you too need in both its forms power,—the power of encouragement afforded by the sight of a definite end or purpose, the power of support giving you at least good hope of attaining it. Now the Resurrection of the Lord Jesus satisfies these conditions, and I add that it does so on a magnificent scale. In the first place, the Resurrection opens out before the eye of the soul its one adequate end in all action and in all endurance,—union of the whole man with God, extending throughout the vast prospectives of a boundless eternity.

It may be asked whether the doctrine of the immortality of the soul would not support this want just as well. The answer is that it would not. First of all, there is the difficulty of procuring general acceptance for it. Revelation teaches it, as revelation teaches with equal clearness the resurrection of the body. If the authority of revelation is good for anything we must listen to it whenever it speaks. But it is of course abundantly notorious that, as in the ancient pagan world so now, there were and are men who, never having heard of or denying the resurrection of the body, would ground the immortality of the soul upon a basis of reason, and their arguments are, as I apprehend, in the main twofold. There is the argument that the soul, being a simple uncompounded substance, cannot be dissolved at the dissolution of the body—an argument stated by Plato, and nobly worked out by Fénelon: and there is the far stronger and moral argument, which insists with truth and force upon the tremendous disproportion in this present life between deserts on the one hand

and rewards and punishments on the other. It may be fairly said that the Almighty Governor of such a world as this owes a future existence to His creatures as a debt of justice to virtue, and as rebuking the triumphs of vice. No thoughtful man will disparage for one moment the force of these arguments. The first goes to establish the permanence of the substance of the soul, the second the permanence of our distinct personality. Yet, strong as these are, they are not such arguments as would carry conviction to the millions of mankind. To appreciate the one, a man must have enjoyed a certain amount of mental culture; to do justice to the other, his own moral sense of right must be clear and strong. If not merely a few thinkers but the many, you and I, are to believe with all our hearts in a future life; if we are to live for it; if we are to feel it as an anticipation shaping and controlling day by day thoughts, and words, and acts,—then something more is needed, something that shall rivet and complete the anticipations of reason by an appeal to experience. Besides this, reason will not always stop precisely at the point which is wanted for the purpose. The arguments which would render the destiny of the soul so entirely independent of that of the body are not altogether true to the facts of human nature. It is said that of late years our highest medical science has established more and more clearly the traces of a correspondence between thought and matter, between the several faculties of the mind and the convolutions of the brain; and this consideration has been generally supposed to show that the soul has no real existence, that it is a mere phosphoric exhalation from matter—in other words, to prove the truth of materialism; but nothing as yet, as I apprehend, has been found by our anatomists which can account in any degree whatever for such a fact as consciousness,—for that power of reflecting on and taking the measure of its own existence, which attests the presence of an immaterial spirit; therefore, the more you demonstrate in other respects this sensitive correspondence between matter and mind, the more certainly do you establish not the perishableness of the soul but the presumptive immortality of the body. Your demonstration goes to show with some of the greatest of the Christian fathers that the personality of man would be impaired if the body could rot in its grave; that the immortality of the soul, if it is to be the immortality of a person, implies also the immortality of the body which has been so intimately, so long associated with its whole life of action and thought and feeling; that the temporary divorce which takes place at death, the few years of dishonour and decay which are covered by the coffin and the grave, must needs give place to a future in which man in his unmutilated completeness again will live—live for ever in the regions of some endless life.

And even if it were true that the immortality of the soul, without implying anything as to the body, could be brought home by sheer reason to the convictions of every member of our race, still this conviction of the reason, if unaided, would not supply what you and I need in the presence of death. In times of sorrow it is the senses and the imagination that take the lead. They bid reason fall into the rear. The eye of sense rests day after day upon the ravages of disease; it rests at length upon the pallor, the chill, the disfigurement, the corruption of death; it scans with something like despair the expressionless corpse which but yesterday was the home, the instrument, of a living spirit. And when all that can meet the eye of sense is at length hidden from sight, the imagination will often wander after the funeral hearse. It will hover around the precincts of the tomb; it will penetrate beneath the soil of the churchyard, beneath the arches of the vault, beneath the boards of the coffin; it will sit there in its dark agony, tracing from stage to stage the fell work of corruption as it breaks up what was yesterday so animated, so beautiful, into the loathsome forms of decomposing matter. You may say that this is morbid, but you are yourself in good health and spirits, and the answer to you is that in hours of deep sorrow all this is profoundly human. Reason may still cherish her abstract arguments for immortality, she may push them to the very verge of the Christian faith itself; but reason cannot hold her own against this energetic agony of imagination and sense, when they inflict upon the soul their profound despondency. "It cannot be," they whisper to us, "that there is really a future. It cannot be that, after all, matter and not mind is really ruler of this universe. Contact with death shatters that phantom of immortality, that phantom which is the creation of your human self-love." So whispers, I say, not reason, but imagination and sense to the afflicted mourner; and something is wanted which shall meet imagination and sense on their own ground,—which shall visibly reverse the impressions of this spectacle of death which so painfully depresses them: something is wanted which shall emancipate reason in its hour of darkest sorrow from the trammels of these lower faculties, and shall roll back the stone from the door of the sepulchre of the very best of human hopes. That something was supplied on the early morning of Easter Day. After preaching to the spirits in prison, the human Soul of Jesus Christ—surrounded we may be sure by a multitude of adoring spirits —moved upwards from the home of the ancient dead and paused by the side of the holy Body; and then the dark sepulchre was illumined by a flash of light, and the vast rock that closed the entrance rolled lightly away, and the soldiers, whom Jewish suspicion had set to watch, were terrified into silence; and, as He passed forth in the morning with His resistless force from His grave, first to teach His disciples how to build His Church, and then to ascend to His throne above, what was the lesson which by His very action He taught to the generations of men? "Some of you," He might seem to say, "know the real meaning of your destiny on the authority of God: multitudes of you do not even suspect it: others have conjectured it, but only to question their conjectures. Henceforth let that future life, which has been an unsuspected or a disputed truth, be raised at once to the rank of a certainty, absolute, indisputable. If heretofore the anticipations of the last hour have seemed to poison all the brightness of life,—if you have looked on the grave only as a conqueror, before whom all that is strongest and most buoyant must bend at last in humiliation and sorrow—here is death robbed of its sting, here is the grave balked of its victory by a triumph visible to your very senses; for 'I am He that liveth, and was dead; and, behold, I am alive for evermore, Amen; and have the keys of hell and of death.'[1] 'I am the Resurrection and the Life: he that believeth in Me, though he were dead, yet shall he live: and whosoever liveth and believeth in Me shall never die.'"[2] It was thus that the Resurrection spoke to the first Christians. They knew that it was not merely the resurrection of the Redeemer. They knew that God, Who had raised up Jesus, would raise us up of His own power with Jesus, Who is indeed "risen from the dead, and become the first fruits of them that slept;" for that "as in Adam all die, even so in Christ should all be made alive."[3] And thus a new power has entered into human life, the vast power of sincere belief in a future world. Every true Christian

[1] Rev. i. 18.   [2] John xi. 25, 26.   [3] 1 Cor. xv. 20.

feels that this life is an insignificant preface to the rest; that it is merely the shadow which precedes the substance, but upon which the attainment of the substance depends; that the longest life is a mere halt upon the brink of the eternal world—that world of awful, unchangeable realities. Here, I say, where a man has a sincere belief, there is a tremendous power,—a power which can invigorate the will, and purify affection, and check the fire of passion, and quicken into life the languor of despair,—a power which elevates the whole aim and scope of life, which forbids petty aims and indulgences, and bids each one of us in success and in failure, in great things and in small, in private and in public, ever to forget the present in the future, to remember "what is the hope of our calling, and what the riches of the glory of our inheritance among the saints."[1]

Not many days ago an eminent historian was addressing a Scotch university, and he is reported to have used these remarkable words:—"From the great houses in the city of London to the village grocer, the commercial life of England has been saturated with fraud. So deep has it gone that a strictly honest tradesman can hardly hold his ground against competition. You can no longer trust that any article you buy is the thing that it pretends to be. We have false weights, false measures, cheating everywhere." Now I do not mean to endorse that indictment against the commercial life of England; but supposing it to be true, or, what is more probable, only very partially true, I ask where is the remedy? Not, I venture to say, in a teaching which shall make it a point of honour to ignore, if it do not deny God, eternity, the Redeemer's Blood, the means of Grace—all that cannot be reached, by touch, or sight, or smell—and then which shall insist

[1] Eph. i. 18.

vehemently, exclusively, upon the practical advantages of honesty in this present visible world. No doubt honesty is the best policy here, but that consideration will not make a man honest when great private advantage is in his opinion to be won by dishonour. No, if you would make men honest or pure or in any way great, tell them of the true dignity of their being; open before their eyes the vast prospects of the eternity which awaits them in that kingdom into which can enter nothing that defileth or maketh a lie,[1] yet into which they may enter if only they will; tell them, though you incur the sarcasms of unbelief, of the presence and Grace of the risen Redeemer; tell them of "the exceeding greatness of God's power" at this moment "to us-ward who believe, according to the working of His mighty power, which He wrought in Christ, when He raised Him from the dead, and set Him at His own right hand in the heavenly places."[2]

"The power of His resurrection." We live in a day when men ask for positive grounds of thought and action, and the power before us—it is my last word—is the power not of a sentiment but of a fact. A sentiment! It has its day, if it be only a sentiment. The phases of mere feeling which pass rapidly over the generation of men are like the forms of the clouds above our heads, beautiful but evanescent; but a fact such as the Resurrection remains. It is like the sun in the heavens, which, though it may be deemed commonplace and uninteresting by a race of barbarians, is the daily study and wonder of your astronomers. It remains through days, through years, almost through lives of neglect, to claim at the last the vast homage of the mind and heart of man which rightfully belongs to it; to make itself felt in thought and in practice; to ennoble our dealings with our fellow creatures;

[1] Rev. xxi. 27.     [2] Eph. i. 19, 20.

to define our true relationship to God. And thus while it hallows the things of time, it unveils, it warrants the true glories of eternity; and, at the least, it loses nothing of its surpassing interest as the years flow on, and we ourselves draw nearer and nearer to that mysterious world whither so many loved ones already have preceded even the younger of us, since more than any other truth in the Christian Creed it bids us wait and work trustfully, patiently, till

> "with the morn those angel faces smile
> Which we have loved long since, and lost awhile." [1]

O thou, Who art indeed risen from the dead, the eternal Jesus, build up and invigorate the faith of this people even at the door of Thy empty sepulchre. Open our earthborn eyes to that mighty world wherein Thou and Thou alone art King; and then crucify us, if need be, to the things of time, that with Thee and by Thee both here and hereafter we may indeed know the truth, the resistless power of thy glorious Resurrection. And to Thee, with the Father and the Holy Spirit, be glory and dominion for ever.

[1] J. H. Newman: Lyra Apostolica, xxv.

# SERMON XI.

## THE INEVITABLENESS OF CHRIST'S RESURRECTION.

### Acts ii. 24.

"*Whom God hath raised up, having loosed the pains of death: because it was not possible that He should be holden of it.*"

THIS is the language of the first Christian apostle in the first sermon that ever was preached in the Church of Christ. St. Peter is accounting for the miraculous gift of languages on the day of Pentecost; and, after observing that it was, after all, only a fulfilment of the prophecy of Joel about the out-pouring of the Spirit in the last days, he proceeds to trace it to its cause. It was the work, he says, of Jesus Christ now ascended into Heaven. "He hath shed forth this, which ye now see and hear."[1] But Jesus Christ, he argues, had really ascended into heaven, because He had first really risen from His grave; and it is to St. Peter's way of accounting for Christ's resurrection that I invite your attention to-day, as being the first apostolic statement on the subject that was given to the world.

My brethren, even if this point were only one of antiquarian interest it surely would be full of attractions for every intelligent man to know how the first Christians thought about the chief truths of their faith, considering the influence that that faith has had, and still has, on the

[1] Acts ii. 33.

development of the human race. But, for us Christians, concern in this matter is more exacting and more urgent. Our hopes and fears, our depressions and our enthusiasms, our improvement or our deterioration, are bound up with it. "If Christ be not risen, then is our preaching vain, and your faith is also vain."[1]

Let us, then, listen to what the apostle St. Peter says about a subject upon which his opportunities—to say nothing of higher credentials—qualified him to speak with authority.

First of all, then, St. Peter states the fact that Christ had risen from the dead. "Whom God hath raised up, having loosed the pains of death." Let us remember that he is preaching in Jerusalem, the scene of the death and resurrection of Christ, and, as his sermon shows, he is preaching to some who had taken part in the crucifixion. Not more than seven weeks have yet passed since those events—just about the time that has passed since Quinquagesima Sunday; and in Jerusalem, we may be sure, men did not live as fast as they do in a European capital in this age of telegraphs and railroads. An event like the Crucifixion, in a town of that size so far removed from the greater centres of human life, would have occupied general attention for a considerable period. It would have been discussed and rediscussed in all its bearings; and all that happened at the time and immediately afterwards— the supposed disappointment of the disciples, the presumed ruin of the cause, as well as the agony and humiliation of the Master—would have been still ordinary topics of conversation in most circles of Jewish society. It was, then, to persons keenly interested in the subject, and who had opportunities at hand of testing the exact truth of what he said, that Peter states, thus calmly and unhesitatingly, the fact of the Resurrection. He states it as just as much a

[1] 1 Cor. xv. 14.

truth of history as the Crucifixion in which his hearers themselves had taken part. " Ye men of Israel, hear these words; Jesus of Nazareth, a Man approved of God among you, by miracles and wonders and signs, which God did by Him in the midst of you, as ye yourselves also know: Him, being delivered by the determinate counsel and foreknowledge of God, ye have taken, and by wicked hands have crucified and slain." And then he adds, " Whom God hath raised up, having loosed the pains of death." "This Jesus," he adds a little afterwards, "hath God raised up, whereof we all are witnesses." Not one or two favoured disciples, but all, even the doubter —all had seen their beloved Master: they had heard the tone of that familiar voice: they had seen the wounds of the Passion: they recognised in repeated conversations the continuity of heart, of thought, of purpose. It was the Jesus of old days, only radiant with a new and awful glory. On the very day that He rose He had been seen five times; and "He showed Himself alive after His Passion by many infallible proofs, being seen of His disciples forty days and speaking of the things pertaining to the kingdom of God."[1] And some twenty-six years later, when St. Paul wrote his first letter to the church of Corinth, there were, he says, more than two hundred and fifty persons still alive who had seen Jesus Christ after His resurrection on a single occasion. The number of witnesses to the fact of the Resurrection, to whom St. Peter could appeal, and whom his hearers might cross-question if they liked, will account for the simplicity and confidence of his assertion. In those days men had not yet learned to think more of abstract theories than of well attested facts. The world had not yet heard of that singular state of mind with which we of to-day are not alto-

[1] Acts i. 3.

gether unfamiliar, which holds that some *à priori* doctrine about the nature of things, or, stranger still, about the temper and moods of human thought, is a sufficient reason for refusing to listen to the evidence which may be produced in favour of a fact which interferes with these theories. Nobody, it may be added—nobody who professed to believe in an almighty God—thought it either reverent or reasonable to say that He could not, for sufficient reasons, modify or innovate upon His ordinary rules of working, if He chose to do so.

St. Peter, then, preached the Resurrection as a fact, and, as we know, with great and immediate results. But how did he account for the Resurrection? What was the reason which he gave for its having happened at all? This is the second point to which I invite your attention, and it will detain us rather longer than the first.

St. Peter, then, says that Christ was raised from the dead because it was not possible that He should be holden of death. Thus you will observe that St. Peter's thought about this matter is the very opposite to that of many persons in our day. They say, in so many words, that no evidence will convince them that Christ has risen, because they hold it to be antecedently impossible that He should rise. St. Peter, on the other hand, almost speaks as if he could dispense with evidence, so certain is he that Jesus Christ must rise. In point of fact, as we know, St. Peter had his own experience to fall back upon. He had seen his risen Master on the day of the Resurrection, and often since; but so far was this evidence of his senses from causing him any perplexity, that it only fell in with the anticipations which he had now formed on other and independent grounds. It was not possible, he says, that Christ should be holden or imprisoned by death.

It will do us good, my brethren, as fellow believers with

St. Peter, to spend some little time upon his grounds for saying this,—to consider, so far as we may, the reasons for this divine impossibility.

And here, first of all, we find the reason which lay, so to speak, nearest to the conclusion, and it was intended to convince the apostle's hearers in the sermon itself. " It was not possible that Christ should be holden of death; for David speaketh concerning Him." It was, then, Jewish prophecy which, if I may say so, forbade the Christ to remain in His grave—which made His resurrection nothing less than a divine necessity. As to the principle of this argument there would have been no controversy between St. Peter and the Jews. The Jews believed in the reality and in the compulsive force of prophecy—of that variety of prophecy which predicts events that are strictly future —just as distinctly as do Christians. The prophets, in the belief of the Jews, were the confidants of God. God whispered into the ear of their souls by His Spirit His secret resolutions for the coming time. "Surely," could exclaim the prophet Amos,—" Surely the Lord God will do nothing, but He revealeth his secret unto His servants the prophets."[1] And when once God had thus spoken, it was felt by Jews as it is felt by Christians, that His word standeth sure, His gifts and calling are without repentance. The prophetical word became, in virtue of the moral attributes of God, a restraint upon that very liberty of God, of which it was the product, until it was fulfilled. It constituted, within the limits of its application, a law of necessity, to which men and events, and, if need were, nature, had to bend. And for all who believed in its Author, the supposition that it would come to nothing after all was, to use St. Peter's phrase, "not possible." That word could not return empty. It must accomplish the work for which

[1] Amos iii. 7.

God had sent it forth, since it bound Him to an engagement with those who uttered, and with those who heard, His message. Of course, my brethren, the true drift of a prophecy may easily be mistaken, and God is not responsible for eccentric guesses as to His meaning, in which well intentioned men of lively imagination may possibly indulge. We have lived in this generation to hear some very confident guesses, based on the supposed meaning of prophecy, respecting the end of the world, or some impending general catastrophe. The dates assigned for such occurrences have passed, and religion would be seriously discredited if indeed the sacred word itself were at fault, instead of the fervid imagination of some apocalyptic expositor. But where a prediction is clear, it does bind Him, who is its real Author, to its fulfilment, which in the event, will be recognized as such; and such a prediction of the resurrection of Messiah St. Peter finds in the 16th psalm, where David, as on a greater scale in the 22nd psalm, loses the sense of his own personal circumstances in the impetus and ecstasy of the prophetic spirit which possesses him, and describes a Personality of which, indeed, he was the type, but which altogether transcends his own. "Therefore My heart is glad and My glory rejoiceth: My flesh also shall rest in hope. For Thou wilt not leave My soul in hell, neither wilt Thou suffer Thine Holy One to see corruption. Thou wilt show Me the path of life: in Thy presence is the fulness of joy; and at Thy right hand there are pleasures for evermore."[1] David, so St. Peter argues, utters these words, but of David himself they are not strictly true. "David," he says, "is both dead and buried, and his sepulchre is among us even unto this day."[2] Or, as St. Paul puts it, when appealing to this very psalm in his sermon at Antioch in Pisidia,

---

[1] Ps. xvi. 9-11.     [2] Acts ii. 29.

"David, after he had served his own generation by the will of God, fell on sleep, and was laid unto his fathers, and saw corruption: but He, Whom God raised again, saw no corruption."[1] And the meaning of the psalm was so clear to one school of the Jewish doctors that, unable as they were to reconcile it with the facts of David's history, they invented the fable that his body was miraculously preserved from corruption. David was really speaking at the moment in the person of Messiah, and his language created the necessity that Messiah should rise from the dead; or, as St. Peter puts it, his language made it impossible that the Christ should be holden by death. God had spoken in other passages, no doubt, but especially in this word: His word could not return unto Him empty.

Observe, my brethren, that St. Peter had not always felt and thought thus. He had known the 16th psalm all his life; but long after he had followed Jesus Christ about Galilee and Judea he had been ignorant of its true meaning. Only little by little it is that any one of us learns God's full truth and will; and so lately as the morning of the Resurrection, St. Matthew says of both St. Peter and St. John that, as yet, they knew not the scripture that Christ must rise again from the dead. Since then, the Holy Spirit had come down. He had poured a flood of light into the minds of His apostles, and over the sacred pages of the Old Testament; and the necessity for the Resurrection, which even Jewish expositors might have recognised if they would, became abundantly plain to them. May that same Spirit teach us, as He taught our spiritual forefathers, the true meaning of His word!

And a second reason which would have shaped St. Peter's language lay in the character of Jesus Christ. It was our Lord's character, not less than His miracles, which drew

[1] Acts xiii. 36, 37.

human hearts to Him—which led or forced them to give up all that the world could offer, for the happiness of following and serving Him. Now, of our Lord's character the leading feature, if I may so speak with reverence, was its simple truthfulness. It was morally impossible for Him to hold out prospects which would never be realized, or to use words which He did not mean. Nay, He insisted upon simple sincerity of language in those who came into His company. He would not allow the young man to call Him "Good Master," when the expression was, in his mouth, a mere phrase. He would not accept pretensions to following Him whithersoever He went, or aspirations to sit on His right hand or on His left hand in His kingdom, till men had weighed their words, and were quite sure that they meant what their words involved. Unless, then, He was like the Pharisees whom He condemned for laying burdens upon others which they would not touch themselves, it might be taken for granted that if He promised He would perform—that His promise made performance morally binding—made non-performance morally impossible. This was the feeling of His disciples about Him—that He was too wise to predict the impossible, too sincere to promise what He did not mean. Now, Jesus Christ had, again and again, said that He would be put to a violent death, and that after dying He would rise again. Sometimes, as to the Jews in the temple when He cleansed it in the early days of His ministry, He expressed His meaning in the language of metaphor. "Destroy," He said, "this temple, and in three days I will raise it up."[1] The Jews rallied Him on the absurdity of undertaking to reconstruct an edifice in three days which had taken forty-six years to build; but the real sense of the words was plain to the disciples by the gesture which had accompanied them.

[1] John ii. 19.

And in later years they understood the full sense in which He termed His human Body a temple, namely, because in Him dwelt all the fulness of the Godhead bodily.

And sometimes He fell back upon ancient Hebrew history, and compared that which was to happen to Himself with the miraculous adventure of the prophet who shrank from the mission which God had assigned to him. When the Pharisees, irritated at His stern rebuke of their blasphemous levity in assigning His miracle on the blind and dumb man to the agency of Beelzebub, asked Him for a sign—that is, for some credentials of His mission—He contented Himself with saying that, as Jonah had been three days and three nights in the whale's belly, so the Son of Man would be in the heart of the earth. In other words, His right to speak and act as He did would be proved by His rising from the dead. But with His disciples He used neither metaphor nor historical parallel. He said simply, on three occasions at the least, as the hour of His sufferings approached, that He should be crucified and should rise from death. Peter himself had, on the first of these occasions, rebuked Him, as we know, and had been rebuked in turn. And thus He was pledged, if we may reverently say so, to this particular act of resurrection. He was pledged to the Jewish people. He was pledged to its rulers and its governing classes. He was pledged, especially, to His own chosen band of followers. He could not have remained in His grave—I will not say without dishonour, but without entailing that revulsion of feeling which is always provoked, and justly provoked, by the exposure of baseless pretensions. It may be, indeed it has been urged, that the resurrection foretold by Christ was not a literal resurrection of His dead Body, but only a recovery of His ascendancy, His credit, His popular authority—obscured as these had been for a while by the tragedy of the Crucifixion—in the apprehension of His disciples and of the world. The word "resurrection," according to this supposition, is, in His mouth, a purely metaphorical expression. It is used to describe not anything which affected Jesus Christ Himself, but only a revulsion of opinion and feeling about Him in the minds of others. Socrates had had to drink the fatal hemlock, and the body of Socrates had long since mingled with the dust; but Socrates, it might be said, had, in a sense, risen—risen in the intellectual triumphs of his pupils—risen in the enthusiastic admiration of succeeding ages; and the method and the words of Socrates have been preserved for all time in a literature that will never die. If Christ was to be put to death by crucifixion, He would triumph, even after a death so shameful and degrading, as Socrates and others had triumphed before Him. To imagine for Him an actual exit from His tomb, is said to be a literalisation natural to uncultivated ages, but impossible when the finer suggestiveness of human language has been felt to transcend the letter. An obvious reply to this explanation is, that it arbitrarily makes our Lord use a literal and a metaphorical expression in two successive clauses of a single sentence. He is literal, it seems, when He predicts His crucifixion. There is no doubt on any side about that. The world has agreed with the Church as to the fact of His being crucified. Tacitus mentions His death as well as the evangelists. But if He is to be understood literally when He foretells His cross, why is He to become suddenly metaphorical when He foretells His resurrection? Why should not His resurrection, if it be only metaphorical, be preceded by a metaphorical crucifixion, too,—a crucifixion of the thought—a crucifixion of the will—a crucifixion of His reputation—not the literal nailing of His human Body to a wooden cross? Why does this fastidious spiritualism, if it be such, which shrinks from the idea of a literal rising out of a literal grave, not shrink equally from a literal nailing to a literal cross? It is impossible, my brethren, seriously to maintain, on any grounds that can be accepted by an honest interpretation of language, that our Lord Himself could have meant that He would be literally crucified, but would only rise in a metaphorical sense. He meant that the one event would be just as much, or just as little, a matter of fact as the other, and any other construction of His words would never have originated except with those who wish to combine some sort of faint, lingering respect for the language of the Master, with a total disbelief in the supreme miracle which has made Him what He is to Christendom. No, it must be said: if Jesus Christ had not risen from the grave, He would not have kept His engagements with His disciples, or with the world. This was the feeling of the men who knew and who loved Him best. This was the feeling of St. Peter, ripened, no doubt, only lately into a sharply defined conviction, but based on years of intimate companionship—that after He, so scrupulously truthful, so invariably wise, had once said that He would rise from death, any other event was simply impossible. All was really staked thus on His really rising again; and when He did rise, He was declared, as His apostle said, to be the Son of God with power, in respect of His higher eternal Nature, by this resurrection from the dead. Those who cling to His human character, and yet deny His resurrection, would do well to consider that they must choose between their moral enthusiasm on the one hand, and their unbelief on the other; since it is the character of Christ which, even more than the language of prophecy, made the idea that He would not rise after death so impossible to His first disciples.

Nor have we yet exhausted St. Peter's reasons for this remarkable expression.

You will remember, my brethren, that in the sermon which St. Peter preached to a crowd shortly after this, after the healing of the lame man at the Beautiful Gate of the temple,[1] he went over a great deal of the same ground as that which he had traversed in this his first sermon on the day of Pentecost. He told his hearers, among other things, that they had killed the Prince of life, Whom God had raised from the dead. Remark, brethren, that title—the Prince of life. Not merely does it show how high above all earthly royalties was the crucified Saviour in the heart and faith of His apostle: it connects the thought of St. Peter in this, the earliest stage of his ministry, with the language of his divine Master, on the one side, and with that of the apostles Paul and John on the other. Our Lord had said, "I am the way, the truth, and the life."[2] He had explained the sense of this last word "life," by saying that as the Father hath life in Himself so hath He given to the Son to have life in Himself.[3] He had complained to the men of His time, "Ye will not come to me that ye might have life;"[4] and St. John had said of Him that in Him was life;[5] and St. Paul, as in to-day's epistle, calls Him "Christ Who is our life."[6] When, then, St. Peter names Him the Prince of life, he is referring to this same truth of his Master, and it is, in fact, the key-note of the gospel. That "What is life?" is a question which, even at this date of the world's history, no man can really answer. We do not know what life is in itself. We can only register its symptoms. We see growth, and we see movement, and we say, "Here is life." It exists in one degree in the tree; in a higher de-

---

[1] Acts iii.     [2] John xiv. 6.     [3] John v. 26.
[4] John v. 40.     [5] John i. 4.     [6] Col. iii. 4.

gree in the animal; in a higher degree still in man. In beings above man, we cannot doubt, it is to be found on a still grander scale; but in all these cases, be it what it may, it is a gift from Another, and having been given, it might be modified or withdrawn. Who is He in Whom life resides originally?—He Who owes it to no patron—He from Whom no other being can conceivably take it? Only He, the Self-existent, lives of right—lives because He cannot but live—lives an original, as distinct from a derived, life. This is true of the eternal Three who yet are as One, but the Christian revelation assures us that it is only true of the Son and of the Holy Spirit, because, by an unbegotten and unending communication of Deity, they receive such life from the eternal Father. And hence our Lord says, "As the Father hath life in Himself, so hath He given to the Son to have life in Himself."[1] Not merely life, let me repeat it, but life *in Himself*." He is thus to be equal with the eternal Giver, Fountain, and Source of life; nay, rather, He is to be, with reference to all created beings, the Life—their Creator, their Upholder, their last End. For, says St. Paul, "By Him were all things created, that are in heaven, and that are in earth, visible and invisible, whether they be thrones, or dominions, or principalities, or powers: all things were created by Him, and for Him: and He is before all things, and by Him all things consist."[2]

Thus, then, this is the full sense of St. Peter's expression—the Prince of life.

And in the truth which it teaches as to our Lord's jurisdiction over life, based on the truth of His eternal Nature, we may trace a third reason for St. Peter's expression in the text. How could the very Lord and Source of life be subdued by death? If, for reasons of wisdom and mercy,

[1] John v. 26.  [2] Col. i. 16, 17.

He subjected the Nature which He had made His own to the king of terrors, it was surely not in the course of nature: it was a violence to nature that this should be. And, therefore, when the object had been achieved He would rise, St. Peter implies, by an inevitable rebound: He would rise by the force of things: He would rise by the inherent energy of His irrepressible life. The real wonder, from St. Peter's point of view, would be if such a Being as Christ were not to rise. The pains of death were loosed not in an extraordinary effort, as in your case or mine, but because it was impossible that He, the Prince of life, should be holden of it.

Observe, brethren, before we leave this point, how St. Peter deals with the subject. He looks at it, if I may so speak, from above rather than from below. He asks himself what his existing faith about the Son of God points to, rather than what history proves to have taken place. He is, for the moment, more concerned for the honour of his Master than for the value and significance of His acts for us. To St. Peter it is less strange that there should be an innovation upon nature, like the resurrection of a dead body, than it would be if a Being like Jesus Christ, having been put to death, did not rise. St. Peter is very far from being indifferent to the proof of the fact that He did rise. He often insists upon this proof. But just as St. John calls Christ's miracles His works, meaning by that that they were just what such a Being might be expected to perform, so St. Peter treats His resurrection from the dead as perfectly natural to Him—as an event which any man or angel, with sufficient knowledge, might have calculated beforehand, just as astronomers predict unerringly the movements of the heavenly bodies. "God hath raised Jesus from the dead," he says, "because it was impossible that death should continue to hold Him." The buried Christ could not remain in His grave. He was raised from it in virtue of a divine necessity; and this necessity, while in its original form it is strictly proper to His case, points to kindred necessities which affect His servants and His Church.

Let us, in conclusion, briefly consider them.

See, first, the impossibility for us Christians, too, of being buried for ever in the tomb in which we shall be laid at death. We, too, shall rise: we must rise. In this, as in other matters, as He is so are we in this world. To us as to Him, although in a different way, God has pledged himself. There is a difference, indeed, such as might be expected, between our case and His. In Him an eternal vital force beside the voice of prophecy made resurrection from the dead necessary. In us there is no such intrinsic force—only a powerful guarantee to us from without. He could say of the temple of His Body, "I will raise it up in three days."[1] We can only say that God will raise us up, we know not when. But this we do know—that "if the Spirit of Him that raised up Jesus from the dead dwell in us, He that raised up Christ from the dead shall also quicken our mortal bodies by His Spirit that dwelleth in us."[2] This we do know—that "we all must be manifest before the judgment seat of Christ; that every one may receive the things done in the body, according to that which he hath done, whether it be good or bad."[3] The law of justice and the law of love combine to create a necessity which requires a resurrection of the dead, both of the just and the unjust.

See, too, here the principle of the many resurrections in the Church of Christ. As with the bodies of the faithful, so it is with the Body of the Redeemer. The Church of Christ is, as St. Paul says, Christ Himself in history. He

---

[1] John ii. 19.     [2] Rom. viii. 11.     [3] 2 Cor. v. 10.

says as much when He tells us that as the body is one and has many members, and all the members of the body, being many, are one body, so also is Christ.'  The Church is Christ's Body—the fulness of Him that filleth all in all. But the force of this language is limited by the fact, equally warranted by Scripture, that the Church has in it a sinful element—a human element which, unlike the humanity of Christ, is weak and sinful. The church of Corinth itself, to which St. Paul wrote the glowing sentence which I have just quoted, was filled, he tells us, with strife, irreverence—worse sins than these. Hence the Church of Christ has, again and again, in the course of her history, seemed to be dead and buried outright—buried away in some one of the lumber rooms of the past; and the world has gone its way rejoicing, as if all was over—as if, henceforth, unbelief and ungodliness would never be disturbed in their reign on earth by protests from Heaven. But suddenly the tomb has opened. There has been a profound agitation in men's consciences—a moral movement—a feeling that all is far from right; and then a new uprising of the spirit of devotion—a social stir—literary, missionary, philanthropic activity—conspicuous self-sacrifice, and the world awakes one fine morning to an uneasy suspicion that John the Baptist has risen from the dead, and that mighty works do show forth themselves in him. The truth is that the Christ Himself has again burst His tomb and is abroad among men.  So it was after the deep degradation of the papacy in the tenth century.  So it was after the accumulated corruptions of the fourteenth and fifteenth centuries.  So it was in this country after the great triumph of misbelief and profanity in the middle of the seventeenth century; and later, after that indifference to all true religion during the greater part of the

---

[1] 1 Cor. xii. 12.

eighteenth. The oppression, the degradation, the enfeeblement of the Church of Christ is possible enough. Too generally the world only binds and makes sport of Samson, because Samson has first yielded to the blandishments of Delilah. But there is a vital force in the Church of Christ which asserts, and must assert, itself from generation to generation. If the Crucifixion is re-enacted in the holy Body—if, as St. Paul phrases it, we will fill up from century to century that which is behind of the sufferings of Christ, the Resurrection is re-enacted, too. It is not possible that the Body of Christ, instinct with His force and with His vital and quickening Spirit, should be permanently holden down by death. Each apparent failure and collapse is followed assuredly by an outburst of energy and moral glory which reveals the presence of the living Christ—His presence, Who, if crucified through weakness, yet lives by the power of God.

And we have here, lastly, what should be the governing principle of our own personal lives. If we have been laid in the tomb of sin, it ought to be impossible that we should be holden of it. I say, "ought to be," because, as a matter of fact, it is not impossible. God only is responsible for the resurrection of His Son,—for the resurrection of the Christian's body,—for the perpetuity through its successive resurrections of the Christian Church: and therefore, it is impossible that either one or the other of these should permanently succumb to the empire of death. But God, Who raises our bodies, whether we will or not, does not raise our souls from sin without our corresponding with His Grace; and it is quite in our power to refuse this necessary correspondence. That we should rise, then, from sin is a moral—it is not a physical—necessity; but, surely, we ought to make it as real a necessity as if it were physical. For any man who feels in his soul the greatness and the love of Jesus Christ, it ought to be morally impossible to remain in this tomb. "Like as Christ was raised up from the dead by the glory of the Father, even so we also should walk in newness of life."[1] If Lent is the time for mourning the past, Easter is the time for bracing, definite resolutions—for vigorous efforts which shall control the future. If we were unaided and alone, such efforts and resolutions would be failures, in that they would be like the vain flutterings of a bird against the wires of the cage which imprisons it. But He Who has broken the gates of brass and smitten the bars of iron in sunder will not fail us, if we seek His strength, and the permanence and the splendour of His life in glory may, and should be, the warrant of our own.

One word more. A real resurrection with Christ will make and leave some definite mark upon our life. Let us resolve this day, brethren, to do, or to leave undone, henceforth, some one thing which will make the needful difference. Conscience will instruct us in this matter if we ask it; and if any of you are looking out for a way of showing gratitude to our risen Redeemer, I would suggest that you should send the best contribution you can afford to the secretary of the Society for the Propagation of the Gospel, in support of the mission at Zanzibar on the east coast of Africa. There a small band of noble men, under the leadership of a bishop of apostolic life, are making efforts, worthy of the best days of the Church, to propagate the faith among races to whom no depths of degradation and misery that are possible for human beings are practically unknown, but races which are as capable as ourselves of rising with Christ to a new life of moral and mental glory. According to the accounts which have reached this country quite recently, just at the moment

[1] Rom. vi. 4.

when new and unlooked-for opportunities are presenting themselves to the servants of Christ, and a real inroad upon heathendom, and upon slavery and the vices which mark its empire, is possible as it has never been possible before since the mission began, their scanty means altogether failed them. They literally have not enough to eat, much less to attempt new enterprises of Christian charity such as the circumstances imperatively demand. Shall we leave them to despondency, to retreat, to failure, with the heathen before them stretching out their hands, almost within sight of the Cross of their Redeemer and their God, with the impure imposture of the false prophet hard by, ready to take advantage of our supineness? Surely it cannot but be that some who hear me will make an effort worthy of Easter gratitude. There will be no collection after the service, but, as I have said, I am sure that the secretary of the Society for the Propagation of the Gospel will gladly receive subscriptions for an object than which nothing more truly Christian and philanthropic, nothing more worthy of men who humbly hope that they have their part in the first resurrection and in its divine necessities, can well be imagined.

# SERMON XII.

## THE VALLEY OF DRY BONES.

**EZEKIEL xxxvii. 3.**

*"And he said unto me, Son of man, can these bones live? And I answered, O Lord God, thou knowest."*

THOSE who have read the prophet Ezekiel—and he is, perhaps, less read than any other book in the Old Testament—will remember this vision of the dry bones. Like many other visions, before and since, it was partly shaped by the circumstances of the times. The horrors of the Chaldean invasion, which had resulted in the carrying away of the Jewish people into Babylon, were still fresh in the memories of men. In many a valley, on many a hill side, in southern Palestine, the track of the invading army as it advanced and retired would have been marked by the bones of the unoffending but slaughtered peasantry. In his work on Nineveh, written some years ago, Mr. Layard has described such a scene in Armenia,—an upland valley covered by the bones of a Christian population which had been plundered and murdered by the Kurds. Such a scene may well have suggested to Ezekiel the background of the vision which the prophetic spirit so shaped as to express a truth which Israel needed to know. Ezekiel, wrapt in a spiritual ecstasy, was set down in the midst of a valley that was full of bones. He was caused to pass by them round about. He marked their great number; he marked their dryness. They were the bones of a multitude of men who had been slain long since. He was asked by the divine Being with Whom he was the while in close communion, "Son of man, can these bones live?" Ezekiel knew that nothing was impossible with God. He knew, too, that what was possible might be forbidden by necessities, by laws, of which he knew nothing, and he reverently answered, "O Lord God, thou knowest." And forthwith he was made the instrument through which the question which had been put to him was answered. "He said unto me, Prophesy upon these bones, and say unto them, O ye dry bones, hear the word of the Lord. Thus saith the Lord God unto these bones; Behold, I will cause breath to enter into you, and ye shall live: and I will lay sinews upon you, and will bring up flesh upon you, and cover you with skin, and put breath in you, and ye shall live; and ye shall know that I am the Lord." And then Ezekiel continues—"So I prophesied as I was commanded: and as I prophesied there was a noise, and behold a shaking, and the bones came together, bone to his bone. And when I beheld, lo, the sinews and the flesh came up upon them, and the skin covered them above: but there was no breath in them." That was the first stage of the revival. It was still incomplete. Something more was needed—something which the prophet goes on to describe. "Then said He unto me, Prophesy unto the breath,"—or spirit—"prophesy, son of man, and say to the spirit, Thus saith the Lord God; Come from the four winds, O spirit, and breathe upon these slain, that they may live." And then he continues, "So I prophesied as He commanded me, and the breath came into them, and they lived, and stood up upon their feet, an exceeding great army."[1] That was

[1] Ezek. xxxvii. 1–10.

the second stage of the revival. And it is followed by an explanation of the purpose of the vision. But let us at this point ask ourselves the question—What are we to understand by the dry bones of the vision of Ezekiel?

The dry bones of Ezekiel's vision are, doubtless, to begin with, the bones of human bodies,—bones from which the flesh had been either stripped or decayed away through exposure to the air. Ezekiel beholds a shaking,—a coming together of these bones. He sees them again clothed with flesh and sinews, and finally the breath comes into them and they live. They stand on their feet.

This is plainly the picture of a resurrection; not, indeed, of the general resurrection, because what Ezekiel saw was clearly limited and local, but at the same time it is a sample of what will occur at the general resurrection. And on this ground the passage is read by the Church as a proper lesson on Easter Tuesday. It may be urged that this representation is presently explained to refer to something quite distinct, namely, the restoration of the Jewish people from Babylon, and therefore that what passed before the prophet's eyes need not have been regarded by him as more than an imaginary or even impossible occurrence intended to symbolize the coming event. But, if this were the case, the vision, it must be said, was very ill adapted for its proposed purpose. The idea of a restoration from Babylon was, humanly speaking—was, politically speaking—sufficiently improbable already, without heightening this existing improbability by what is thus supposed to have been a greater improbability still. Men do not learn to accept difficult or unfamiliar truth through the assistance of truth still more unfamiliar, still more difficult. The fact is that the form of Ezekiel's vision, and the popular use which Ezekiel made of it, shows that at this date the idea of the resurrection of the body cannot have been a strange one to religious Jews. Had it been so, Ezekiel's vision would have been turned against himself. The restoration from the captivity would have been thought more improbable than ever, if the measure of its probability was to be found in a doctrine unheard of as yet by the people of revelation. We know, in fact, from their own Scriptures, that the Jews had had, for many a century, glimpses, more or less distinct, of this truth. Long ago the mother of Samuel could sing that the Lord bringeth down to the grave and bringeth up; and Job could be sure that though worms destroyed his body, yet in his flesh he would see God; and David, speaking for a higher Being than himself, yet knows that God will not leave the soul in hell or suffer His Holy One to see corruption; and Daniel, Ezekiel's contemporary, or nearly so, foresees that many of them that sleep in the dust of the earth shall awake, some to everlasting life and some to shame and everlasting contempt. And later on the courageous mother of the seven Maccabean martyrs cries to her dying son, "The Creator of the world, Who formed all the generations of man, and found out the beginning of all things, will also of His own mercy give you breath and life again, as ye now regard not your own selves for His laws' sake."[1] Undoubtedly there was among the Jews a certain belief in the resurrection of the body—a belief which this very vision must have at once represented and confirmed. Men shrink from admitting the idea that there will be a resurrection of the dead, on the ground, mainly, that it involves an exertion of divine power to which nothing exactly corresponds within the range of every day experience. Whether it is quite wise to make the range of our experience a measure of what God can do, may be more than questionable. But, at least, the doctrine of the resurrec-

[1] 2 Macc. vii. 23.

tion of all men from the dead involves no greater difficulty for a thoughtful man than that which he already encounters if he believes seriously in God at all; for belief in God involves, as a necessary part of itself, a belief in the creation of the universe out of nothing. However you may multiply the centuries during which man is supposed to have existed on the surface of this planet—however vast may be the tracts of time which you may demand as theoretically necessary to fill up the interval between some primary chaos and man's first appearance on the scene—say what you will about the date of the solar system or of the fixed stars, or of the presumable history of their evolution—still in the last resort, in the rear of all these theories amid which the scientific imagination may run such splendid riot, the question of questions awaits you. It can not be ignored; it can not be eluded. How did the original matter out of which all that we see around us took shape—how did this originally come to be? That is the question into which all others ultimately resolve themselves, and upon the answer which is given to it depends no less an issue than belief or disbelief in the existence of God; for if you say that original, unformed, unevolved matter always existed, then you deny the existence of the Being Whom we call God. God—He is nothing if He is not the alone Everlasting,—if He is not the Source of all else that is,—if He is not in His essence altogether spiritual, immaterial. If there existed from everlasting side by side with God, a something which you call matter which was not Himself,—which was in itself distinct from Himself—which did not owe its existence to Him, and which, as being itself presumably eternal, contradicts the first law of His Being as the Source of all that is beside Himself, then God the Creator of all things has no existence. But if, having on independent grounds a clear and strong belief in God, you deny, as you must deny, the eternity of matter, then you must trace the origin of the raw material out of which this universe has been fashioned, in whatever way, back to God. How did it come from Him? If it escaped from Him—and what would be this escape of matter from the immaterial?—if it escaped from Him without, or against, His will, then He is no longer Master, not merely in His creation, but of Himself. Being God, He must have summoned it into being by a free act of His free will. There was nothing out of which to frame it, and therefore He must have summoned it out of nothing. There was vacancy, and He bade the rude elements of matter to begin to be. It was something to fashion man out of the existing dust of the earth; but to give existence to the dust of the earth when as yet there was nothing, was an infinitely higher exercise of power. Think, my brethren, what this means,—creation out of nothing—that act with which every thinking and sincere believer in God must necessarily credit Him—and then compare it with the relatively puny difficulties which we are told ought to arrest the hand of the great Creator on the day of the general resurrection. It is not for us to trace His methods of procedure by audacious guesses, or to say how He will restore to each human body such of its proper materials as may have drifted away into subtle connections with other forms; but this I take it is certain to any reasonable man,—that no difficulties about the resurrection of the body can seriously suspend our belief in it, if we do believe already in God as really God, that is, as the Creator, and believe further that He has told us that He will one day raise the bodies of all men from the dead.

Ezekiel's vision, then, may remind us what Christ our Lord has taught us again and again, in His own words, of the resurrection of the body. But its teaching by no means ends with this; for the dry bones of Ezekiel's vision may well represent the lifeless condition of societies of men at particular times in their history,—the condition of nations, of churches, of less important institutions. Indeed Ezekiel, as we have seen, was left in no kind of doubt about the divinely intended meaning of his vision. The dry bones were a picture of what the Jewish nation believed itself to be in consequence of the captivity in Babylon. All that was left of it could be best compared to the bones of the Jews who had been massacred by the Chaldean invader, and which bleached on the hillsides of Palestine. "He said unto me, Son of man, these bones are the whole house of Israel: behold, they say, Our bones are dried, and our hope is lost: as for us we are cut off."[1] Certainly, in the captivity little was left to Israel beyond a skeleton of its former self. There were the sacred books; there were royal descendants of the race of David; there were priests; there were prophets; there was the old Hebrew and sacred language not yet wholly corrupted into Chaldean; there were the precious and loved traditions of the past great days of Jerusalem. These were the dry bones of what had been Israel. There was nothing to connect them. They lay on the soil of heathenism. They lay apart from each other as if quite unconnected. Nay rather—for the form of the representation changes as the explanation succeeds the vision—they now lay buried beneath the soil,—beneath the thick layer of pagan life, of pagan worship, of pagan oppression, of pagan vice, which buried them out of sight. To the captive people Babylon was not merely a valley of dry bones, —a social and political neighbourhood which was fatal to the corporate life of Israel as the people of revelation— Babylon was a grave. And accordingly the prophet was

[1] Ezek. xxxvii. 11.

desired to address his countrymen, "Thus saith the Lord God; Behold, O my people, I will open your graves, and cause you to come up out of your graves, and bring you into the land of Israel. And ye shall know that I am the Lord, when I have opened your graves, O my people, and brought you up out of your graves."[1] And this is what really did happen at the restoration of the Jews from Babylon. Each of the promises in Ezekiel's vision was fulfilled. First, the divine breath came upon the bones and they lived. The remains of the past of Israel—its sacred books, its priests, its prophets, its laws, its great traditions, its splendid hopes—these once more moved in the soul of the nation. As if with the motion of reviving life, they came together. They were readjusted into an harmonious whole. They received the clothing of bone and sinew which originally belonged to them. And the nation thus reconstructed in the days of its captivity was lifted by the divine power, when the moment came, out of the grave, and restored to the upper air of its ancient home in Palestine. It was a wonderful restoration; almost, if not altogether, unique in history. We see it in progress in such a psalm as the 119th, which doubtless belongs to this very period, and which exhibits the upward struggles of a sincere and dutiful soul at the first dawn of the national restoration; and we read of its completion in the books of Ezra and Nehemiah. It was completed when the temple, the centre of the spiritual and national life, was fully rebuilt, and when the old life of the people in its completeness was thus renewed upon the spot which had been the home of their fathers from generation to generation.

And something of the same kind has been seen in portions of the Christian Church. As a whole we know

[1] Ezek. xxxvii. 12, 13.

the Church of Christ can not fail; the gates of hell shall not prevail against it; but particular churches may fail in very different degrees. National churches, provincial churches, local churches—these, like the seven churches in Asia, which stand as a warning for all the ages of Christendom, may experience very varying degrees of corruption, of ruin, and of the moral insensibility which precedes death. So it was with the Church of Rome so long ago, even, as in the tenth century. Those who know the history of that century know that no man could ever have violated the spirit and the law of Christ more flagrantly than did the rulers of the Roman Church in that dark and miserable age. And yet this age was succeeded by a striking moral and religious restoration. And so it has been, although in a somewhat different sense, with the Church of England, and more than once since the Reformation. During the past week we may have seen in the public prints accounts of the completion of a new college at one of our universities, which has been erected on a more splendid scale than anything of the kind in England for at least two hundred years. What has been the motive for this enterprise? This college bears the name of a quiet country clergyman, whom during his lifetime nobody in authority thought worthy of patronage or notice. After a short career at his university, he died at a country parsonage. And it may well be asked, What was the work which has earned for him, at the hands of his fellow-churchmen, this unprecedented distinction after his death? The answer is, that when John Keble entered on the work of his life, the Church of England was, to a considerable extent, in a condition which answered to Ezekiel's vision of the valley of dry bones. She had succeeded to a splendid inheritance, but she understood her privileges very imperfectly. By large numbers of her people, the higher, nobler sides of the Christian life—its pathos, its awfulness, its risks, its strength, its capacities for heroism, its capacities for sacrifice, its secret powers derived from communion with the unseen, its magnificent prospects which dwarf down into insignificance all that merely meets the eye of sense—this had been forgotten. For them the kingdom of heaven had come to be almost as one of the kingdoms of this world. The Episcopate was merely the form of church government approved of by the state in this part of the empire. The Sacraments were old ceremonies pleasing to the religious sentiment, but very far indeed from being necessary to salvation. The Bible was a venerable book—the most venerable of books; but nobody knew exactly what criticism would presently say of it. And as for the Prayer Book, it was described as a human compilation just three hundred years old. Think of the case of a soul which might hope, from the echoes of the gospel resounding down the centuries, that a home had been found for it on earth—a home in which its sorrows might be consoled and its aspirations encouraged—and then wending its way into a Church which had so largely forgotten its first love as this! There are those still living who can say what has happened to such souls in that dreary period; but it was the high privilege of the man whom we are thinking of, more perhaps than of any other man, to bring the remedy. Not from any position which of itself commanded attention, but as relying on the native force and beauty and majesty of truth, he published a collection of poems, unwillingly enough, which has had more effect than a thousand volumes of more pretentious character. No one could think less highly of the "Christian Year" than did its humble-minded author; and it was in the judgment of very competent judges inferior as poetry to other works of his pen. It was merely fugitive.

It was careless of finish and of symmetry. It was indistinct. It was hard to be understood by those who had not the key to understand it. It was eminently a book which was not made, but which grew, and was marked with the rude irregularities of growth as distinct from the polish and the finish of mere manufacture. But underneath its language—above and beyond its literary faults whatever they were—there was a subtle, fine, penetrative, —I may dare to say a divine,—spirit, which belonged to religious genius of the very highest order, and which has renewed the faith of the Church of England. It breathed through this book upon the dry bones around it. It clothed once more the chief pastors of the Church in the garb of apostles. It traced beneath the form of the Sacraments the inward Grace which unites with Christ. It supplied a point of view for reading the sacred Scriptures intelligently, and yet as an inspired whole, and with a constant sense of their profound, their unfathomable meaning. It lighted up the Prayer Book as a beautiful relic of the best work of the primitive Church, upon which the sixteenth century, while removing blemishes and corruptions, has after all only lightly laid its hand. It did this after such a fashion that at last we understand it. Even yet we are too near the date of the publication of this book to take an accurate measure of all that it has done for the English Church; but we can see enough to be sure that through it breathed the breath of heaven by which dying churches are renewed,—by which the dry bones of past ages of faith and love are again clothed upon with the substance of life.

And some of us may have noted a little resurrection in some institution, neither as divine as a church nor yet so broad, so inclusive as a nation—in a school, a college, a hospital, a charitable guild, a company. It is the creation

—it is the relic—of a distant age. It is magnificent in its picturesqueness. It lacks, alas! nothing but life. It treasures up statutes which are no longer observed. It observes ceremonies and customs which have lost their meaning. It stoutly upholds a phraseology and livery which tell of a past time, and of which the object has been forgotten. On certain days in the year its members meet. They go through the accustomed usages. They signalise their meeting, it may be, by a splendid banquet, by commanding oratory; but in their heart of hearts they know well that they are meeting in a valley of dry bones. The old rules, usages, phrases, dresses—these are scattered around them like the bones in the valley of Ezekiel's vision. The life which once animated and clothed them has long since perished away. They lie apart without connection with each other, without attempt at arrangement, without the decencies of order; and the question is, Who shall bring them together? Who shall restore to them movement and power? Who shall clothe them with flesh and blood, and make them once more what they were made to be? And on such occasions there are always those who would cry with a modern prophet of despair—

> "Poor fragments of a broken world
> Whereon men pitch'd their tent,
> Why were ye, too, to death not hurl'd,
> When your world's day was spent?
> That glow of central fire is done,
> Which, with its fusing flame,
> Knit all your hearts and kept in one;
> But ye—ye are the same."

But we can think, it may be, of cases where a nobler spirit than this has prevailed—where a man has appeared, who, instead of contemptuously sweeping away what the past has left, sets himself to gather, to arrange, to combine—if it may be, to reconstruct—sets himself above all to invoke that divine Spirit of life and Grace, Who alone can restore life to the dead and inaugurate a moral and social resurrection. Before he began his work, the thought came to him too, "Can these bones live?" But believing that resurrection is the will of God, the Author of Life whether moral or physical, he went forward. It was enough for him to say, "O Lord, thou knowest." And he heard not long after the divine command, "Son of man prophesy unto the breath, and say, O breath, come unto these bones that they may live."

And lastly, the dry bones of Ezekiel's vision may be discovered, and that not seldom, within the human soul. When a soul has lost its hold on truth or grace—when it has ceased to believe, or ceased to love—all the traces of what it once has been do not forthwith disappear. There are survivals of the old believing life, fragments of the skeleton of the old convictions, bits of stray logic which once guarded a creed, phrases which expressed the feeling which once winged a prayer. There may remain on in the arid desolation a very valley full of dry bones; of aspirations which have no goal; of opinions which have no real basis, no practical consequences; of friendships which are felt to be hollow, but which are still kept up; of habits which have lost all meaning, but which it is hard to surrender. Not seldom may we meet with writers, and with talkers, with historians, with poets, whose language shows that they have once known what it is to believe, but for whom a living faith has perished utterly, and left behind it only these dried up relics of its former life. Such a case —it may be, partially at least, that of some who hear me— such a case must suggest the solemn question, can these bones live? Can these phrases, these forms, these habits, these associations which once were part of a spirit's life—can they ever become what they were? Is it worth while to treasure them? Were it not better, were it not more sincere, to have done with them altogether—to disavow what we no longer mean—to abandon habits of devotion which have become for us only forms—to break with practices of piety, of benevolence, which are only due now to the surviving impetus of habit? Why should the soul be thus a charnel house of the past? Why not clear it out and begin afresh with some such new life as may yet be possible? Brethren, it is better, believe me, to respect the dry bones, though they are only dry bones. They have their value in that they witness to a loving past. They have their value in that they point on to a possible restoration in the future. On them, too, the breath of God may light. Into them may yet be infused a new quickening force. It is easy enough to decry religious habit as only habit,—as motiveless, soulless, unaccepted service. Doubtless habit which is only habit is not life, but it is better, I dare to say, than nothing at all—better, if not in itself, yet surely for the sake of that which it may lead on to. A man may have ceased to mean his prayers. His prayers may now be but the dry bones of that warm and living communion which he once held with God. But do not let him, on that account, give them up. Do not let him break with the little that remains of what once was life. It is easy to decry habit, but habit may be the scaffolding which saves us from a great fall. Habit may be the arch which bridges over a chasm that yawns between one height and another on our upward road. Habit without motive is sufficiently unsatisfactory; but habit is better, better far, than nothing.

Some of us it may be, surveying the shrivelled elements of our religious life cannot avoid the question which is borne in upon us from heaven, "Can these bones live?" They seem to us in our best moments so hopelessly dislocated, so dry, so dead. And to this question the answer always must be, " O Lord God, thou knowest." Yes, He does know. He sees, as He saw of old into the grave of Lazarus. He sees, as He saw into the tomb of the Lord Jesus, so into the secrets of a soul of whose faith and love only these dry bones remains. And He knows that life is again possible, ay, that it is much more than possible. The word of His power may again clothe with form and with flesh. The breath of His Spirit may again impart animation, warmth, movement, growth. The quickening power of Christ's resurrection, from which all recovery, whether moral or social or physical, must go forth—this may assert itself victoriously in that desert soul, so that like as Christ was raised up from the dead by the glory of the Father, even so this soul should walk in newness of life.[1]

[1] Rom. vi. 4.

# SERMON XIII.

## THE ADEQUACY OF PRESENT OPPORTUNITIES.

### LUKE xvi. 31.

*" And He said unto him, If they hear not Moses and the prophets, neither will they be persuaded, though one rose from the dead."*

ON this the first of the long line of Sundays after Trinity, the parable of the rich man and Lazarus opens the lessons on Christian duty, which are set before us in the successive gospels, with a force and a pathos which we feel from our early childhood—at least, if I may trust my own experience. The three vivid contrasts of this parable are among the very first features in the gospel to take possession of the imagination and the heart.

First there is the contrast between the rich and the poor —that great contrast which is apparently rooted in the nature of things, which reappears in all ages and countries wherever there is a settled order of human society. Dives, with his outer robe of purple wool and with his under tunic of fine linen—Dives, with his table furnished day after day with every delicacy that money can buy—he is always here. And Lazarus, thrown down—such is the original expression—thrown down, to lie at the gate of the outer court of the rich man's mansion—Lazarus who feeds upon the crumbs which the slaves of Dives, half contemptuously, throw to him—Lazarus so unclothed that his very wounds are without bandages, and the dogs that roam through the streets of the eastern city stop for a moment as they pass to lick his sores—he, too, is always here; a contrast, I say, as old and as lasting as society, a contrast which met the eye centuries ago in Rome and in Jerusalem, just as it meets it when we walk from the east to the west end of London; a contrast, it must be added, which social science and wise legislation and above all the divine charities of Jesus Christ our Lord filling the regenerated hearts of men, make less harsh, less shocking, but the cause of which they cannot really remove.

And there is a second contrast—that of the living and the dead. The parable places us face to face with Dives and Lazarus, first in life, and then in the world which follows. This is a more solemn contrast than that between the rich and the poor. It is a contrast between that which passes and that which lasts—between appearance and reality. Lazarus—so we are told—dies in time, worn out, no doubt, by want and sickness. Nothing is said of his burial: perhaps he was not buried at all. And after a while Dives dies too, and of course is buried—buried with all due respect and ceremony. And after the brief sleep of death they wake, as we shall all one day wake, in a new world. The life of that world is a continuation of the life of this. Circumstances are altered: characters remain. Enough now to repeat that what we see here is the apparent: what we shall see there is the real. And this contrast between the living and the dead is much more rooted in the nature of things than that between the rich and the poor. It is as old, it is as wide, it is as enduring, as the human race. Day by day men and women around us are exploring it: day by day they are passing the line which separates the living and the dead, and sounding the heights and depths of its stern, of its blessed, significance.

And the parable brings before us a third contrast, differing from the two former in this,—that whereas they belong, the first wholly, and the second in part, to this present world, this third is altogether concerned with the next. In the next world there are two companies of beings, the miserable and the blessed. All are not blessed: numbers, thank God, are certainly not miserable. There Lazarus rests in the bosom of Abraham: there Dives lifts up his eyes being in torment. And between the two there is a great gulf fixed, "so that," in Abraham's words, "they which would pass from hence to you cannot; neither can they pass to us, that would come from thence."[1] A contrast, my brethren, yet more solemn than that between the living and the dead—a contrast which will still endure when all that now meets the eye of sense shall have passed away.

As we dwell on our Saviour's words we are, perhaps, tempted to say to ourselves, "After all, it is only a parable." Well brethren, it is a parable, although it is possibly also a history. There is something, at any rate, to be said for the opinion that Dives and Lazarus were real persons with whose earthly circumstances our Lord's hearers were acquainted, and whose destiny after death He authoritatively proclaims. But, however this may be, a parable, though it be a purely fictitious narrative, teaches something when it comes from the mouth of the Master of eternal truth. Its imagery, its rabbinical phraseology, its incidents—these all, each of them, do mean something. They may be translated into corresponding realities. And this parable, I submit, if it teaches anything at all, can certainly teach nothing less than these three contrasts—the contrasts between the rich—the selfish rich—and the poor, the suffering poor; the contrast between the living and the dead; the contrast between the happy and the miserable in another world.

Now it is to the last of these three contrasts that our

[1] Luke xvi. 26.

text belongs.  Dives and Lazarus are now among the dead, not yet separated, as they will be after the final judgment, but separated, we are told by an impassable gulf.  They are in that sphere of being into one district of which our Lord descended after His death, and which we call "hell" in the creed,—which contains, on the one hand, paradise and Abraham's bosom—anticipations, these, of a perfect happiness to come; and which also contains that which is already the portion of Dives while he awaits the final judgment.  Yet between Dives and Abraham, it would seem, some sort of communication is still possible; and in this report or representation of the divine Teacher we have put before us two separate conversations.

First of all Dives petitions Abraham, as the father of all faithful Israelites, that a drop of water may be sent him by the hand of Lazarus; and Abraham tells his son—(mark the tragic irony of the expression)—that this cannot be, partly because an absolute justice is redressing the inequalities of that life on earth, and partly because there is a great gulf fixed: the divine award is irreversible.  Then, since nothing can be done among the dead, Dives thinks of the living.  Dives is ruined, as he now knows, not because he was rich, but because he abused his wealth. He has five brethren who are living as he once lived on earth.  He thinks that if Lazarus could visit them, speaking of what happens beyond the grave with the authority of experience, they would be changed men.  Abraham answers, "They have Moses and the prophets; let them hear them."[1]  Dives remembers that he in his earthly days had Moses and the prophets too, close at hand, and yet that he had died as he had lived; and so he pleads with Abraham that, if only a visitor from the realms of death should see them, these five brethren would really repent.

[1] Luke xvi. 29.

And to this Abraham answers again that, "if they hear not Moses and the prophets, neither will they be persuaded, though one rose from the dead."

Now perhaps if we were to say out what we really think,—some of us—we should say that it seems to us, at first sight, almost hard in Abraham to answer Dives as he does answer him; for, after all, Dives was doing all that it was still possible for him to do. For himself, he was ruined—ruined irretrievably; but these five brethren—could nothing be done for them? If Lazarus might not cross the great gulf fixed, with a drop of water for the tongue of Dives, might he not visit the world of living men, to speak a word of warning to the rich man's five surviving brethren? No, Abraham will not allow that this demand is justified; for, if we translate the parable into the meaning which the divine Speaker and His hearers would alike put on it, what is this demand of Dives, virtually, but an indictment against God for not having furnished the rich Israelites of that day with sufficiently strong motives to holiness and amendment of life? The Jewish opponents of Jesus Christ our Lord were continually asking in this way for signs and wonders, and our Lord was constantly replying that there were proofs enough and to spare, of His mission, in the law, in the prophets, in His own works, in His own words—proofs enough to dispense with anything of the kind. Dives talks still like the ordinary Pharisees of the day. When he asks that Lazarus may be sent to his brethren, he implies, you observe, that if he himself had been visited by one who had seen the realities of the other life he would have lived and died quite differently. As it was, he had only had the old Book to fall back upon—only Moses and the prophets. There was something, he tacitly suggests, there was something to be said for him, after all; and therefore when Abraham refers to the five brethren he means Dives himself as well. If Dives had not heard Moses and the prophets, neither would he have been persuaded, though one had risen from the dead to warn him.

Now this answer to Dives is undoubtedly meant to represent the mind and judgment of our Lord Himself. Abraham in the parable declares the will of God, just as Dives puts into words the thoughts of the Pharisees of the day. Let us, then, consider this reply of Abraham somewhat more at length. What does it teach us?

It teaches us, first of all, how far the actual sight of a miracle would be likely to produce real faith in the unseen world. Dives let Lazarus lie at his gate. Why? Because he had no true belief in the unseen. The brethren of Dives would do their duty by such as Lazarus if they only could see, in all His perfections, Him Who is invisible —their present Master—their future Judge. Hundreds of men in our day, who have lost living faith in the religion of Jesus Christ our Lord, think that if they could only witness a miracle they could not help believing again—believing at once. "It is all very well," they say, "to read in the gospels about the stilling the tempest, about feeding the five thousand, about the raising three persons from the dead, about the resurrection of the Lord Himself. More than eighteen centuries have passed since those events, and there are no miracles, it seems, now. Let us see a miracle," they say; "let us have it examined and approved by competent persons, and, depend upon it, it will not fail in its effect. People will then believe, because they will not be able to help believing in the truth of the creed which the miracle is intended to attest." This, you observe, is exactly what Dives thought and said about the five brethren, if Lazarus were allowed to appear before them. The apparition, he thought, must make them live for another life—that is to say, live by faith. Moses and the prophets, he implied, had lost their power: they were old books dealing with matters which had been said and done hundreds of years ago. They were books which Dives and his brethren had known from childhood, and familiarity had bred indifference, or something worse. And men ask now, in the heart of Christendom, "Is there not something in this?" Is not that which appeals to sense more powerful with most of us than that which appeals to thought? Is not the present more moving than the past—a witnessed action than a written testimony or an abstract argument? Would not a dead man standing before our eyes, telling us that he had revived to come from the regions of the dead, with an appearance and other evidences that justified his assertion, have, of necessity, an influence upon us which a Bible read quietly in our church, or in our bedroom, or a Christian teacher listened to under accustomed circumstances, could never command? Would not a preternatural apparition exert over us a sway immediate, resistless, making us believers—earnest, clear-sighted, impartial believers—in spite of our very selves? All these questions our Lord answers now, and for this answer the reasons are not hard to find. Miracles are called in the Bible, with reference to their effect upon the human mind, "signs and wonders." They excite astonishment: they call attention to the mission or message of the worker. A miracle is intended, first of all, to startle the beholder: it is a wonder; and it is intended, next, to point towards the unseen and the eternal: it is a sign. But even if the sight of a miracle produces these effects,—if it first startles the man, and next suggests that there is something which he does not see and which is worth his attention and belief—this does not amount to actual faith. It is one thing to be convinced of the truth of the unseen; it is another thing to be startled. At some time in our lives we must all of us have been startled by occurrences which, although unaccustomed, at least to us, could not be deemed miracles. A friend has died without any sort of warning. We have been in a railway accident in which several persons have lost their lives, and we have escaped—we know not how—through a series of unforeseen contingencies. Or some historical catastrophe, like the surrender of Sedan, or like the recent tragedies at Constantinople, has happened, and for the moment the world holds its breath, and seems to feel that God is passing along the corridors of human history. And events like these, on a small scale or a great, are intended to remind us that what we see and are is very insignificant indeed, compared with what we do not see and what we shall be. Events like these, though occurring in a strictly natural way, do, up to a certain point, the very proper work of miracles. They flash upon our minds for a moment the truth that God is, not now only but always, near, with His eye upon us, guarding us, judging us in His perfect truth, His perfect love, His perfect justice.

Ah, these occurrences startle us, but what does it amount to? A momentary sensation; a mental, a moral spasm, which comes and goes and leaves us as we were, or perhaps, religiously speaking, if it goes, not quite so well off as we were. Of course a shock of this kind, like St. Paul's great experience on the road to Damascus, may be our very door of entrance into the life of faith; but the shock of itself does not insure these consequences. Utter astonishment and bewilderment is one thing; faith in the unseen is another. A swift succession of several new phases of thought and feeling, produced by a grand catastrophe and compressed into a single minute, may be the turning point of an existence, or only a strange experience. No doubt the five brethren and Dives too in his earthly lifetime would have been startled by the appearance of Lazarus, fresh from the scenes beyond the grave; but this does not at all prove that they would have been endued with that new and vivid perception of unseen things which we call faith.

For, secondly, a miracle is only likely to have real and lasting effect when it is addressed to a particular set of men. A sonata of Beethoven means nothing for a man who has no ear for music. A picture of Raphael is lost upon the observer who has no sense of colour, of proportion, of artistic beauty. And, in the same way, the mind of the man who witnesses a miracle must be predisposed in a certain way, or the miracle will altogether fail of its intended effect. The observer must, in the psalmist's words, have an eye to God, if he is to be enlightened by the miracle. He must be already looking out for God—looking out for some token of the will of God. He believes, we will suppose, in a vague way, that there is a Maker and Ruler of the world. He believes that there is an Author of the law of right and wrong which he recognizes within himself. Now, depend upon it, the more he makes of this law of right and wrong, the more disposed he will be to make the most of what will be told him on authority about the Being Who gave the law. In this state of mind he will watch anxiously for any sign that the Lord of nature may deign or seem to deign to make on the surface of nature, with a view to showing that He is also the Lord of conscience and the Lord of revelation. But if the man has no such interests, no such anticipations, to begin with, then the miracle says nothing to him; for him the miracle is a mere curious irregularity observable upon the surface of nature. It arrests his attention; perhaps it excites his apprehension for a moment; but that is all. And if he has already made up his mind against the truth of which the miracle is the divine certificate, then the miracle must be powerless to move him. "If they hear not Moses and the prophets, neither will they be persuaded, though one rose from the dead." This was actually the case with those Jews, to whom our Lord was speaking, not long after. Moses and the prophets had foretold Him—the true Messiah. "Search the scriptures—your own scriptures" He had said,—for in them ye think ye have eternal life: and they are they which testify of Me."[1] But Moses and the prophets had written in vain, as far as that generation of Israelites was concerned. "Their table"—as prophet and apostle had said—"their table was made a snare to take themselves withal; and the things which should have been for their wealth were unto them an occasion of falling."[2] Scripture had failed. Could miracle succeed? Jesus Christ died in public; He was buried; on the third day He rose from the dead. His resurrection was a well-attested fact. Those who had known Him best saw Him singly—saw Him with others. He was seen again and again during the period of forty days. On one occasion he was seen by five hundred persons, half of whom were living some twenty-five years afterwards. But were the Jews as a people convinced? On the contrary, they set themselves at once to get rid of this stupendous miracle, intended though it was to convince them that He to Whom their whole history pointed had really come, by every explanation they could devise. The disciples, they said, had stolen the Body. The disciples had conspired to palm off an imposture on the world. Our Lord might as well have remained in His grave, as far as the great men in Jerusalem were concerned. They began, you see, by refusing to hear Moses and the prophets; they were not persuaded though He, their true King, had risen from the dead.

[1] John v. 39.  [2] Ps. lxix. 23: P. B. Version; Rom. xi. 9.

Remember this, brethren, when you are tempted to think that faith would have been easier in the days of the apostles than it is now. "If a miracle could only be worked before my eyes," it is sometimes said, "I should have believed without difficulty." Would you? The probability is that the very temper of mind which makes you ask for the miracle would kill belief in the presence of the miracle. Miracles are intended to assist those who are already seeking God. They are not intended to inflict the sense of God's power and presence and truth on those who do not wish to know more about Him. A miracle cannot force a soul to believe: it does not act like a machine or like a chemical solvent, producing the specific effect whether men will or not. There are many ways of neutralising this proper effect; and if we have heard Moses and the prophets,—if we have listened to evangelists and apostles, and to the Lord of life Himself, to no real or lasting purpose,—we should not, of necessity, be persuaded, though the floor of this abbey were this evening to break up beneath our feet, and the buried dead were to come forth to tell us that the world to come is an awful and overwhelming reality.

And next, Abraham's reply to Dives teaches us how far circumstances can be presumed to determine conduct. What a miracle is to faith, that favourable circumstances are to duty. As a miracle makes faith easy, so favourable circumstances, good examples, encouraging friends, the urgency of great opportunities, the inheritance of a noble name—these make duty easy. But duty is no more necessarily forced upon us by circumstances than faith is forced upon us by miracle. Yet if there are hundreds who say, "I should be a sincere believer in Christianity if I could only see a person who had come from the dead," there are thousands who say, "I should be a better woman or man than I am if only I were differently circumstanced,—if I were not tempted by poverty or tempted by wealth,—if I had religious and high-minded friends about me,—if I lived near a church, or knew a good clergyman,—if I had lived in other ages, the ages of faith, as they are called, when all the controversies that fill the air in modern times were quite unknown, and everybody was of one mind as to the best way of getting to Heaven." My brethren, it is not the same thing to any one of us whether we have good friends or bad,—whether we have religious privileges at hand or are quite without them,—whether we can resort at will for counsel or comfort to the servants of Christ, or are debarred from doing so,—whether we are exposed to the temptations of luxury or to the temptations of want, or are blessed with that amount of competency which saves us from these temptations. Circumstances are judgments, or they are blessings, from God; and when He surrounds us with such circumstances as to make it easier for us to live for Him and to attain the true end of our existence, we have, indeed, great reason to bless Him for the blessings of this life, since, like all other good things, they come from Him the Fountain of all goodness. But these blessings do not of themselves make a moral, religious, beneficent, Christian life necessary. They do not act upon us as the rain or the sunshine or the atmosphere act upon plants. Under favourable circumstances a plant cannot help growing. It obeys the law of its kind by an inevitable necessity. But under favourable circumstances,—nay, under the most favourable that we can possibly conceive—a human soul can refuse to grow—can remain resolutely stunted, dwarfed, misshapen—can resist triumphantly, ay, to its final ruin, all the blessed influences that might draw it upwards and onwards,—all that might purify, invigorate, transfigure, save it. Felix was not compelled to be a Christian by the apostle's burning words about righteousness, temperance, and judgment to come, though he felt their awful force. Demas was not cured of his love of this present world by the sight and friendship of Christ's aged servant Paul, now in chains at Rome, and on the eve of his martyrdom. Nay, if circumstances were ever favourable—so we may well think—to the wellbeing and growth of any human soul, they were the circumstances of the unhappy Judas, blest as he was with the daily visible divine companionship of the Saviour of the world. They did not arrest the commission of two tremendous crimes,—first, that of betraying the Most Holy into the hands of His enemies, and next of rushing by his own act, impenitent, into the presence of his Judge.

Certainly let us admit that if favourable circumstances do not force holiness upon us, they may and do often protect us against monstrous vice—against the outcome of passions and dispositions which, it may be, are still unsubdued within us, though kept more or less in check. When we read of a great crime how rarely does it occur to us to ask ourselves, with Augustine, whether, but for God's protection and Grace, we too might not have been the criminal. We read in boyhood the histories, no doubt, of the early Roman Emperors—of Caligula, of Nero, of Domitian, of Commodus; and we said to ourselves that it was wonderful that men so lost to the better instincts of our common nature should have been permitted to cumber the high places of the earth. But should we have been better in their circumstances? With unlimited power of gratifying our own selfish instincts, and of making all others with whom we came into contact the slaves of our will,—without the fear of another world before our eyes, the fear of judgment, the fear of God,—without the light which streams—more or less of it—upon the most benighted consciences in Christendom from the radiant Figure of our Lord Jesus Christ, should we have been better than they? Should we have been capable of unselfishness, or disinterestedness, or largeness of heart, or self-discipline, in that place of dizzy, awful elevation, with all the world at our feet,—with every incentive to indulge the whims and passions of self at the cost of others? Should we have been capable of the splendid natural virtues—I will not say of Antoninus or of Marcus Aurelius, but even of Trajan—even of Hadrian? In our Lord's day the Jews of Palestine used to compare themselves with their forefathers who had a hand in murdering the prophets. They said that had they been there they would not have killed the prophets. But He Who knew what was in man saw them through and through. He knew that they would have done just what their fathers had done before them. He looked onwards a few months into the future; He knew what was coming; He saw the Jewish mob which would arrest Him in the garden; He heard the insults in the house of Caiaphas; He witnessed the long tragedy of the Way of Sorrows—the hours which He would spend on the Cross of shame. "Fill ye up, therefore, the measure of your fathers.[1] Do not criticise men whose conduct would have been—whose temper and principles were—exactly your own."

Yes, circumstances have an immense restraining power, but they have of themselves no active power to change the heart. Dives and his brethren knew that divine code, the tenderness and mercy of which for the suffering and the poor had been so fully drawn out by the great Jewish teacher Nimonides. They were flooded with the light of God's moral law. Israel was the very home of the traditions of compassion and mercy that were to be found in

[1] Matt. xxiii. 32.

the ancient world. Its higher conscience—this, as always, was on the side of the suffering and the poor. "Be merciful after thy power. If thou hast much, give plenteously; if thou hast little, do thy diligence gladly to give of that little."[1] "Give alms of thy goods, and never turn thy face from any poor man; and then the face of the Lord shall not be turned away from thee."[2] These were among its later utterances. The Synagogue could name teachers famous for their tenderness, famous for their generosity and compassion; but Dives thought that these examples and motives were quite insufficient. We marvel at Dives; but, brethren, is it otherwise with ourselves? Do we not dwell on the difficulties of serving God in this as in other matters, and forget the Grace, the light, the strength, the examples, the encouragements, which He has given us in the kingdom of His Son? What might not heathens have done with our measure of opportunity—with our measure of light? There were towns in Israel of old the streets of which were trodden by the feet of the Saviour of the world, and He pronounced with His own blessed lips their condemnation on this very ground: because pagan cities with their advantages would have been very much more responsive to His presence and His words. "Woe unto thee Chorazin! woe unto thee Bethsaida! for if the mighty works, which were done in you, had been done in Tyre and Sidon, they would have repented long ago in sackcloth and ashes."[3] No, it is something else than circumstances which makes us do God's will, just as it is something else than miracle which makes us believe His word. Miracle and circumstances do their part. They assist the heart; they make the task of the will easier; they do not compel obedience. He who has made us free

---

[1] Tobit iv. 8, 9, P. B. Version in Office of Holy Communion.
[2] Ibid. iv. 7.     [3] Matt. xi. 21.

respects our freedom even when we use it against Himself —even when we resist His own most gracious and gentle pressure and choose to disbelieve or to disobey Him. If Moses and the prophets are to persuade us—if we are not to be beyond persuasion, though one rose from the dead— there must be that inward seeking, yearning after God, that wholeness of heart, that tender and affectionate disposition towards Him Who is the end as He is the Source of our existence, of which the Bible is so full from first to last—which is the very essence of religion—which He, its Object and its Author, gives most assuredly to all who ask Him.

My brethren, few of us, it may be, are exactly in the case of Dives. Probably at least nine-tenths of those who hear me have something to give, if they will make an effort at self-denial, in order to meet the claims of Lazarus. And to-day is a great occasion for discovering how far we are capable of persuasion by the love of God, by the claims of humanity, by the example and precepts of our divine Lord and Saviour, to say nothing of Moses and the prophets. We have many of us, it may be, in our time, had before our minds visions of doing splendid deeds of benevolence, —visions which belonged not to our actual means or circumstances, but to those of others, or to a fancy world. We have said to ourselves, "If I had the fortune of such and such a nobleman at my command, and if such and such a catastrophe were only to occur, how I should delight at laying out a hundred thousand pounds or half-a-million of money for the relief, the pure relief, of human suffering." Oh, admirable aspiration! But the worst of it is that the occasion and the means of meeting it are alike hypothetical; and this purely hypothetical benevolence is like a certain sort of novel: it taxes our sympathy without resulting in any real good either to our own characters or to other people. Do not let us wait to do what good we can till some one comes from the dead: do not let us wait till our circumstances change. Ere they change all may have ended with us in this life of probation. "Though one rose from the dead." A Lazarus has risen before now in history, not to persuade the selfish possessors of property to recognise their responsibilities towards human want and pain around them, but to judge. He has risen from the oppressions, from the neglect of a thousand years; he has risen, it may be, more than once in history amid scenes of blasphemy and violence and blood, but he has risen in the name of a forgotten justice to plead the cause which has been pleaded in vain by his open sore for ages, lying as he was at the gate of Dives. The spectre of a social revolution has been happily unknown in England—unknown for this among other reasons—that the duties of the wealthy towards the suffering classes have been—I dare not say adequately, but largely—recognised among us for a great number of years. But the immense disparities of our society—its masses, its increasing masses, of poverty—its vast accumulations of wealth—present a contrast which year by year may well cause, as it does cause, increasing anxiety; and this anxiety can only be lessened, if those to whom God has given wealth and influence lose no opportunity at their disposal of supplying the wants and bettering the position of their poorer fellow countrymen.

Here is Hospital Sunday upon us—a great, a blessed occasion for the fruitful exercise of pure benevolence. All the common objections to charitable effort are silent here. The social and political economists do not warn us to-day that we demoralise the poor when we bring them the highest medical skill and knowledge as they lie on their bed of pain. The financiers do not suggest that our alms are spent partly or wholly on the way to the object for which we give them. And at the gates of the hospitals, those true temples of compassion, our controversies are silent. Those who know most of our Lord and Saviour—those who know less or least about Him—those even who do not own the empire of His ever blessed Name—agree as to the urgency of His precept and His blessing, " Blessed are the merciful, for they shall obtain mercy." Lazarus is close to us. Hundreds of thousands in this vast city have succeeded to his inheritance; and if we, the servants of Christ, would not be as was Dives here and hereafter, we must not wait for larger means, for more striking occasions, for more commanding motives to self-sacrifice than we have. We must enter now the secret chambers of our own hearts. We must listen to all that God has taught us individually of His own astonishing mercy to us in Jesus Christ—of our utter need of it. For us Christians, Christ is Lazarus to the end of time, coming to us from the dead to warn us of our duty, receiving in the persons of His poor what we give as given to Himself. Surely no social catastrophe, no unforeseen providence, no palpable miracle, could constrain us more effectually than His boundless, His patient, His unmerited love—than those divine words of His which faith, it seems to me, must trace over the door of every hospital: " Inasmuch as ye have done it unto one of the least of these My brethren, ye have done it unto Me." [1]

[1] Matt. xxv. 40.

# SERMON XIV.

## NAAMAN'S EXPECTATIONS: A REPRESENTATIVE CASE.

### 2 KINGS v. 11, 12.

*"But Naaman was wroth, and went away, and said, Behold, I thought, He will surely come out to me, and stand, and call on the name of the Lord his God, and strike his hand over the place, and recover the leper. Are not Abana and Pharpar, rivers of Damascus, better than all the waters of Israel? may I not wash in them, and be clean? So he turned and went away in a rage."*

NAAMAN the Syrian, the proud noble, the brave soldier, the afflicted leper, is in these several capacities a representative man. His peers, his comrades, his fellow-sufferers, may well have been proud of claiming his friendship. But it is not these particulars which should engage our attention most earnestly this afternoon. Naaman, as he waits, disappointed and indignant, before the door of Elisha's house in Samaria, represents human nature in presence of some higher truth than it has yet mastered—in presence of revelation; and from this point of view he may be studied with no little advantage.

Let us, first of all, glance at his history. Naaman, I have already said, was a brave and skilful soldier. The Bible tells us that by him the Lord had given deliverance unto Syria; and some recently discovered inscriptions make it at least probable that he had distinguished himself in a campaign by which the Syrians of Damascus were freed from the oppressive power of the Assyrian kings. The successful soldier naturally stood high in the favour of his sovereign, and in the opinion of his countrymen; but his life was embittered by the humiliating and painful disease which in those ages was so prevalent throughout the East, and in which the Israelites had learnt to trace a material shadow or symbol of moral evil. Naaman's leprosy cannot have been of the severest type, or it would have interfered with his duties in the palace and in the camp—duties which, as it would seem, were never interrupted. Had he been an Israelite, his illness would have shut him out altogether from human society; but a pagan Syrian could still hold his position as a public man, although he must have felt keenly the distress and the loathsomeness of his malady. It is plain, too, that his master, the king of Syria, felt and expressed strong sympathy with his distinguished officer, and that he was looking out for a remedy, if one only could be had.

How then did Naaman, commanding the Syrian forces in Damascus, come to find himself waiting in the city of Samaria outside the door of a prophet of the Lord? The explanation, my brethren, is instructive because it shows the sort of channels along which, in all ages of the world's history, religious truth has filtered itself through the great fabric of human society; and it anticipates almost exactly what happened again and again in the earliest days of the Church of Christ. The Syrians, without being exactly at war with Israel, were on very bad terms with it ever since the failure of Ahab's expedition; and, from time to time, raids were made into the two territories from either side, and such booty as could be laid hands on was carried off. And in one of these raids, the Syrians had carried away from her home a young Israelitish girl, who was now a slave in Naaman's palace, and in attendance upon his wife. Like Daniel, like Esther, like that late psalmist who has told us how by the waters of Babylon he sat down and wept, this maiden cherished a loving and tender memory of the religious blessings of her distant home. Often, no doubt, like another captive or exile, she would have exclaimed, "Why art thou so vexed, O my soul? and why art thou so disquieted within me? O put thy trust in God; for I will yet thank Him, Which is the help of my countenance, and my God." [1] In all ages there are persons who, without being slaves, live perforce in situations of dependence which often seem to cut them off from religious privileges, or from opportunities of religious usefulness. This is often the case with governesses, and, in another sense, with maid-servants among ourselves. Many such an one thinks it very hard to have to consult, at all times, the whims of a thoughtless mistress, and to pass what she deems an obscure and fruitless life. Depend upon it, where there is integrity of principle and simplicity of purpose, the time comes sooner or later for doing the act, or for saying the word, which gives dignity, greatness, sanctity, to any life,—which redeems it altogether from being barren or commonplace. So it was with the little slave girl in the palace of Naaman at Damascus. She saw day by day her master's sufferings uncured, and, so far as Syrian skill went, incurable. She had heard in her young days, in her beloved home, of the prophet who had succeeded Elijah, and who lived in great consideration and wielded immense authority in Samaria. She ventured to whisper to her mistress, in one of those moments of intimacy to which even slaves were not unfrequently admitted, that she wished her lord could only see the great prophet who dwelt in Samaria, and who, she felt sure, would cure the leprosy. Her words were re-

[1] Ps. xlii. 14, 15: P. B. Version.

peated to Naaman, and Naaman in turn repeated them to the sovereign; and the king of Syria at once resolved to make the most of the suggestion. Naaman in person was ordered to leave at once for Samaria. He took with him money and presents, amounting to more than twelve thousand pounds of our money, and he was also the bearer of a letter which requested that the leper who bore it might be cured. The king of Israel himself was neither a physician nor a prophet, and he saw, or chose to see, in the despatch of the Syrian monarch, only one of those impossible demands with which ambitious sovereigns are wont to preface a declaration of war.

But Naaman's arrival, and all that had followed it, were reported to Elisha. With the freedom and authority of his great mission, he rebuked Jehoram for his unbelief and his alarm. Why could not Naaman be sent on to him, that he might learn that there was a prophet in Israel? And so Naaman obeyed. The great Syrian left the palace of the monarch, and he drew up with his long line of horsemen, and in his splendid war chariot, before the humble dwelling of the prophet. He waited; but although the prophet was within, a servant only presented himself, and that not to invite him to enter Elisha's dwelling, but to bid him journey more than thirty miles across the country, and then bathe himself seven times in the stream of the Jordan. If he would do that, he would recover. It was this message which led to the outbreak of temper and language described in the text. "Naaman was wroth, and went away, and said, Behold, I thought, He will surely come out to me, and stand, and call on the name of Jehovah, his God, and strike his hand over the place, and recover the leper. Are not Abana and Pharpar, rivers of Damascus, better than all the waters of Israel? May I not wash in them, and be clean? So he turned, and went away in a rage."

Here, I say, Naaman represents human nature, anxious to be blest by God's revelation of Himself, yet unwilling to take the blessing except on its own terms; for Naaman saw in Elisha not merely, or chiefly, a master of the healing art, but the exponent and prophet of a religion which was, he dimly felt, higher and diviner than any he had encountered before. Like the sculptor of what is called the Moabite stone, heathen though he was, Naaman was acquainted with the sacred Name of Israel's God, and indeed he expected that Elisha would cure him by invoking that Name. And thus, you observe, his bearing has a distinctly religious interest, and his treatment of Elisha's message has been repeated, and is repeated continually, under other circumstances, by thousands upon thousands of human beings. And our business, my brethren, is not to judge a man who, with scanty advantages, failed on a critical occasion in temper and in judgment,—failed when dealing with a very serious subject. But his conduct, like all else in holy Scripture, was certainly written for our learning, and we shall do well to see how far he may possibly have anticipated some of either our temptations or our actual failings in the great work of dealing with religious truth.

In Naaman's language, then, we see, first of all, a sense of humiliation and wrong. Naaman feels himself slighted. He had been accustomed at the brilliant court of Damascus to receive a great deal of deference and consideration,—more, probably, than any one else except the monarch himself. He had made a long journey into what he probably considered a vassal kingdom; and here one of its religious ministers treats him as if he were in a position of clearly marked inferiority. "Behold, I thought, He will surely come out to me." And Elisha's conduct cannot reasonably be ascribed to the legal prohibition of intercourse with lepers, or to any wish to magnify the miracle in the eyes of Naaman,—still less to any fear of infection. Elisha divined Naaman's state of mind. He knew what was the first lesson that Naaman needed to learn. Elisha acted as the minister of Him Who resisteth the proud, and giveth grace to the humble.[1] It is so in our own day. Here, for instance, is a man who feels instinctively that Christianity can give him that which, in a lasting form, is attainable nowhere else—purity in his heart, peace in his soul. The man has tried Syria in all its forms,—society, philosophy, pleasure, every kind of occupation; but there the sore remains. He has heard that Israel's true prophet still cures the leper, and he too comes for the remedy. But then he comes to Jesus Christ our Lord in an easy, confident spirit, just as though he were doing the gospel a good turn by conferring upon it the distinction of his splendid patronage. He comes for a blessing, no doubt; but then he believes himself to be giving something like an equivalent. He comes, in short, in his inmost heart to treat with our Lord as if He were a sort of equal; not to bend utterly before the Holiest as a repentant sinner. And, therefore, the first duty which religion has to discharge towards him, is to convince him of the true state of the case. He has to be undeceived as to his own condition; he has to learn that he, as all else have, has sinned and come short of the glory of God, and that, if justified at all, they are justified freely by His Grace through the redemption that is in Jesus Christ.

Certainly Christianity does not take a flattering view of fallen human nature. The first three chapters of the Epistle to the Romans stand at the portal of the very fullest statement which we have in the whole of the New

[1] Jam. iv. 6; 1 Pet. v. 5.

Testament of our Lord's redemptive work; and when men are going about to establish their own natural righteousness, not submitting to the righteousness of God,—when they are forgetting or slurring over the moral evil which has established a barrier between themselves and the All-holy,—when they would deal with Christianity just as if it were only a philosophy, truer, no doubt, and more comprehensive, and more adequate to deal with the facts, as they say, than other philosophies, but not entitled to set up a tribunal of judgment within the conscience, or to investigate and probe the secrets of the heart,—then the message which is sent out to them runs thus, "Because thou sayest, I am rich, and increased with goods; and knowest not that thou art wretched, and miserable, and poor, and blind, and naked: I counsel thee to buy of Me gold tried in the fire, that thou mayest be rich; and white raiment, that thou mayest be clothed, and that the shame of thy nakedness do not appear; and anoint thine eyes with eye-salve, that thou mayest see. As many as I love, I rebuke and chasten."[1]

And we see, secondly, in Naaman's language, the demand which human nature often makes for the sensational element in religion. Naaman expected an interview with the prophet that should be full of dramatic and striking incident. He knew perfectly well how the priests and magicians of his native Syria would have acted, had they possessed a tithe of Elisha's power. They would have set it off by all the arts that could possibly impress the imagination. "I thought, He will surely come out to me, and stand, and call on the name of Jehovah, his God, and move his hand" (so it is, quite literally) "up and down over the place, and recover the leper." And, instead of this, how tame and prosaic and business-like is the pro-

[1] Rev. iii. 17–19.

ceeding. Naaman, the great prince and soldier, is put off with a curt message. He is told, just as any peasant might be told, to bathe seven times in the stream of the Jordan—a proceeding which was open to all the world besides. If the prophet had bidden him attempt some great thing, something corresponding to what he believed to be the general proportions of his station and his character, something verging upon the limits of the superhuman and the impossible, would he not have done, or tried to do it? Of course he would. But to drive some thirty miles across the hills in order to bathe in the national river of Israel at the end of the drive—the proposal was too commonplace: it was simply intolerable.

And here, I say, Naaman is human nature in all countries and all times. The striking, the impressive, the sensational, as a test of truth, are as much in request here and now as they were in Elisha's day in Samaria. A man is feeling his way, I again suppose, towards practical Christianity. He has lived on excitement all his life, and he expects still to find that which will gratify it to the full, although in another shape, at the door of the Church of Christ. It is a sort of necessity of his nature. And if he is not greeted by something that is exceptional and brilliant, he is quite prepared to go away in a rage; and then he is almost necessarily disappointed. "I thought," he says to himself—"I thought that He Whom I am seeking to cure me of my leprosy would surely come out to me, presenting Himself in some splendid literature, in some world-wide, spotless, undivided Church, proclaiming truth by voices of matchless eloquence, inviting to worship by ceremonies of graceful and imposing magnificence. And yet, what is the case? The world which I have left does better, and after my experience of its charms I find the Church tame and insipid. Compare its hesitating, its stilted utterances," he continues, " with the freedom, with the resource, with the bold and fearless impetuosity, of worldly genius lavishing itself over the fields of poetry and philosophy, taking the human mind captive by its many-sided attractiveness. Compare its feeble, its unconnected and often disorganised or self-neutralising action, with the decision and the power which characterise the work of great worldly potentates and representative statesmen. Nay, how little do its most characteristic rites respond to the just expectations of my soul!" It is a hard thing when a man is waiting to be touched by the fire of prophetic utterance, that he should be sent in an official way—(no doubt Naaman thought so) —to bathe seven times in the stream of the Jordan. It is hard when a man is expecting some new and brilliant theory that shall take account, in its majestic compass, of all the facts that disturb, or that are supposed to disturb, all the possible relations of religion and philosophy, to be told simply, in the old way, that the Blood of the Atonement alone cleanses, and that the water in the Font is still efficacious. So men speak. It is the voice of Naaman: it is the voice of human nature, which expects that, when it is in contact with revealed religion, it must necessarily find the sensational.

No doubt at times true religion does, to a certain extent, in condescension to our weakness, meet this deep craving of our nature. They who witnessed the Transfiguration, or the Ascension, or the tongues of fire as they descended on the Day of Pentecost,—they who heard Paul speak on the strand at Miletus, or who listened to the speakers in the mystic languages at Corinth, or who in the first fervour of their conversion would have plucked out their eyes and given them to the apostle who had brought them to the feet of Christ—they, assuredly, must have felt in varying degrees something of its power. And it is undeniable that again and again, in the later ages of Christendom, vast enthusiasms have swept over the Christian populations,—that Elisha has, as it were, come out to the door of his house, and has passed his hand again and again rapidly over the sores of society, and has recovered the leper. But, on the whole, the strength of revealed religion is seen in its power of dispensing with efforts of this kind; for its force resides, not in the earthquake which occasionally shakes, not in the fire which at times consumes the heart of the Church, but in the still small voice which speaks to conscience. The power of producing a great sensation is no test of truth or of goodness. The power of controlling passion and of quickening conscience is a test. But then this is achieved in quietness and confidence,—achieved often most successfully in the discharge of routine duties, in the formation and the strengthening of quiet and deep convictions, in that inner life of affection for our Lord which risks its excellence by rude exposure, by eager demonstrativeness. An early Communion, where ten or twelve assemble in the twilight to receive the Sacrament of the Divine Redemption, is likely, often, to be much more useful than attendance at an evening sermon in a crowded church.

And, once more, Naaman represents prejudiced attachment to early associations, coupled, as it often is, with a jealous impatience of anything like exclusive claims put forward on behalf of the truths or ordinances of a religion which we are for the first time attentively considering. Naaman will forget the prophet's disappointing reserve. His mind rests for a moment on the prophet's command. What is he to do? He is to bathe, it appears, in some distant stream, and then the leprosy will disappear. Will not the rivers of his native Syria suffice,—the clear, cool stream of the Abana or Barada, rushing down from the Antilibanus, and forming the oasis on which his native Damascus is built, or, farther to the south, the Pharpar, flowing from the plain into the desert lake? If the cure is to depend on any such conditions at all, why will not these historic waters achieve it? Why must he be asked to bathe in the turbid and muddy brook which he had passed on the road to Samaria, and which was bound up with the history of an alien race? "Are not Abana and Pharpar, rivers of Damascus, better than all the waters of Israel? May I not wash in them, and be clean?" My brethren, few things can be more precious than early associations when we have been nurtured, through God's mercy, in a Christian home, and when memory treasures up actions and persons on whom Christ our Lord has shed the light of His countenance. But it is otherwise when this unspeakable blessing has been denied us,—when the heart has given of its freshest and its best to that which is erroneous or is wrong. Then, if we ever reach the door of Elisha's house, there is an inevitable struggle, and men ask why Grace, of which, as yet, they know so little is, after all, so efficacious and so necessary; and they ask why nature, of which they may or may not really know more, cannot do the work of cleansing them from their defilement. "Look at nature," they say; "look at its beauty, its freedom, its resource. Can it be the impotent, the fruitless thing that you say? Has it not its points of superiority to the hard, stiff, formal teaching of your theologians? Are not the green fields better than the close air, and the dingy aspect, of your churches? Is not a good library, or a brilliant conversation, or a scientific lecture, more to the purpose than your dull and uninteresting sermons? Why are we to believe that your Sacraments are the especial channels of any regenerative efficacy,—

that a little water and a few words can make, as your Catechism says, 'a member of Christ, a child of God, and an heir of the kingdom of heaven'? High intellectual gifts, great moral ascendancy—these things, we believe it, these things may compass the regeneration of the world. For the rest, it has been well said that a good national literature is much more to the purpose than all or any of the gifts of Christ."

Nature, no doubt, my brethren, can do much. We may admit it, because all that is great, beautiful, productive in nature comes most assuredly, like the gifts of Grace, from the good God, the Fountain of all goodness. But nature can no more rise above its level than water can. Nature can civilise, undoubtedly: that is one thing. It can not regenerate: that is quite another. He who made us can alone remake us; and He is perfectly free to choose the channel of this His last, His choicest gift. He might have made the Syrian waters the means of His healing power; He might have denied forever any efficacy to the waters of the Jordan. There was no physical quality inherent in the Jordan water that wrought the cure. The cure was wrought by the divine Will connecting its efficacy with this one particular instrument. Of themselves, neither Syrian nor Jewish streams had, let me repeat it, any healing properties at all. By a particular choice, God made the Jewish river the means whereby His healing virtue was to be dispensed to Naaman. The question is not, whether man's natural life in thought and action has not a force and a splendour that is all its own. Of course it has. The question is, whether anything in it can render unnecessary or superfluous that stupendous act of power and of love which was achieved on Mount Calvary. Of itself a little water applied to a child's forehead, while a few words are repeated at the moment, could not possibly convey any spiritual gift. To suppose this would be simply to believe in a material charm. But if, choosing this out of a thousand possible acts or symbols, He to Whom all power is given in earth and Heaven has indeed attached to it a specific spiritual efficacy, then, I say, the case is utterly different. Nature may be, in itself, more graceful, more fertile, more persuasive. She is comparatively powerless to touch, to remould the soul of man, because she lacks that which gives power to what in themselves are weak and beggarly elements: she lacks the chartered presence of the world's Redeemer, the presence of Christ.

But to go, lastly, to the root of the matter. Naaman's fundamental mistake consisted in his attempt to decide at all how the prophet should work the miracle of his cure. He plainly, in reason, had no means of doing this. He only knew, or had reason to suppose, that the religion of Israel was higher and diviner than his own. He came to it for that which his own could not give him; and he, suppliant and leper as he was, was in no position to determine what would or what would not be appropriate action or advice on the part of its ministers. If it did its work, if he obtained the cure he needed, that would be enough. To decide upon its method of procedure was beyond his power. Yet how often is this fundamental mistake repeated! Men who know themselves to be lepers, who have lived all their lives far on the wrong side of the frontier of the Christian Church, and who at last, through God's mercy, have come to it for that which neither civilisation nor culture can possibly give them,—men who have come, it may be, thus far, at very considerable sacrifices, with their ten talents of silver and their six thousand pieces of gold and their ten changes of raiment,—men who have discovered that a Jehoram, a mere worldly compromise with religion, cannot help them, and have pushed their way on resolutely, persistently, to the very door of Elisha—they yet strangely, conceive themselves able to determine what their great Benefactor ought to do in order to achieve their cure. Christian evidences, they say, ought to be mathematical; moral evidence will not do. Christian doctrine must include these elements, it must exclude those. Christian worship must be either the exaggeration of slovenliness, or the exaggeration of ceremony. Christian philanthropy must make a compact with our political economy. Christian philosophy must come to an understanding with this or that writer who is at issue with its first postulates. Christian morals must have an eye to detail, and yet must avoid becoming casuistry. Christianity as a whole must respond to our expectations without violently exceeding them. In short, Christ must come out to meet the man; He must stand; He must move His hand, just as the man desires, over the place, and must recover the leper.

Do I say, my brethren, that Naaman has no duties except those of simple submission? Do I say that there are no conditions with which a faith claiming to come from God must comply, in order to claim the allegiance of the human soul? Far from it. Apart from the evidences which lead a man up to faith, there are two tests of a true revelation which can never be dispensed with. It must not contradict the highest, purest, clearest voice of natural conscience: it must not contradict itself. Our sense of primary moral truth is just as much God's voice as His revelation of truth without us. He cannot unsay without what He has already told us within. Our conscience, of course, may be misinformed. We must look to that: it is a grave matter. But if, for instance, it were true that the doctrine of the Atonement contradicted the true idea of justice—not of justice between one creature and another creature, but of a very different thing, justice as between the creature and the Creator,—then that would be a reason for rejecting the doctrine. And if we are told that a series of teachers who, unless history is worthless, contradict each other on important points, are all equally infallible, that certainly is a reason for distrusting the system which makes the assertion. But beyond this, in the purely spiritual and supernatural sphere, we are not at all able to say beforehand what a religion coming from God ought to do, ought to teach, ought to be like. The finite cannot measure the Infinite or His work. To attempt to do this is to be exposed sooner or later to the shock of certain disappointment. A German poet satirises the writers of his day who say practically, "What I would have done had I only been the Christ!" And an apostle, when he closes his account of the dispensation of mercy, exclaims, "O, the depth of the riches both of the wisdom and knowledge of God! how unsearchable are His judgments, and His ways past finding out!"[1]

Naaman, we know, thought better of it. After his recovery he showed that he had a grateful and a simple heart by returning to Samaria, by making his acknowledgments to Elisha, by making his profession of faith in Elisha's God. And the general lesson of his history is plain. We are lepers. We need the healing virtue that goes forth from our Lord and Saviour, however, whenever, through whomsoever, He may bestow it. We know that He, the true prophet of all the ages, heals souls in the midst of Israel. We know that His Blood cleanses, that His Spirit sanctifies, that there are appointed channels of His grace and His power. If we are satisfied that the

[1] Rom. xi. 33.

general evidence for this revelation of love and mercy is at all sufficient to live by, to rest upon in life and in death, do not let us dream of the folly of improving upon His work in detail,—of asking for, or of creating, new organs of infallibility, or of depreciating old and assured means of sharing His redemptive grace. It is unpractical as well as irreverent to discuss what has been settled by the infinite Wisdom, and therefore settled irrevocably. The true scope of our activity is to make the most, the very most, day by day, of His bounty and His love, that by His healing and strengthening Grace we too may be cured of our leprosy,—may so pass through things temporal, that we finally lose not the things eternal.[1]

[1] Collect of the 4th Sunday after Trinity.

# SERMON XV.

## THE CALL OF ELISHA.

### 1 KINGS xix. 19, 20, 21.

*" So he departed thence, and found Elisha the son of Shaphat, who was ploughing with twelve yoke of oxen before him, and he with the twelfth: and Elijah passed by him, and cast his mantle upon him. And he left the oxen and ran after Elijah, and said, Let me, I pray thee, kiss my father and my mother, and then I will follow thee. And he said unto him, Go back again: for what have I done to thee? And he returned back from him, and took a yoke of oxen, and slew them, and boiled their flesh with the instruments of the oxen, and gave unto the people, and they did eat. Then he arose, and went after Elijah, and ministered unto him."*

HERE, my brethren, we see one of the methods by which the prophetical ministry was propagated and maintained in Israel. It was not, you will have remarked, like the Jewish priesthood, a matter of hereditary descent. The son did not become a prophet because his father had been a prophet before him. Like Jeremiah, each prophet was the subject of a special predestination to his work. "Before I formed thee in the belly I knew thee; and before thou camest forth out of the womb I sanctified thee, and I ordained thee a prophet unto the nations."[1] But each prophet was called to his work by some especial token or influence; and then, either as a student in one

[1] Jer. i. 5.

of the colleges or schools of the prophets, as they were called, or as an attendant upon a great teacher, he received a kind of education for his future life.

Elisha appears to have been a man of substance. He was ploughing in the field with twelve yoke of oxen at Abel-meholah in the valley of the Jordan, when Elijah passed on his way back from the great vision which he had received in Horeb. Elijah does not seem to have spoken; he merely cast his mantle on Elisha and passed on. This act, indeed, was symbolical. It had, like many of the formal actions of the prophets, such as rending the dress or putting ashes on the head, an ascertained and recognised meaning. The prophet's mantle was a visible sign of the robe of spiritual power which encompassed him; and to cast the mantle on another was to call him to share the labour, the glory, the responsibility, the danger of the prophetic office. Although Elijah had not spoken, this significant action was perfectly understood. Elisha obeyed its purpose. He ran after the silent prophet who was already vanishing from his sight. He had one, only one, petition: he would just take leave of his parents and receive their blessing, and then he would follow. Elijah consents, but Elisha must return soon, considering the greatness of the destiny before him. The original would here better be rendered, "Go, return, for how great a thing have I done unto thee." Elisha is bent upon shewing the undivided allegiance which he owes to the prophet, the completeness of his self-surrender. Up to that moment his farm on the banks of the Jordan had been his all, as in a later age their boats and nets had been everything to those fishermen on the Sea of Galilee who were predestined to the apostolate of the world. Elisha does not linger to drop regrets over the cherished past from which he is passing forever. He forthwith slays the oxen with which he had just been ploughing; he takes the plough tackling for fuel that he may boil their flesh; he gives one parting entertainment to his acquaintances, to the neighbourhood, that they may have no doubt either about his goodwill towards themselves, or of his fixed and lofty resolutions; and then he leaves the scene of his labours,—he leaves his field, his home, his all, to become the servant of Elijah.

Is this, think you, to be looked upon as only and strictly an incident in the life of an ancient prophet? Has it no permanent, no wider application? Has it no human significance? There is some risk, my brethren, of blinding ourselves to the real meaning of the Old Testament—of its urgent and striking appeals to the Christian, to the human conscience and life—by saying that this and that in it is only oriental, and has, therefore, no relevancy for a modern European. Certainly there is a superficial element of custom and of ceremony in the life described in the Old Testament which does belong to the ancient East, and which is untransferable to the circumstances of our own day and country; but human nature, on the one side, and the great laws of God's providential dealings, on the other, were in the East, two thousand eight hundred years ago, exactly what they are now, and what occurred then was, as an apostle says, "written for our learning, that we through patience and comfort of the scriptures might have hope,"[1]—hope as well as other virtues which are to be won from their perusal. The call of Elisha has its place not merely in the history of his order, not merely in the history of his country, but in the history of humanity, and as such it must be regarded as an astonishing instance of the power of religious influence. The silent prophet passes; he drops his mantle; and the

[1] Rom. xv. 4.

life of another fellow man is agitated to its centre, to its inmost depths. Its whole current and direction is from that moment changed. He yields to an attraction: he does not analyse it; he obeys. And it may be well to ask ourselves in what—putting aside for to-day, but by no means ignoring it, the great question of God's supernatural Grace—in what did this influence, viewed on its human side, in what did this attraction, consist? For it is not to be supposed that the obedience of Elisha had nothing to do with those motives and laws of conduct which govern the actions of thoughtful and conscientious men now. It is not to be supposed that Elijah put forth some force which was literally magical—magical in such sense that it exerted upon Elisha's will an influence for which no account could be given in reason—a magnetic influence which could not—*could not*—but be obeyed. Had, indeed, this been the case, the interest of this history would have been shifted from the department of spiritual and moral life to the department of physics, and it would be, perhaps, more properly investigated in some lecture-room at St. Bartholomew's Hospital than from the pulpit of this Cathedral. No; mighty as was the influence of Elijah, Elisha's liberty was not suspended, still less destroyed by it. He was perfectly free to have resisted it. If he did not do so, if he yielded at once, if he decided instantaneously on an obedience which, as we may for the moment think, ought to have been preceded and justified by an exhaustive discussion, this was because there must have been a preparatory educational process going on for some time within him. He must have had thoughts, affections, aspirations, which only waited the occasion to be combined, to be expressed in action; and so when the great prophet passed by him, all the scattered reasons for being drawn towards him coalesced into a single ray of moral light and moral warmth, and determined his future disciple's course, impelled him to an act of such unreserved obedience.

It is, then, material to ask what must have been at least some of the motives which led Elisha thus to obey.

And, first, Elijah would have represented in Elisha's eyes a great cause, a great or imperious idea or truth which had been lodged for centuries in the soul of every Israelite. That idea was the existence, the claims, of the one living and true God Who had revealed Himself to Israel. While the surrounding nations were in different degrees of heathen darkness and degradation, Israel by a singular exercise of God's favour had been chosen, indeed, to know His will, and in that knowledge to learn much, although by no means all, that we Christians know of Himself, of His character, of His nature, of His attributes. To treasure that knowledge, to hand it on from generation to generation, to make it the inspiring principle of national as well as individual thought and life,— this was the appointed task of the consecrated people, again and again prescribed in their law, again and again enforced by the exhortations of their prophets, again and again illustrated by the lives and by the works of their most representative saints and leaders. In quiet times not merely every prophet, every member of the priesthood and of the Levitical tribe, but even every Israelite, in some sense represented this great truth; for every Israelite was admitted by circumcision into a covenant with God which bound him to loyalty to God's revelation of Himself, just as every baptised Christian in this Cathedral bears the sacred Sign, as our baptismal service expresses it, " in token that hereafter he shall not be ashamed to confess the faith of Christ crucified, but manfully to fight under His banner against sin, the world, and the devil, and to continue Christ's faithful soldier and servant unto life's end." In quiet times this representative duty of every believer towards the Revelation which he believes is accepted, at least in terms, without difficulty. It is only, as our Lord said, "when tribulation or persecution ariseth because of the word"[1] that certain classes of character are, as a matter of course, offended. When Elijah appeared upon the scene of history it seemed as if the Revelation committed to Israel were on the point of being trodden out by a young and vigorous idolatry. The marriage of Ahab, king of Israel, with Jezebel, the daughter of Ethbaal, the king of Sidon, had led to the propagation of the queen's religion, the worship of the Phœnician Baal,—one of those seductive varieties of worship of the vital forms of nature in a personified shape which exercised so extraordinary a sway over the imagination and reason of the ancient world, and which, although in modern times they have adopted a more refined guise, are by no means strange or unwelcome to the modern world. So seductive was the superstition, so commanding the influence of the court, so vigorous, so trenchant the policy of the queen, that seven thousand was the total number of Israelites who had escaped the taint—who had not bowed the knee to the image of Baal.

And, at great trial times like this, great causes become almost necessarily identified with the names of individuals. Truths are, for the time, impersonated in single men. Elijah was, to the Revelation of the one God, Maker of heaven and earth, what at a later age St. Paul was to the truth of man's justification through Christ's merits without legal obedience—at least in certain portions of the Church,—what St. Athanasius was, during the great Arian struggle, to the true Godhead of Jesus Christ

[1] Matt. xiii. 21.

as it had been taught by the apostles. When men looked at Elijah moving rapidly from one scene of danger to another in those troublous times, the whole history of Israel, the whole Mosaic revelation, seemed to live again—seemed to speak in him. Behind his individual voice and gesture there was the felt presence of a great and living cause,—of a mighty and eternal truth; and, as a consequence, he exercised an influence quite out of proportion to his personal position. It was not the man himself, it was the divine cause, it was the Heaven sent Revelation which he represented, which won, which enchained to him, the hearts of those who still believed in it. Elisha bent before the truth of which his master was himself the servant.

My brethren, the first condition of a deep religious influence, proceeding whether from individuals or from Churches, is a clear positive creed,—clear and positive whether it be large or small. The man must know, at least, what he does believe. Elijah would have been powerless, had he only insisted on the falsehood of the superstitions of Jezebel and her prophets. He would have been powerless, had he merely surrounded the Revelation of Sinai with a garniture of the finest sentiment and poetry, leaving it doubtful whether he himself believed it to be true or not. He was powerful because men knew that he had no sort of doubt about his creed,—about its exact frontier, about its absolute certainty; and Elisha felt the presence not of a mere man, but of a mighty cause or truth represented in the man, and he obeyed it.

But then, secondly, in representing a great cause, official representation is not enough for religious influence. Personal qualities are needed—qualities in harmony with the requirements of the cause or truth represented. Eli and his sons represented the Mosaic Revelation in Israel in their day, but they only made the Lord's people to transgress. Alexander the Sixth and Leo the Tenth represented Christianity, in the official sense of the term, to western Christendom. They certainly did not recommend it to the consciences of men. The ordinary Hanoverian bishops of a century ago were, by their office, representatives of Christianity in the Church of England; but with a few splendid exceptions their representation, too, was strictly heartless and official and powerless, where it was not, as in Hoadley's case, utterly repulsive. In order to reach hearts and to move convictions, some sort of personal conformity to the idea represented is needed, as well as the official right to represent; and Elijah would have been felt by Elisha to have this personal title to represent the cause of God superadded to the official one. Every Israelite, we may be sure, whether friend or foe—whether in open league with the apostate court of Jezebel, or in secret correspondence with the scattered schools of the prophets—every Israelite had heard of the stern mien and lofty proportions of the character which seemed to its contemporaries to belong to another world. They knew that, if anywhere, here was perfect simplicity of purpose, here was determination to live and to die for the glory of the God of the patriarchs, Who had brought Israel out of Egypt, Who had spoken from Sinai. They knew that here was an unflinching courage which shrank not from encounter with the cruel, the wily, idolatress who ruled the policy of Israel. They must have been well aware that the ties of flesh and blood did not fetter the great prophet's liberty, for, like John the Baptist nine centuries later, he had prepared for his ministry in the solitude of the desert. He then had suddenly appeared in the very palace of the weak and apostate monarch to denounce his sins, to foretell the judgments which awaited him. In an age of decaying faith, in an age of progressive moral deterioration, in an age of general apostasy, Elijah stood forth from among the mass of men in almost solitary grandeur. He must have been felt to be the typical saint and hero of the old theocracy. He must have been recognised as embodying in the highest degree the moral power which belonged to a life so shaped, so led, as to express before men's eyes his firm conviction of the truth of the Sinaitic Revelation. True it was, as we have heard in this afternoon's lesson, that Elijah too was at times subject even to the deepest discouragement. When, after his great victory over the assembled prophets of Baal upon Carmel, it seemed as if the tide of public feeling in Israel had really turned, men cried in their enthusiasm, "The Lord He is the God! The Lord He is the God!"[1] But the change was but of short duration. The day of Carmel was soon forgotten, and Ahab was still Ahab, and Jezebel had not ceased to be Jezebel; and the multitude, which, for a moment had obeyed with fervour the authority of the prophet, soon fell back to the sanguinary voluptuous rites of the Phœnician god with a new enthusiasm. And then Elijah felt that despondency of which great and ardent souls alone are capable. God seemed to be hiding His face. The prophet's faith was almost slipping from him. The whole order of the moral world was, in his eyes, for the moment confused, dark, incomprehensible, out of course. Jezebel was again in power. She was menacing his life; and he, in truth, is weary of his life—weary of the apparently hopeless struggle which is its condition. He returns to the southern desert in which he had learnt his earliest lesson, where he is well out of the way of the levity, of the frivolity, of his

[1] 1 Kings xviii. 39.

apostate countrymen,—where he is face to face with the savage desolation of nature in a scene that seems to correspond to the blank of his own inward misery. He fain would die; and when a voice from above reaches his conscience in his retreat—" What doest thou here, Elijah?"[1] he can only reply by a bitter complaint that God has abandoned His cause,—that He has left His prophet to struggle unbefriended, alone, vanquished. Does this forfeit the prophet's influence? Is it fatal to the commanding, to the unique, greatness of his character? Certainly we must admit it had been a more perfect course to have trusted God throughout—to have trusted Him in failure not less than amid success; but Elijah, great as he was, was yet not the All-perfect, and his failure was itself one of those forms of failure which are only possible to faith and devotion. They to whom life seems worthless because God's cause—not theirs, but God's—is imperilled or defeated for the time, are, in all generations, among the few. To the many, the whole question is of no great concern. Whether the Church of Christ is winning her way among human souls, or losing it,—whether she is extending the frontiers of the Redeemer's kingdom, or barely maintaining them,—whether her ministers are speaking boldly in the name of Jesus, or are pandering weakly to the popular unbelief,—all this troubles them not. They eat, they walk, they sleep, as if all were well, just as did their fathers in the quiet days before them. The anguish, the discontent, the fierce desperation of Elijah, are the products—it may be that they are the unregulated and disordered products, but they are the products—of a noble passion whereof they know nothing,—the noble, the generous passion, which is careful only for the honour of God, which is uncontrollable when He

[1] 1 Kings xix. 9.

seems to be defeated or disowned. No; if Elisha did know of Elijah's retreat in profound discouragement, almost in despair, to the rocks of Horeb, he would not have been (we may dare to say it) less open to the great prophet's influence. The poignant despondency of a great faith is almost its virtue. Elisha would have felt not the less drawn to the solitary at Horeb than to the conqueror at Carmel.

There is a third element of influence beyond: the influence which belongs to a soul often in communion with God. This is less easy to seize, to describe, to measure than the weight which belongs either to the representation of a great cause or truth, or to personal elevation of character. This cannot be mapped out in words or in actions. It is nothing exactly tangible. It is an atmosphere which hovers around the life, and which we are conscious of breathing, but that is all, when we approach it. It is not a matter of manner, of gesture, of expressive words, of expressive and studied silences. It is not to be precipitated into any outward form. It is too volatile,—if you like, it is too strictly supersensuous,—it is too altogether appertaining to the region of spirit, to be registered by any definite tests and marks in the sphere of matter. Yet who has not sometimes felt it—this indescribable influence—this sure certificate of nearness to God, which some few privileged souls of both sexes, in all stations of society, unconsciously to themselves but most surely, exert? It is a something beyond character; it is tone. It is something beyond goodness; it is holiness. It needs no language to express it; it is felt instinctively. Elisha may well have felt it (as we read the narrative we know it) as Elijah passed the field of Abelmeholah.

And this history suggests two sets of considerations,

one for those who exert religious influence, the other for those who yield to it.

And for those who exert it, all wise and thoughtful people may well shrink, my brethren, from the great but unavoidable responsibility of doing so—the responsibility of saying (whether in words or by acts to others, it little matters) "Follow me! Follow me upwards through this path or that, in the light of this or that creed, towards the throne of light." Many men profess altogether to decline any such responsibility; and yet it is certain that, do what we will, we cannot, any one of us, but exert some religious influence. Every man is assuredly the apostle of something—of evil, if not of good. Our very presence is of itself the propagation of some faith. Whether we will or not, we are leading men; we are leading those around us in some direction.

> "We scatter seeds with careless hand,
>   And dream we ne'er shall see them more;
>     But, for a thousand years,
>     Their fruit appears
>   In weeds that mar the land,
>   Or healthful store.
>
> "The deeds we do, the words we say,
>   Into still air they seem to fleet.
>     We count them ever past,
>     But they shall last
>   In the great judgment-day,
>   And we shall meet."

It is better, then, to make a virtue of what is already a necessity,—to wield a talent usefully of which we cannot dispossess ourselves altogether if we would. Some of us are teachers: what is the influence we are exerting on our pupils? Many of us are masters and mistresses: what is the influence we are bringing to bear upon our servants? Others are parents: How are we influencing—(in some important way we must be influencing)—the future of our children? "Ah," we say, "we wish we could be of use in this way; but then it is an affair of temperament. Some people seem to understand it; others do not, and we are among the number." No, brethren, the explanation is simpler, it is juster, than this. If when Elijah casts his mantle upon Elisha—the mantle of his creed, of his conduct, of his life—Elisha does not respond, there may be another explanation of the failure than that which you are thinking of. Success is impossible if Elijah represents nothing clear and certain,—if he does not know his own mind,—if he is only trying to win acceptance for a few private guesses or crotchets of his own instead of for a Creed which has come from Heaven. Success is improbable, again, if Elijah's life is quite out of keeping with his Creed,—if he is felt to be incapable of that which he recommends,—if he has done and has ventured nothing for the cause he advocates. It is improbable, too, if he has about him nothing of the air and bearing of an envoy of God,—if he is obviously devoted to this world, and only alludes to the next in an official and formal way, and without the accent of a man to whom it is a serious reality. Doubtless, God may make His truth do its own work through His Grace in hearts, in spite of the inconsistencies of its representatives. But then I am speaking of what is probable; and, as a rule, God works through instruments—as a rule. Elisha is won by the decision, by the consistency, by the unearthliness of Elijah, as much as by the intrinsic claims of that which he represents.

And, lastly, there is instruction here for those who yield to religious influence. Some of us, I suppose, at least, have known in life something like the passage of Elijah in our past lives. A religious influence has swept across our path, placing truth, placing duty, more clearly before us than we ever knew them before—recommending them by an example of high-minded devotion, of simple, of disinterested life. We have felt its power. Have we obeyed it? It may be after a legitimate, a wise hesitation, such as was Elisha's; but still, have we obeyed it? Had Elisha refused to acknowledge what was meant by the casting of Elijah's mantle, we know how vast would have been the difference to the kingdom of Israel, to the kingdom of Judah, to the kingdom of Syria, to the kingdom of God in each, to himself above all. He was no longer in the same moral position after the divine call had reached him. He could no longer survey, if he would, his twelve yoke of oxen with a perfectly easy conscience, as if he had really no duty, no destiny, excepting that of ploughing up the field in Abel-meholah. A spell from Heaven had crossed his path, and he must decide either deliberately to acknowledge or deliberately to ignore it. So it may be or has been with us. The history of this afternoon's lesson will have recalled, to those of us who know our Bibles, at least two passages in the life of the divine Redeemer: the call of the disciples, and the call of the man who wished first to bury his father. In our Lord's case it is observable that the call to instant obedience is much more peremptory than in Elijah's. He commands in terms, "Follow me!" Elijah only suggests by a symbolical action. Our Lord will allow of no delay even to perform the last duties to a parent's memory. Elijah has no hesitation in allowing Elisha to take leave of his father and mother before entering on the prophetic life. The difference is to be explained by the intrinsic difference between the person of the prophet and the Person of the Redeemer. Elijah did but represent the cause of God. In Jesus, as His apostle said, there dwelt the whole fulness of the Godhead bodily. Elijah's conduct, although that of a saint and hero, was not absolutely perfect. In the life of Jesus no trace of shortcoming could possibly be detected by the most cynical criticism. They who came near to Elijah came near to one who was irradiated by constant communion with God. They who came near to Jesus were, as the seraphim and the cherubim around the throne, close, whether they knew it or not, to the very Form which the All-holy had assumed in time. The greater urgency of our Lord is proportioned to His unspeakably higher and more imperative claim. And it is with Him—not with His prophet, not with any of His creatures—that we have to do. Amid our most trivial duties, on days which are passing in the usual round of uneventful routine, He may speak to us as never before. A quiet word may be dropped by a friend,—a sentence read in a book,—a thought lodged, we know not why or how, in the mind. We are laid under obligations to a new and more imperious view of life and duty. Not Elijah, but Elijah's Lord, has passed and cast His mantle.

There is, of course, room for self-delusion of many kinds in the supposed visit of the heavenly call. We may read our fancies in the skies, if we do not take care. We may transfigure our own wishes into divine voices, by a process so subtle as to impose upon ourselves. But we are tolerably safe if two conditions are observed,—if, first, the duty or line of life prescribed is unwelcome to our natural inclinations; and if, secondly, it does not contradict what we know God has taught us hitherto,—if it is an extension of His earlier teaching, not its condemnation. No one who believes that our Lord Jesus Christ is present by His Spirit in His Church, can doubt that He will, from time to time, speak thus to souls in virtue of

His own promises. No one who knows anything practically of the lives of earnest Christians will question the fact of His having done so. And to listen for the footsteps of the divine Redeemer passing by us in the ordinary providences of life is a most important part of the probation of every man. How much may depend on following when He beckons us to some higher duty, to some more perfect service, we shall only know when we see all things as they really are in the light of His eternity.

# SERMON XVI.

## THE INVISIBLE WORLD A REALITY TO FAITH.

### 2 KINGS vi. 17.

*"And Elisha prayed, and said, Lord, I pray thee, open his eyes, that he may see. And the Lord opened the eyes of the young man; and he saw: and, behold, the mountain was full of horses and chariots of fire round about Elisha.*

MEN who read their Bibles least carefully must, I should think, have observed the remarkable number and character of the miracles which cluster around the lives of the great prophets Elijah and Elisha. There is nothing exactly like it in the case of any of the other prophets, if perhaps we are to except Daniel.

And the reason is not difficult to see. Great outbursts of the miraculous, attesting God's energetic presence at particular times in particular places, appear to recur in the sacred history in cycles, when truth has to be announced—when it has to be promulgated afresh—when it has to be saved from extinction. One such there was in the days of Moses, when Israel was delivered from Egypt and the faith of Sinai was proclaimed; another in the days of Joshua, when the promised land was solemnly taken possession of; another in the time we are considering, the days of Elijah and Elisha, when the belief and law of Sinai were threatened with nothing less than extinction by the apostasy of the court of Israel and the attacks of the powerful monarchs of Syria; another during the Babylonish captivity, when Israel sat down and wept over the memories of Zion by the waters of her heathen exile; and a last great display of God's miraculous power was made in the days of His incarnate Son Jesus Christ and His apostles—the days in which He Who had, "at sundry times and in divers manners, spoken aforetime unto the fathers by the prophets,"[1] spoke finally, spoke fully, in and by His Son—the epoch of His largest and of His last unveiling of His Name and will to the intelligent and moral creatures of His hand.

Now, the miracles belonging to these different periods are, up to a certain point, as would be expected, unlike each other. Each period has, if I may so express myself, its characteristic miracles. But, on the other hand, there is a likeness between them arising from their having more or less of a common object and purpose which cannot be mistaken. Not to go beyond our text, this miracle of Elisha is peculiarly evangelical. It is just such a miracle as befits the drift and purpose of the Gospel considered as an unveiling of the unseen world to the soul of man. It especially anticipates such miracles of our Lord as that by which, as St. John describes it, He healed the man born blind; in which at one and the same time, you will remark, He gave the gift of natural sight and the higher gift of spiritual sight—the two gifts together—the lower gift being at once a type and an earnest of the higher.

Let us briefly recall the circumstances under which this miracle was worked.

Elisha was on good terms with Jehoram, then king of Israel, and Jehoram was at war, as his father and his grandfather were before him, with the Syrians of Damas-

[1] Heb. i. 1.

cus, the inveterate enemies of the kingdom of Israel. The Syrians of this latter period seem to have carried on their war by a system of predatory incursions into the territory of Israel; and on several occasions Elisha warned king Jehoram of the place which the Syrians intended to surround, and by thus putting him on his guard enabled him to escape, or at any rate enabled him to defeat, the measures of the enemy. The king of Syria suspected, naturally enough, that a failure which occurred so often must be due to some secret treachery on the part of his own officers; but on his making inquiry they told him that the prophet Elisha possessed such powers as to be able to keep the king of Israel accurately informed of the Syrian king's most secret counsels. "The prophet that is in Israel," they said, "telleth the king of Israel the words that thou speakest in thy bed-chamber."[1] The Syrian king was, therefore, resolved to capture the prophet if it was possible to do so, and with this view he sent a large body of troops by night to surround Dothan, a small town some twelve Roman miles north of Samaria, where Elisha was residing at the time; and when Elisha's servant went out in the morning and found that the town had been during the night completely invested by the Syrians, he returned to his master in something very like despair. Escape seemed impossible. "Alas! my lord," he said, "what shall we do?" The prophet simply remarked that he should not fear, "since they that are with us are more than they that are with them." This statement must, at first, have seemed nothing less than absurd to the servant, who compared the few Israelites shut up within the small town with the numerous Syrian host outside it. But Elisha prayed the Lord to open the servant's eyes that he might see something more than the world of sense,—that

[1] 2 Kings vi. 12.

he might see that world which is above, around, beyond the world of sense. The servant accordingly beheld what was really a repetition of Jacob's vision, who, when he was threatened by Esau, had seen a double army of angels encamped around him. "The Lord opened the eyes of the young man; and he saw: and, behold, the mountain was full of horses and chariots of fire round about Elisha."[1]

What is meant by opening the eyes of the young man? Clearly it was not the gift of natural sight, since the young man saw the Syrian host round Dothan and was terrified. It was some higher gift, analogous probably to clairvoyance. It was a supernatural ecstacy which laid open to him, for the time being, as to St. John in Patmos, the world of spirits under such form as his intelligence could bear. The same thing had occurred in an earlier age to Balaam. His eyes, we are told, were opened, and he saw an angel stopping his path,—an angel who was there, but whom his natural eye had not seen. It was the gift, you see, of a new and more piercing sense reaching into a sphere of being that was previously out of reach. It was like a natural discovery by the aid of a powerful telescope—the discovery of a planet unseen before, but of the existence of which an astronomer is or might have been certain by calculations that could not fail him. Elisha's servant knew full well—knew from the terms of his creed—that there were such beings as angels. God, at Elisha's prayers, gave him a new power of spiritual vision, and he saw them.

What did he see? "He saw: and, behold, horses and chariots of fire, round about Elisha." The chariots and horses are not here, as in the account of the ascent of Elijah a few chapters before, vehicles for a glorious passage to the skies, but simply symbols of the divine power

[1] 2 Kings vi. 17.

and protection. But in both passages the highest intelligences are represented as taking shapes, like the forms in Ezekiel, which imply that their true nobility is always service. The immaterial spirits became cognisable by the servant of Elisha under forms of active power best calculated to reassure his fainting faith. Fire is the symbol of the Godhead, because fire is the most ethereal of the earthly elements. The gift of Pentecost sat as tongues of fire on the heads of the apostles. God is said by His prophet and His apostle to be a "consuming fire."[1] The seraph is, properly, the "burning spirit." The horses and chariots mean, therefore, warlike force. Still, what the servant sees is not a material — it is a spiritual reality, taking a form which assures him of God's sure protection through the agencies of those "ministers of His, that do His pleasure,"[2] and at a time when all was dark to the eye of faith.

Now here we see, as if through a microscope, the act or process of faith in the human soul. What is faith? It is, says the apostle, "the substance of things hoped for, the evidence of things not seen."[3] That is to say, it is the faculty which reaches to that which is beyond the senses, yet which apprehends it as certain,—as being at least as certain as the things which we see. Now, let us pause to consider a little at length what faith is, by considering what it is not.

Faith, then, first of all, is not an act of the natural imagination. It is necessary to say this, because a great many persons constantly allude to faith in terms which imply that it is. They speak of "a person of great faith," meaning that he is a very imaginative person,—that he has quite an unusual share of that privileged, of that versatile, faculty which does, indeed, achieve so much in society, so much for literature,—which is the very well-spring

---

[1] Heb. xii. 29.   [2] Ps. ciii. 21.   [3] Heb. xi. 1.

of poetry,—which is the soul, the genius, of constructive art, but which is less welcome in the sphere of religious truth because its highest efforts result in surrounding us with the unreal, while investing it with the attributes of reality. No; faith is not another word for a vivid imagination. Imagination deals with that which is not, faith with that which is; imagination with fiction, faith with facts. The objects of faith and the objects of imagination may have this, if you will, in common, that they are both beyond the reach of the natural sight; but then there is this difference, that the objects of faith, being, as they are, real, may become visible to a higher sense than the bodily eye, while the objects of imagination can never be thus visible to the soul. Being fictions, however beautiful, they occur to the soul always as fictions,—as fictions, it may be, of its own creation, not as realities. When men speak of faith as a vivid and energetic form of imagination, they mean to deny this without stating in terms that they do so. They mean to imply that just as the poet Virgil projected a picture of the nether world out of the immense wealth of his fancy, so evangelists and apostles have traced their own beautiful pictures of Heaven and their awful descriptions of Hell and of Judgment on the pages of our Testaments by the aid of an extraordinary variety of the religious imagination. Evangelists and apostles, whatever else they were (I say it with reverence) were not poets. They were eminently prosaic; and the remark of Rousseau, that the inventor of the Gospel history must have been not less wonderful than its Hero if he were entirely unassisted from above, is at least a satisfactory reply to this theory of faith doing the work of pure imagination. Why, the apostles say with St. Peter, "we have not followed cunningly devised fables."[1] The

[1] 2 Pet. i. 16.

apostles exclaim, with St. John, "That which we have seen and heard declare we unto you."[1] And among ordinary Christians is it not a matter of daily experience that the most earnest, the most practical, believers are constantly persons who are exceptionally wanting in the faculty of imagination, and who look at all the concerns of life in a matter of fact way which forbids the idea of their ever under any circumstances giving the reins to fancy? In the case before us, Elisha's servant did not create by an act of imagination a splendid picture in the air, after the manner of a Milton or a Reubens—a picture of fiery beings circling round the form of his beloved, of his imperilled, master. The thing was psychologically impossible. He had his eye upon the hard and menacing fact before him,—upon the lines of the Syrian troops who were sent to capture the prophet, his master. He could for the time see nothing beyond the sphere of sense. He was terrified at what he saw; and then Elisha prayed that he might see farther, higher, into another sphere; and then he saw the world of spirits. But the world of spirits was a thing utterly independent of his imagination. It would have been none the less there if he had never seen it, just as the Syrian troops would have been none the less there if Elisha's servant had been born blind and he had never seen them. His new power of seeing the horses and chariots of fire sweeping round Elisha did not create these spiritual forms and beings. There they were, whether he and other men saw them or not, just as—to recur to an illustration which I have already employed—just as the more remote planets were certainly revolving in their orbits during the centuries when our science had not yet reached them by her reckonings and her telescopes. Elisha had been just as much encompassed by the spirit-world the

[1] 1 John i. 3.

moment before his servant saw that this was the case as he was the moment after. The man's new sight could not create, as his blindness could not have destroyed, the supernatural reality.

"Yes," I hear it whispered, "yes, but there is a common sense, based on our ordinary experience, which resists these notions of an invisible world actually around and about us." But what, my brethren, is the real worth of this so-called "common sense?" When the comet of October, 1858, appeared, a lecturer made a tour of some country villages in Devonshire with a view to telling the country people some facts about the beautiful object which night by night attracted so much of their attention; and among other points he touched upon the calculations which astronomers had made as to the enormous length of the tail of the comet. I recollect hearing a countryman who treated this part of his lecture with contemptuous incredulity. "I saw the comet myself," said the man to a sympathising crowd of villagers, "I saw the comet myself, and its tail was *just four feet long;* and how are we to believe this man, who comes down here to tell us that it is ever so many millions of miles?" Now that was the "common sense" of ordinary sight pitted against the common sense of that higher insight into nature which is won by scientific investigation. But science, too, as she is sometimes misrepresented—never when she is true to herself—science can sometimes be guilty of an appeal to common sense of this sort, against the assertions of a still higher insight into the supersensuous realities than is her own—against the assertions of faith. The astronomer with Lord Rosse's telescope at his disposal sees—he does not imagine—the heavenly bodies which are utterly out of the reach of your ordinary sight or mine; and the servant of Elisha, when the eyes of his spirit are open, sees, by the aid of a new spiritual faculty, what he would not, what he could not, have imagined,—sees the world of spirits floating in all its power and its beauty round his endangered master.

Nor is faith only the conclusion, the final act, of a process of natural reasoning. If this were the case—if faith were merely the conclusion of a syllogism—it would follow that all people with good understandings must necessarily be believers in Christianity. We know, my brethren, that this is not the case. We know, alas, that many persons of good natural abilities, such as was Voltaire, are and have been unbelievers; and this alone would seem to show that something besides intelligence is implied in an act of faith. No man whose mind was not impaired could go through a proposition of Euclid and refuse to assent to the conclusion; but many people do read Paley's Evidences, or, what is more to the purpose, what St. Paul himself says about the Resurrection, and yet do not admit Paley's and St. Paul's conclusion that Christianity comes from God. If believing in Christianity were simply an affair of the natural understanding, this could not be. It would be just as inevitable to believe St. Paul as it is, intellectually, to believe Euclid. Why is this so? Why is the acceptance of religious truth not just as imperative upon the human understanding as the acceptance of mathematical truth? Because the act of faith is not merely the act of the intelligence,—because it is an act of the whole inward nature, an act of the affections and the will as well as an act of the understanding. "With the heart," says St. Paul, "man believeth unto righteousness."[1] The affections and the will have a great deal to say in every pure act of faith. The understanding cannot compel faith. The evidence at the disposal of the understanding is always less than absolutely mathematical.

[1] Rom. x. 10.

It does not convince unless the moral nature is in such a condition that it is possible for it to be convincing. The evidence of religion at our disposal is, further, designedly less than strictly irresistible, in order that there may be room for the play of our moral nature; so that the act of faith may be a test not of the goodness of our natural understandings, not of the advantages which we have had in education, but of the state of our moral dispositions. If faith were merely an assent of the understanding to a conclusion warranted by sufficient evidence, it is plain that St. Paul could never speak of it as he does when writing to the Romans and the Galatians. He tells them that it is that which justifies before God. Why, goodness of understanding could be no more a reason for our acceptance than strength of the limbs or retentiveness of the memory. Faith is thus spoken of in the New Testament because it is a test of the moral nature,—because a man believes upon adequate although not absolutely compulsory evidence, in obedience to the promptings of his heart and will. A man who has made the most of the natural light which God has given him will look out for, will desire, the light of Revelation. He will believe that the Author of that law of right and wrong within himself, with which during all his life he has been more or less familiar, is likely to unfold to him something more about Himself. But then what is it that, at the decisive moment, makes the moral nature capable of this supreme act? What is it which makes the desire of the heart on the one side, and the evidence at the disposal of the understanding on the other side, result in the complex, in the perfect act of faith? What is it which strikes the sacred sparks,—which thus combines the action of the understanding and the yearnings of the heart into the single act which supersedes while it combines them? "The Lord opened the eyes of the young man; and he saw: and, behold, the mountain was full of horses and chariots of fire round about Elisha."[1]

Faith is, in the last resort, the fire which is lighted up in the soul by a ray from Heaven—by a ray of Grace. It is a gift from God; it is a fresh gift, which nature can neither rival nor anticipate. Elisha might have insisted upon many considerations which ought, in reason, to have satisfied his servant that God and His holy ones were now, as of old, near at hand,—that the near presence of the Syrians did not amount to a real reason for despair. Had not God helped the patriarch Jacob? Had He not delivered Israel in the wilderness, and David from the wild beasts and from the hand of Saul, and Elijah quite recently from all the power of Ahab and of Jezebel? Was it to be supposed that He would desert His prophet now, or that, happen what might, He was unconcerned and powerless? Elisha did not argue. There are times when argument is most precious; there are times when it is worse than useless. Elisha prayed; he prayed that the Lord would open the eyes of the young man to see things, not as they appear to sense, but as they are—to see not merely the world of sense but the world of spirit. And his prayer was granted. Now this exactly agrees with what we are taught about faith in the New Testament. Faith is there represented as a new spiritual sense,—as an endowment or gift bestowed upon the soul by the Holy Ghost. It is contrasted with natural sight. "We walk by faith, not by sight,"[2] says St. Paul. It is contrasted with natural reason. "The natural man," says St. Paul, "perceiveth not the things of the Spirit of God: neither can he know them, because they are spiritually discerned."[3] It is a higher reason than the reason which nature gives.

[1] 2 Kings vi. 17.   [2] 2 Cor. v. 7.   [3] 1 Cor. ii. 14.

It is a higher and more perfect sight which God gives, over and above the sight of nature, which nature cannot, if she would, achieve. "Faith," says St. Paul again, "Is not of yourselves: it is the gift of God."[1] And thus it happened that when the Lord had opened the heart of Lydia, she believed the things that were spoken by Paul; and thus St. Paul prays that the Ephesians "May know what is the hope of their calling, and what the riches of the glory of their inheritance in the saints."[2] He does not for a moment expect them to know this by nature, but only when the eyes of their understanding are enlightened; that is, as a consequence of the gift of faith.

Do not misunderstand me. Do I say that natural reason has no office whatever to discharge in the work of establishing our religious convictions? Very far from it. If this were so, not merely the evidential theology of the Church, but much of the language of the Bible itself, which unmistakably appeals to reason, would be a vast mistake. Reason can do very much for faith. Reason stands to faith just as did the Baptist to Christ our Lord. She is the messenger which goes before the face of faith to make ready its path within the soul. Reason can explain; she can infer; she can combine; she can reduce difficulties to their true proportions; she can make the most of considerations which show what, upon the whole, is to be expected. But here she must stop. She cannot do the work of God's grace; she cannot change, she cannot transform the moral nature, so as to enable it to correspond to the conclusions of the illuminated intellect; she cannot open the eyes of the young man and make him see. If this triumph is to be achieved, it must be by Grace given in answer to prayer.

Let us see in this history, brethren, a remedy against

[1] Eph. ii. 8.     [2] Eph. i. 18.

despondency such as good Christians often feel on contemplating the state of the world at particular periods. All seems to be going against the cause of right, of truth, of God. "The enemy crieth so, and the ungodly cometh on so fast; for they are minded to do me some mischief, so maliciously are they set against me."[1] The Psalmist's cry is echoed by the Church kneeling at the foot of the throne of Christ; it is echoed throughout the centuries. Intellectual assailants, political adversaries, all the passions, all the prejudices, all the misapprehensions of an unregenerated humanity, come down and besiege the prophet in Dothan. All might well seem to be lost again and again, if it were not that again and again the eyes of the spirit are opened to perceive that they which are with us are more than they which are with them. Courage! The unseen is greater than the seen; the eternal will surely outlive the things of time. An act of faith may cross the threshold of the door which separates us from that world which is beyond the senses, and may at once correct the apparent preponderance of evil by a vision of the throne, of the resources, of the All-good.

And see, too, in this history our true patent of nobility. It has been a common saying, quoted again and again of late to justify changes on the Continent that have taken place within the last ten years, that it is better to be the citizen of a great state than the citizen of a small one. Brethren, it is better for many reasons,—for this among the rest: there is an inspiration for good which comes from the sense of wide and noble fellowship—of high and distinguished associates and guardians—which is denied to those who are members of a small society and have it not. And in His kingdom God has provided us with this. All the races of the world furnish their contributions to the

[1] Ps. lv. 3; P. B. Version.

universal Church, but the frontier of sense is not the frontier of the Church of Christ. It embraces both worlds—the unseen world as well as the visible. "Ye are come," says the Apostle, writing to Christian converts,—"Ye are come by your conversion unto Mount Zion, unto the city of the living God, the heavenly Jerusalem, and to an innumerable company of angels, to the general assembly and the Church of the firstborn, whose names are written in Heaven, and to God the Judge of all, and to the spirits of the just made perfect."[1] The Church thus is, according to the Apostle, a mixed as well as a world-embracing society, consisting here of the faithful, there of the blessed angels and of the spirits of the dead, united in the bonds of one indissoluble communion and all ranged beneath the throne of thrones—the throne of God, the throne of Jesus. Does this lofty conviction, think you, inspire nothing like hatred of sin—no longing for a higher life—no wish to live as should the companions and beings who constitute the household of God, and who are our predestined fellow citizens? The Syrian host may press us hard—the host of temptations, of bad thoughts, of bad acquaintances, of haunting memories; but when at the voice of prayer—the prayer of the Church or our own—our eyes open upon the realities around and above us, we must remember that we have a destiny before us, and means at hand to prepare for it. "To have no sense of the invisible," said a great writer, "is the ruin of art." To have no sense of the invisible, it may be most certainly added, is the ruin of virtue.

Lastly, we see here the secret of real effective prayer. O my brethren, why is prayer—public prayer especially—in so many cases nothing better than the coldest of cold and heartless forms? For two reasons, especially. Men

[1] Heb. xii. 22, 23.

enter on it without having any true knowledge of themselves whatever,—of their sins and wants as well as of their hopes and fears,—of their real state before God as well as of their reputed character in the eyes of men. In a word, they have no true knowledge of that for which prayer wins something like a remedy; and thus they have no personal interest of their own, which they can import into and identify with the public language of the Church. They do not, for instance, know enough about themselves to say, with anything like sincerity before God, that they have erred and strayed from His ways like lost sheep, or that there are certain things which for their unworthiness they dare not, and for their blindness they cannot ask.

This is a first reason. But there is a second. Prayer is so cold and heartless a thing, in numbers of instances, because men see nothing of Him to Whom prayer is addressed—nothing of God, nothing of Jesus; nothing of the spirit-world around the throne, nothing of the majesty, the beauty, the glory, which encircle God, such as is possible, really possible, to our finite and purblind gaze; nothing of the everlasting worship which surrounds Him, nothing of the "ministers of His that do His pleasure." Until this is the case, at least in some degree, what a torrent of unmeaning verbiage is—must be—the public language of the Christian Church! Take that glorious hymn in which the Morning Service culminates, the *Te Deum*. If the soul sees nothing beyond the veil, what must be meant when the lips repeat such phrases as that—" To Thee all angels cry aloud: the Heavens and all the Powers therein. To Thee Cherubim and Seraphim continually do cry, Holy, Holy, Holy"? or when, after the first ascent towards the throne of the Thrice Holy, there follows a second,—" The glorious company of the Apostles praise Thee. The goodly fellowship of the Prophets praise Thee: the noble army of

Martyrs praise Thee; the Father of an infinite Majesty; Thine honourable, true, and only Son; also the Holy Ghost, the Comforter"? or when all is finally concentrated on Jesus as the King of Glory, as the Father's everlasting Son, with Whom we may indeed, if we will, plead for help because, when He took upon Him to deliver man, such was His love, His condescension, that He did not abhor the Virgin's womb,—because, when He had "overcome the sharpness of death," He remembered us, even us, and "opened the Kingdom of Heaven to all believers." How unutterably piteous for us, my brethren, if, when such words as these are sung, we are only relieving the weariness of mental contact with vacancy by dwelling on the triumphs of a great composer, on the skill of a trained choir, on the associations of a splendid historical building, or, it is possible enough, by thinking of something worse than this—a something that should have been dropped out of thought long before we crossed the threshold of the sanctuary! There are, believe it, few better prayers on entering a church than Elisha's—" Lord open mine eyes that I may see! I do not wish to mock Thee by a lip service: I do not wish to pile up my ordinary business thoughts, or any thoughts of pleasure, on the very steps of Thy throne. Open mine eyes, then, that I may see Thee in Thy beauty, and in Thy glorious presence may lose all relish for that which belongs only to the things of time." It is when the soul struggles thus, in an honest spiritual agony, that it is really emancipated from the tyranny of sense, and, like the young man in the history of to-day, or, rather, like the dying martyr of the Gospel times, sees the heavens opened —sees Jesus standing at the right hand of God.

To Him, with the Father and the Holy Ghost, be ascribed all honour, power, might, majesty, and dominion, henceforth and for ever!

# SERMON XVII.

## JUSTIFICATION BY FAITH.

### Gal. iii. 24.

*"Wherefore the law was our schoolmaster to bring us unto Christ, that we might be justified by faith."*

LAST Sunday we were considering the place and use of the law of Moses in the religious education of the people of Israel. The law, it appeared, was a tutor entrusted with the responsible duty of bringing Israel down to the school of Jesus Christ; and this duty was discharged, partly by the voice of prophecy, partly by the symbolic teaching of the sacred ceremonies, and, partly, or rather chiefly, by the sense of guilt and the sense of weakness in the conscience of the people of Israel—by the moral precepts given by God to Israel, but which Israel could not keep. This threefold guidance of the law was not, by any means, irresistible. It was actually declined by a majority of those for whom it was intended, but it was sufficient for all sincere souls looking out for traces of God's will, and anxious to make the most of anything they could find.

And so in the treatment of our subject last Sunday afternoon the law had brought its pupil to the door of the school of Christ; and to-day we have to consider what Christ, our Lord, will do for him that the law could not do; in other words, what is meant by the justification by faith which the apostle says was the final purpose of this long providential guidance. "The law was a tutor to bring us unto Christ, that we might be justified by faith."

"That we might be justified by faith." Truly, these are words across which the fierce passions of controversy have swept for centuries; and controversies are apt to leave deposits which obscure, even in sincere and simple minds, the sense of the sacred writer when he wrote the words. What does the apostle mean by "justified?" He means made just or righteous. And what is righteousness or justice? As applied to man, it means a man's being as he should be; it means the conformity—the inner and true conformity—of his life with the standard of that which is good—absolutely good and true. One of the questions which prominently engaged the attention of the Jewish doctors was this: How it was possible for men to attain to righteousness or justice? And their answer always was, "By keeping the law." For them the law was the rule of righteousness. The Jew who kept the law was righteous. But then, the question which St. Paul pressed on them, again and again, was whether any Jew did really keep it; or rather, as we said last Sunday, he quoted the law itself with very great effect to show that, so far from being kept, it was as a rule neglected. "There is," said the law, "none righteous, no not one;" and, "therefore," concludes the Apostle—"therefore, by the deeds of the law shall no flesh be justified in God's sight, for by the law is the knowledge of sin."[1]

And thus the question arises whether any other method of justification—that is, of becoming what we should be—is attainable. And St. Paul answers that question in the text. The law, he said, led its best pupils down to the school of Christ, that they might be justified—not by their

[1] Rom. iii. 12, 20.

own efforts to obey its precepts, but by a very different process, which would in the end, indeed, secure obedience and a great deal else—that they might be justified by faith.

And here a difficulty presents itself, which has very naturally and very seriously exercised thoughtful minds in successive ages, and not least in our own. How is it possible, men ask, that such a mere motion or emotion of the soul, as faith, can achieve this startling and solid result—the making a soul to be as it should be before a holy God? A change of conduct—yes, that, they conceive, may make the necessary difference. Conduct is something tangible, something producible. Conduct is a thing which can be weighed and measured. But faith—how airy, how unsubstantial, how disconnected from any solid, permanent results on character. How nearly allied to the fanciful, to the imaginative. How can faith justify? How can so serious an effect be traced to so inadequate or ineffective a cause? Now the answer to this enquiry can only be given by stating what faith really is. And perhaps we shall best state what faith really is while we proceed to answer the question, how it is that faith justifies or makes men as they should be before God, the All-seeing, the All-holy.

Now here we may observe at the outset that, looking at the surface of the matter, faith does, for the believing man, at least one great and striking service, which of itself goes some way to making him what he should be. Faith raises the aims, the purposes, the thoughts of man from the seen to the unseen—from the material to the immaterial—from earth to, or towards, Heaven. What is man's condition without faith—without that world of glorious but unseen realities which faith makes present? It is the condition of a slave. Unbelieving man is always a slave—the slave of nature, the slave of matter. When no higher world than the world of sense is open to man's view, he falls back under the cruel and exacting bondage of sense and nature. His horizon is that of his bodily senses—neither more nor less. His thoughts and feelings are bounded by that which he can see—can taste—can handle or claw—can smell. To him the visible world is the universe. To him, he himself and his brother man is but an animal—a magnificent animal, no doubt, yet nothing but an animal. He notes with eager and jealous accuracy how the processes of birth and growth, and disease, and death, and decomposition, are the same in his own case and that of the brutes around him. With him, feeling is only nervous sensibility; thought is only phosphorus; the soul, a non-existent abstraction which man in his petty vanity has coaxed out of the higher illusions of his senses. And thus he buries his thought deep in the very folds of matter. And his thought, mark you, may be all the while exceptionally keen and strong, yet not therefore the less enslaved to matter. Perhaps he has a turn for abstract speculations, and nevertheless in the absence of faith he is still occupied—nearly or wholly occupied—by that which comes in contact with the senses. His shop, or his broad acres, or his family circle, or his enjoyments, are for him the universe; he sees no horizons beyond. And since nothing is more certain than the law whereby we men—each one of us—become likened to that on which we gaze—heavenly, if we are looking upward—earthly, or worse, if we are looking downward—it follows that the man who lives in and for matter will gather more and more of its thick grossness around his spirit.

And if his understanding warns him that the material world, which is his all, will pass, and if, in his higher moments, voices sound from out of the depths of his being to protest impatiently that matter does not satisfy; still the motto of those who are taking their fill of sense, whether in its grosser or more refined forms, is, in the last resort, always this, "Let us eat and drink; for to-morrow we die." [1] The nobler minds of every generation have felt the misery of this. They have felt that man was meant for a higher destiny than this enslavement to nature, to matter, to sense; and, in the absence of any better expedients, they have endeavoured to provide an escape by the exercise of the intelligence, and the exercise of the imagination—in other words, by poetry and by philosophy.

Poetry is, at least very frequently, the endeavour to invest human life with the glow and beauty of a higher sphere. Poetry is the protest of the human soul against enslavement to the prosaic uniformity of materialised existence. Poetry is the effort of the imagination to provide an outlook for all in man that will not, that cannot, consent to believe that man is nothing but a highly organised animal. And philosophy is the endeavour to ascend without the emotion which is characteristic of poetry—to ascend from that which meets the senses to that which is beyond the senses—to mount always from the observed effect to the hidden and producing cause—to construct, if it may be, an account and a theory of universal being, and, in the process of doing so, to provide for the thought of man an asylum, or rather a throne, beyond and above the frontiers of matter. And thus, in their different ways, philosophy and poetry imply the degradation of merely materialised life by their efforts to better it. And I am very far from denying that they have, each of them, made noble contributions to the higher side of human existence. Sometimes, indeed, in the great Christian ages, they have been the willing handmaids of faith herself; but, even in the centuries when this was impossible, they have done something to raise the human spirit out of the narrow

[1] 1 Cor. xv. 32.

prison-house of matter. And Homer, and Æschylus, and Socrates, and Plato, with whatever reserves, will be names held in high honour to the end of time. But, whatever poetry and philosophy might achieve for a few individuals, or in the hands of great masters, they do not, in the long run, free the minds of men from the tyranny of matter. Indeed, their fitful efforts to achieve this may remind us of the flying machine which it was attempted to construct some thirty years ago on the banks of the Thames. Imagination—such is the verdict of experience—imagination, if unsustained by a heaven-born companion like faith, does but mount upwards in one generation to surrender itself in the next, almost at discretion, to the grossest suggestions of the senses. And philosophy, if not based on certainties beyond the reach of sense, does but construct its imposing abstractions in one age to shatter them into fragments in the next; and then it ends, as with the Epicurians of antiquity—as with the school which has last appeared on the scene, in Germany—it ends by plunging headlong into matter with a new and impetuous enthusiasm, and prostituting its powers to reconstructing the very fetters from which, centuries ago, in its fresh and early youth, it promised us emancipation.

No, brethren, if man is to be freed from the empire of sense and nature, it must be through his endowment with a new faculty, such as is faith; and faith is a new kind of sight which opens upon the soul a world wholly beyond the reach of the bodily senses. Faith is practically a new sense—a sense whose business it is to discern God, and all that teaches His nature and His action upon the world and upon mankind. Faith makes the man who possesses it to differ from the man who has it not, much as a person in the enjoyment of good bodily sight differs from a blind man. Faith, as the apostle puts it, is the substance of things hoped for; it is the evidence of things not seen.¹ It is evidence to itself, sufficient evidence, of the reality of its object; and thus faith cannot but at least elevate man, with the unseen world spread out before him—the magnificence, the infinitude of the Divine Being—the glory of our Lord Jesus Christ upon His throne, both God and Man—the unnumbered angelic intelligences around the throne—the little suspected, but constant, incessant, communications passing between earth and heaven. Faith introduces the soul of man to a new sphere in which the soul is insensibly bettered, if only by this, by having its attention distracted from the petty material interests of daily human life, and fixed on the splendours of the unseen, of the eternal; and thus faith does raise the soul of man heavenwards, and this elevation of the soul, more solid and permanent than anything which can possibly be provided by poetry or philosophy, in that it brings the soul face to face with the true and the unchanging Being, is of itself a considerable step in the direction of making a man what he should be—in other words, of his justification.

And a second service which faith renders to man, is this: it expands and strengthens all the departments of his spirit's life—his will and his affections not less than his understanding. And this wide and comprehensive scope of its action upon the soul of itself does much to make man to be what he should be, since not one power or faculty is invigorated by it, but all. There we come face to face with a great and common misconception; the mistake, I mean, of supposing that faith is only a bare act of apprehension—only a simple movement of the understanding apprehending truth beyond the province of sense. My brethren, such an act of apprehension as this can only be faith by courtesy; for faith in its origin, as well as in

¹ Heb. xi. 1.

its growth and vitality, is a prompting of the heart and the will, at least as much as of the understanding. "With the heart, man believeth unto righteousness,"[1] and this moral element in faith is the guarantee of its power to change the character. If we doubt this, let us try to explain to ourselves how it is that of two heathens similarly circumstanced, to whom the Gospel is preached by a Christian missionary, one accepts, and the other rejects it; or how it is, as we may see in many an English home, that, of two brothers who have had equally the same education, one is a devout Christian and the other an unbeliever. The explanation which is often given refers this difference to God's secret and eternal predestination of souls. The old words, "He hath mercy on whom He will have mercy, and whom He will He hardeneth,"[2] seem to yield a stern but an adequate solution. But God's predestination of souls, however true and solemn a fact, is only half of the truth which explains the soul's destiny. It is equally true —though we may be unable to reconcile this truth with the foregoing—it is equally true that every soul determines its own destiny, and that God's predestination is never really arbitrary in the sense of being independent of the soul's secret, self-determined history. When, of the two heathens I am considering, one man accepts the faith as it is proposed to him, and the other rejects it, this, we may be sure, so far as the man is concerned, is not an accident: it is an effect of causes which have been already long in duration. If these two men have known from infancy nothing else, they have known this,—that there is a distinction between right and wrong, since this knowledge is part of the human soul. What is right and what is wrong—that, they may have apprehended very imperfectly. They cannot have been ignorant that this primal distinc-

[1] Rom. x. 10.     [2] Rom. ix. 15; Exod. xxxiii. 19.

tion exists. And this distinction of itself, observe, this distinction implies a law—a law of right as distinct from wrong; and a law implies a lawgiver. Who is he? What is he? What can be known about him? Will he ever reveal himself? These are questions which will be repeated again and again in the one mind, eager, by searching, to find out God—ready to make the most of anything which He may disclose about Himself; but they will be repressed and silenced in the other mind, as if they were the mere echoes of some stupid superstition. The distinction between right and wrong itself, it has been said by one who felt thus in the midst of Christian civilization, can only be upheld by a man with a bad digestion. Well, then, on this original difference in the way of treating the sense—the implanted—sense of right and wrong, will subsequently depend the different kinds of welcome given to the missionary—nay, the grave difference between faith and unbelief. The one man wishes to know nothing of the Author of the moral law that haunts him. The other wishes to know as much as he can. And thus, to the one man, the evidence that God has revealed Himself, will appear wholly insufficient. To the other, it will seem to be nothing less than overwhelming.

And thus we see how faith is originally prompted by the moral affections, and the will—how, in point of fact, it grows directly out of these. Men believe, because they wish to believe, if they can, and think that the evidence they have warrants them in doing so. They reject belief, as a rule, because there is a secret warp in their will against the truths which are the objects of faith. "Light," said our Lord—"Light is come into the world, but men love darkness rather than light, because their deeds are evil."[1] And as faith is cradled in the heart and the will, so it is

[1] John iii. 19.

never independent of them. It is an act of the moral nature, as well of the understanding, from first to last. No doubt the word, "faith" is used, by an accommodation, of mere unfruitful knowledge of divine things, as when St. James says, that the devils believe and tremble. The devils think of God just as a scientific man might think of a natural catastrophe, which he was certain would occur— say the outbreak of a volcano, or a hurricane. They think of God with intelligence, with curiosity, but also with aversion. Having, as they have, at command the opportunities of disembodied spirits, whether good or evil, they cannot close their eyes to God's existence—to His power; but they recognise Him only to fear and to hate Him. They believe, and yet tremble. This is an extreme example of the apprehension of God divorced from love. But something like it may be observed in all who hold the truth in unrighteousness. The faith of which St. Paul says so much in his epistles is inseparable from love—inseparable in life and fact, though quite separable in idea, in our way of looking at it. As the illuminated understanding gazes on the majesty and on the attributes of God—on the Person and the redeeming work of Christ —the heart is withal kindled, and the will is braced. Faith which deserves the name worketh ever, and it worketh by love. Faith may be taken to pieces by students and divines; its elements may be sorted out; its mental element may be studied apart from the ingredients of love and of resolution which go to make it up, just as the anatomist in our hospitals may treat the arterial system apart from the nervous system of the human body, although, in the living subject, each is essential to its vitality. We may, if we like, fix our eyes only on the concave, but it always implies the convex. Those who have gone farthest in the direction of saying that faith, considered as pure mental apprehension of the person and merits of Christ, can justify before God, have not, so far as I know, ventured to say that any one human being is justified who is quite without a ray of the love of God in his soul. No. Read through the 11th chapter of the Epistle to the Hebrews, to see what faith is in itself—how practical, how productive a thing it is—how much it leads those who really possess it, upon occasions, to do and to suffer; and then you will understand how it enriches the whole inward life—how powerfully it contributes to make man what he should be—in other words to his justification.

But, thirdly and finally, the greatest service which faith renders is this,—it receives at God's hand the perfect righteousness of Christ. Faith is itself a hand which the soul extends towards the heavens, or with which it grasps the Redeemer's cross. My brethren, that which really makes us men what we should be is not—cannot be—in or of ourselves. It comes to us from without—from the one perfect and sinless Being. And faith is the receptive faculty, or the receptive act, whereby the soul makes this prerogative gift of justification altogether its own. St. Paul is never tired of saying that man cannot be as he should be—that he cannot be just or righteous—without Jesus Christ. The Jew cannot, because, although he had a revealed law, he did not keep it. The heathen cannot. He, too, has a natural law written on his heart, but he falls short of it. The heathen does not seem, as far as the apostle's experience goes, to have supposed that he was absolutely righteous. The Jew did go about to establish his own righteousness, not submitting himself to the righteousness of God. But the hard fact is that "all have sinned, and come short of the glory of God;"[1] and, therefore it is that justification, properly speaking, can only

[1] Rom. iii. 23.

come to us from without. Faith itself would not justify. Faith would lack its elevating, its productive power, if it had not before it an Object utterly independent of human sin and of human weakness—an Object divine, unchanging, immaculate. We cannot raise ourselves from the dust. A moral law of gravitation keeps the fallen race down. We must be lifted, if at all, by a hand reached out to us from above. If justified at all, we must be "justified freely by God's grace, through the redemption that is in Christ Jesus."[1]

Yes, Christ Jesus, Who alone of those who have worn the human form is as He should be—Whose life, public and secret, conforms perfectly to the absolute rule of right—Christ Jesus, the beloved Son, in whom the all-perfect Father is well pleased—is the source of justification to all His brethren. He has done away with their imperfections by bearing their sins in His Body on the tree. He has given them a share in His obedience, His transcending and prevailing merits. He is their peace. He is made to them wisdom, and righteousness, and justification, and redemption. It is not that His righteousness is accredited to them by a kind of fiction, without being conveyed. It is accredited or imputed because it is already in His purposes of mercy conveyed—because, in His generous love, He consents to share it with the poorest and the weakest of His brethren. On His part, this great gift, purchased in its completeness on His cross, is conveyed by His Spirit and by His Sacraments. His Spirit is called the Spirit of Christ, because it is His work to make us partakers in the perfect Manhood of the divine Redeemer. His Sacraments could have no place at all in a religion like His, unless it were a place of the very first importance. Mere graceless forms would be intruders in a dispensation where forms

[1] Rom. iii. 24.

and shadows have given place once for all to the everlasting realities. It is through these channels that He dispenses what He has won—nay, rather, what He is. "As many as have been baptised into Christ have put on Christ."[1] "The bread that I give is My Flesh, which I will give for the life of the world."[2]

But, on our part, how are these treasures to be claimed? How is the human soul to grasp this righteousness of God in Christ? The answer is, "By faith."

Faith is the hand which the soul holds out in order to receive the gifts of heaven. In the case of every adult it is indispensable. God may, in His mercy take infants up in His arms and bless them. The grace of regeneration, like the gift of natural life, may be conferred on those who are as yet unconscious of its greatness. But, as Augustine has said, "He Who made us without ourselves, He Who re-made us without ourselves—will not save us without ourselves,"—without our conscious and deliberate acceptance of His salvation. And this acceptance of God's final gift is effected by faith. Faith is the spiritual act whereby the soul associates itself with the perfect moral Being, Jesus Christ—whereby it makes His righteousness, His obedience, His sufferings, its own—whereby it lays strong hold upon His cross, as on the very source and warrant of its victory—whereby it draws from His Sacraments the virtue which He in His redemptive love has lodged in them—whereby the sinner, penitent and self-renouncing, is forthwith clad in His garments of salvation, and covered with His robe of righteousness, and bidden to sit down in the heavenly places in the eternal Father's home. Yes, faith is the action of the awakened soul, consciously face to face with its Redeemer and its God. In a being capable of it, it is indispensable. Without faith

[1] Gal. iii. 27.     [2] John vi. 51.

there may be vigorous physical and mental life, but the spirit is dead. It must raise us from the dust of earth. It—the product of affection and of will—must rouse will and affection to renewed activity. Above all, it—faith—the spirit of prayer—must be a suppliant, an importunate suppliant, kneeling on the steps of the throne of Heaven to receive for man—we may dare to say, to claim for man—the perfections which man cannot himself command, and which alone can make himself to be what he should be—the priceless gift of his justification through Christ. "Verily, verily, I say unto you, he that believeth on Me hath everlasting life." [1]

Let us rouse ourselves before we leave this church to beg God to give us in new measure this great and necessary Grace, without which, as His apostle has said, it is impossible to please Him. Now, as in bygone days, faith is given—faith is strengthened—in answer to prayer. "Lord, increase our faith." [2] "Lord, I believe; help Thou mine unbelief." [3] These breathings of the human soul eighteen centuries ago are not less powerful with God now, than in the days of old, nor are the issues which depend upon their being answered less momentous, whether in time or in eternity.

[1] John vi. 47.     [2] Luke xvii. 5.     [3] Mark ix. 24.

# SERMON XVIII.

## THE RELATIVE FUNCTIONS OF THE SPIRIT AND THE UNDERSTANDING IN PRAYER.

1 Cor. xiv. 15.

*"I will pray with the spirit, and I will pray with the understanding also."*

TO enter into this saying of St. Paul we must remind ourselves of those supernatural gifts which were bestowed in such abundance on the first members of the Church of Christ at Corinth. Among these, two were especially remarkable, and they gave rise to some troublesome controversies which St. Paul had to settle. These two were the gift of prophecy and the gift of tongues. The gift of prophecy was not merely or chiefly the power of predicting future events. "He that prophesieth," says the apostle, "speaketh unto men to edification, and exhortation, and comfort."[1] No doubt it included upon occasions the power of foretelling future events. It was a great deal besides. It was the general power of influencing others by means of inspired language. And the gift of tongues was not always, or usually, the power of employing a foreign language which had never been learnt by the speaker. This particular power was, indeed, exercised by the apostles, certainly on the day of Pentecost, and prob-

[1] 1 Cor. xiv. 3.

ably on many subsequent occasions; but the gift of tongues in the Church of Corinth was apparently a mystical language, intelligible only to the utterer and to God. "He," says the apostle, "that speaketh in a tongue edifieth himself. He that speaketh in a tongue speaketh not unto men, but unto God: for no man understandeth him; howbeit in the spirit he speaketh mysteries."[1]

Now, there was a great controversy in the Church of Corinth as to which of these two gifts was to be thought most highly of. Each gift had its advocates, and no doubt the advocacy was strengthened in either case by the force of personal considerations. The friends of a Christian who could utter inspired speech with great effect and power, as possessing the gift of prophecy, thought little of another Christian who could only utter what HE had to say in terms which were UNINTELLIGIBLE to the world at large; and the admirers of a holy man who could hold constant converse with God in inspired and mystic language—they, too, had their own opinion of the comparatively humble and undistinguished gift of addressing congregations in their mother-tongue with useful but not extraordinary results. St. Paul decides this controversy by pronouncing in favour of the gift of prophecy. "I would that ye all spake with tongues, but rather that ye prophesied: for greater is he that prophesieth than he that speaketh with tongues." Again: "I thank my God, I speak with tongues more than ye all: yet in the church I had rather speak five words with my understanding, that by my voice I might teach others also, than ten thousand words in a tongue." And his concluding advice is that the Corinthians should "covet to prophesy," but merely "forbid not to speak with tongues."[2]

The reasons for this decision are very instructive—

[1] Cor. xiv. 4, 2.     [2] 1 Cor. xiv. 5; 18, 19; 39.

more instructive for us than the decision itself, which has ceased to have any direct practical application in these later ages of the Church. The gift of prophecy is, in St. Paul's eyes, the higher gift, because it is more useful to members of the Church at large. "He that speaketh in a tongue edifieth himself. He that prophesieth edifieth the Church." The effect of the two gifts is contrasted most emphatically by the apostle, as follows:—"If the whole Church," he says, "be come together into one place, and all speak with tongues, and there come in those that are unlearned, or unbelievers, will they not say that ye are mad? But if all prophesy, and there come in one that believeth not, or one unlearned, he is convinced of all, he is judged of all: and thus are the secrets of his heart made manifest; and so falling down on his face he will worship God, and report that God is in you of a truth." The gift of tongues was of great interest, great value, to the soul endowed with it. As a rule, it did nothing for others, unless it was accompanied by another supplementary gift of interpretation. St. Paul himself asks, "Now, brethren, if I come unto you speaking with tongues, what shall I profit you, except I shall speak to you either by revelation, or by knowledge, or by prophesying, or by doctrine?" He points out that musical instruments and military signals are useless, unless there is a distinction in the sounds; and then he adds, "So likewise ye, except ye utter by the tongue words easy to be understood, how shall it be known what is spoken? for ye shall speak into the air. If I know not the meaning of the voice, I shall be unto him that speaketh a barbarian," or foreigner, "and he that speaketh shall be a barbarian unto me." And thus he concludes, "Let him that speaketh in an unknown tongue pray that he may interpret;" and, generally, he advises the Corinthians, forasmuch as they are desirous of spiritual gifts, to neglect the more showy and attractive endowments, and to seek that they may excel to the edifying of the Church.[1]

St. Paul's principle in deciding upon the relative worth of these two gifts, would be called, nowadays, religious utilitarianism. We shrink from a word like this in such a connection, but it accurately expresses the facts of the case. Prophecy was a useful gift to the Church at large. The gift of tongues was comparatively useless. That was the ground of the apostolic decision. And St. Paul's decision is not at all inconsistent with that other great rule of his, "Whatsoever ye do in word or deed, do all to the glory of God."[2] The glory of God in this matter is best promoted by securing the improvement and edification of man. St. Augustine has said, "God has united His own glory with our highest advantage." Accordingly, in the apostle's estimate, spiritual gifts take rank according to their capacity for bringing men near to God; and on this ground prophecy is ruled to have precedence of the gift of tongues.

Let us pause for a moment to observe that we have a principle here which should govern our judgment in a great many matters which are often under discussion. The real question is not, What is most brilliant and attractive? but, What is, spiritually speaking, most useful, most edifying? We admire this book, it may be, which everybody is talking about; but that simple manual which we have known from our childhood brings us closer to the realities of conscience and of God. We are delighted with some splendid musical service; but those simple chants and hymns in which we can join do really make divine worship more easy, more genuine for us. We are impressed by the conversation of some man of great

[1] 1 Cor. xiv. 4; 23–25; 6; 9; 11; 13; 19.   [2] 1 Cor. x. 31; Col. iii. 17.

ability and reputation ; but, somehow, a quiet prosaic person, whom we have known for years, does us more real good—makes us feel less satisfied with ourselves, more anxious to be at peace in our conscience and with our God. It is the old question between the gift of tongues and the gift of prophecy. We know how St. Paul decided the question. How do we?

Now St. Paul's language about prayer is to be explained by what he has been saying about these two gifts of tongues and of prophecy. "I will pray with the spirit: I will pray with the understanding also." In the word "spirit" he glances at the gift of tongues, in the word "understanding" at the gift of prophecy. The gift of tongues was a spiritual impulse, conferring, no doubt, great happiness, great sense of power and expansion, upon the soul which possessed it, but, seemingly, unaccompanied by very distinct ideas, or, at any rate, by any power of distinctly conveying them. Prophecy, on the other hand, was nothing if it was not active or, rather, aggressive intelligence. Prophecy was spiritual understanding in full play upon the souls of others. We know what a difference there is between feeling strongly on a subject and having that command of the subject which enables us to instruct or to convince others with respect to it. The gift of tongues was highly spiritualised feeling, taking unusual forms of expressing itself. The gift of prophecy was highly spiritualised thought, devoting itself to the instruction of others. But then this distinction was not so sharp and exclusive as to deprive the first gift of every element of intelligence, or the second of every element of emotion. In the text St. Paul implies that prayer, to be good, must combine that which is essential in both gifts—the warmth of the one with the light of the other. But then he lays a stress which we can hardly miss upon the last. "I will pray with the spirit: I will pray with the understanding also."

"I will pray with the spirit." Observe the order of these two elements of prayer. St. Paul does not say, "I will pray with the understanding, and I will pray with the spirit also." That would have been a common, modern way of putting it. "First let us have intelligence," men say, "and then spirituality, if it is to be had." St. Paul, on the other hand, does say, "I will pray with the spirit, and I will pray with the understanding also." The first ingredient in prayer is not intelligence, but movement of the soul—movement of the spirit. The raw material of prayer, so to put it, is a vague aspiration of the soul towards its true object. "Like as the hart desireth the water-brooks, so longeth my soul after Thee, O God. My soul is athirst for God, yea, even for the living God: when shall I come to appear before the presence of God?"[1] And the motive of this movement is a sense of need. It is a sense of weakness; it is a sense of dependence. It is perfectly compatible with very shadowy and imperfect perceptions of God. It is the cry of a child towards its Parent, Whom it sees only indistinctly in the twilight or through the mist. It is an impulse; it is an enthusiasm; it is an emotion; it is, as I have said, a breathing—an aspiration. The raw material of prayer is not—never was —its intellectual element. It is its element of impulse, of love, of moral movement, vigorous and resolute in its upward endeavour, yet vague and indeterminate as to its course and its object. Undoubtedly, very earnest prayer is often compatible with a very slight exercise of the understanding. "I will pray with the spirit" is a resolution which can be carried into practice, if it stands alone, more easily than "I will pray with the understanding" can be

[1] Ps. xlii. 1, 2.

carried into practice, if it stands alone. For the understanding alone does not pray; it only thinks; and thought is a very different thing indeed from prayer. Thought about God, about our Lord Jesus Christ, about ourselves, about the eternal future, is not of and by itself that inward ascensional movement towards God, which is always, at bottom, a creation of Grace, an impulse from on high, which is the first and essential thing in real prayer. The uninstructed, the young, the very ill, the almost despairing, the broken-hearted—these can say after the apostle, when they can say but little else, "I will pray with the spirit."

But then he adds, "I will pray with the understanding also." Although the understanding cannot, as we have seen, give the first impact to prayer, it can supply guidance to it. It is very needful, if the original impulse, which is the essence of prayer, is to be brought into shape—is to be made permanently serviceable to the soul. The original energy of prayer is, indeed, supplied by—it *is*—emotion. Its regulation is secured by the understanding; that is to say, by the understanding illuminated by divine Grace. Without this understanding, the spirit of prayer is like fluid metal, which runs into irregular forms for want of a mould. Without the understanding, the spirit of prayer is like great natural ability which is misused, or is wasted, only from want of proper training. Without the understanding, devotional impulse will easily pass into boisterous and even irreverent rhapsody, or it will shrink back into the lifeless monotony of mere form. The understanding takes the devotional impulse or spirit in hand,—rouses it to a jealous and vigorous consciousness,—bids it consider Who that awful and majestic Being is Who is the object of prayer, what it is that is sought of Him, why He is applied to for this particular benefit, what are the fitting steps or processes in the application. And the understanding thus secures a double result. It introduces point, purpose, order into what without it would be aimless and unregulated impulse. And it does more: it secures reverence. Without injuring the tenderness of the original relations which bind every living soul to its God and its Redeemer, the understanding is there as the perpetual reminder of God's unapproachable majesty, and of the nothingness of every created thing before Him. Nowhere, perhaps, in the Church services do we feel the action of the understanding keeping steadily in check the forward impulsive tendencies of spirit and emotion more than in the Collect which is used this very week, when we address God as a Being Who knows our necessities before we ask, and our ignorance in asking, and then beg Him to grant, for the sake of His divine Son, those things which, for our unworthiness, we dare not, and, for our blindness, we cannot ask.[1]

And here, brethren, we may see our way to one or two conclusions of importance. It can hardly be doubted that the apostle who placed the gift of prophecy higher than the gift of tongues, and who insisted that prayer must be intelligent as well as devout, would have advised the Church of Christ to offer its public prayers to God in the mother tongue of each nation within its fold. Before the Reformation, as you know, the public prayers of the Church were either altogether, or for the most part, in Latin. In the early ages of the Church, when Latin was spoken throughout the Roman Empire and was a living language, this was a very natural arrangement in these western countries; but as time went on, and the old Empire fell to pieces, the people at large ceased to speak Latin. They spoke the languages of the races which had

[1] 4th Collect at the close of the P. B. Office for H. Communion.

overthrown the Empire; and thus it came to pass that the language of the Church services was no longer the language of the people, although undoubtedly in the southern countries of Europe the difference between the two was, and is, much less than in England or in Germany, where the national language, instead of being formed out of the Latin, comes from quite a different stock. We can well understand that, when this change was made three centuries ago, many good people were most unwilling to give the old Latin up. They themselves had been accustomed to it from their earliest years in every parish church in England. It had been used in England since England was Christian. On this very spot, in the two cathedrals which preceded that in which we worship this afternoon—on this very spot, as we cannot but remember—it had already been used for some nine hundred years continuously, before the change was made; and those who loved what they were accustomed to might have pleaded with reason that Latin, if any language, is the language of devotion. Its terseness, its resources, its majesty, make Latin prayers welcome to any man who knows the language well, as was the case with the whole educated class at the time of the Reformation. But the people at large—the women, the children, the poor—what of them? They had a first right to consideration. "To the poor the gospel is preached,"[1] was to be from the first a sign of the kingdom of the redemption; and to the poor, Latin was a dead language. The sounds might be familiar: they were familiar only as sounds. They were not the vehicles of distinct thoughts—the channels of distinct ideas, of living, energetic convictions. Of course when the people came to Church they knew in a general way perfectly well what was going on. Of devotion, of

[1] Luke vii. 22.

tender apprehension of a majestic Presence which they sought and found, those forefathers of ours had, if the truth is to be spoken, often more than we of these later ages. They prayed with the spirit. But then how about the understanding? They could not enter into the words, the sentences, of the public Church language. They could only associate themselves devoutly with its general drift and purpose. They knew that something infinitely good and holy was going forward, but beyond this, there was indistinctness. They could and did pray with the spirit. It was the object of the change made at the Reformation that they should pray with the understanding also. It is not possible to doubt, my brethren, that that change was of very great value. It was a real return to the mind of the apostle. It was a reassertion for the understanding of its rights and duties in public prayer, side by side with those of devotion of the spirit. It reinforced the ardour of devotion by the activity of intelligence. The Latin language was, like the tongues at Corinth, magnificent, but too generally unintelligible; and when she translated the old Latin services which she had used for centuries into the common prayer-book of our own day, the Church of England said with the apostle, "As heretofore, let me pray with the spirit, but I and my children will endeavour hereafter to pray with the understanding also."

Here, too, we may see the value of a fixed order of prayer. A fixed order of divine service is a guarantee of the rights of the understanding as against the eccentricities of unregulated spirit, or enthusiasm, or ill-considered petitions. Undoubtedly mental prayer—prayer without words—prayer prompted from within at the moment, and seizing any words that comes to hand—has a lawful or, rather, a necessary place in the life of the individual

Christian. While private prayer must always have certain fixed elements—acts of faith, hope, charity, repentance, the Creed, the Lord's Prayer, petitions for protection, for guidance, for perseverance, intercessions for those who have a claim on us, self-surrender to the divine will—(fixed features of all good private prayer, these, no one of which can be omitted without serious loss to the soul)—it may also well have a variable element, the nature and extent of which will be determined by the need and temper of the individual. There are many things which every soul can only say to God in its own words—many things between God and the soul which will not go into words, but can be prayed somehow notwithstanding. "The Spirit helpeth our infirmities: for we know not what we should pray for as we ought: but the Spirit Himself maketh intercession for us with groanings which cannot be uttered. And He that searcheth the hearts knoweth what is the mind of the Spirit."[1] The best servants of Christ in all generations have devoted time and efforts to the cultivation of this unspoken, unwritten mental prayer; and these silent hours of intercourse between their souls and the Father of spirits have done much to make the greatest of the saints of Christ what they actually were. But the introduction of extempore prayer into common or public worship is a very different matter. Not to dwell on the fact that it is unknown to the usage of the early Church, it is, I believe, in not a few cases, quite fatal to praying with the understanding; which is not, perhaps, the risk which would be most generally attributed to it. In the first place, this kind of prayer is apt to become merely rhapsody, when feeling outruns thought very rapidly, and the necessity of saying something—something to God—is more strongly felt than the

---

[1] Rom. viii. 26, 27.

necessity of considering well what is said to Him. In the next place, in joining in an extempore prayer, uttered by another, we put ourselves to a very undesirable degree into his hands. The case is very different from that of a sermon, since in listening to a sermon we are only listeners; and if there may be statements which, rightly or wrongly, we are unable to follow, no great harm is done by our dissent. But common prayer is a united address to God, and to maintain a reserved or defiant attitude of mind, while all around us are speaking to God, is very damaging to us and to them, and very dishonouring to Him. And yet how is it always to be avoided in the case of extempore public prayer? The congregation does not know what is coming. Perhaps from minute to minute the minister himself does not know. There are many petitions about which there can be no question amongst Christians; but there are also petitions addressed to God, commonly, in prayers like these, about which there is room for a great deal of question; and a long extempore prayer is apt to cover a great deal of ground—some of it very debatable ground. It follows, naturally enough, the paths which are traced by the feelings, by the interests, by the convictions, of the person who offers it. It wanders from the region of the purely spiritual into the region of contemporary human society, or conduct, or politics. There is much to be prayed about in all of these, and thus it sometimes will, in practice, assume the shape and proportions of a long, argumentative dissertation—I had almost said of a leading article in a paper—with the unusual characteristic of being thrown into the form of petition, and being addressed to the Almighty. Such a prayer naturally contains a great many statements as to the accuracy and advisability of which we may well have failed to make up our minds. But then, before we have time to think, these statements are upon us, challenging not merely our assent, but our willingness to second them in the presence of the All-wise and the All-holy. The alternative is to cease to pray—to separate ourselves from the company of souls gathered in the house of prayer—or else pray with the spirit without the understanding, to join vaguely in a devotional movement going forward around us without stopping to think what it is precisely that we are asking, or why we ask it. From these embarrassments we are saved by the public formularies of the Church. They are in the hands of everybody. We have ample opportunities of considering their exact drift before we use them; and they are no new experiment in devotion. Most of the collects in the Prayer-book have been in use for some fourteen centuries at the least. We, as we join in them, associate ourselves with multitudes of souls who live far from us both in the present and in the past; and this tried, this familiar language, warranted by the experience of believing Christendom, may assuredly be trusted. When we hear it in Church we have not to consider for the first time whether we can agree with it. Our duty is simply to throw into it all the determination and spirit we possibly can, for it does the fullest justice to the warmth and movement of the ascending soul; but it also provides adequately for the demands of the understanding. In using it we know what we are about. We have our thoughts and our feelings, both of them, under control. We pray with the spirit: we pray with the understanding also.

And, lastly, we see here the importance of preparation for prayer, especially for those most solemn and effectual of all prayers which are associated with the Holy Communion. The precept, "Keep thy foot when thou goest to the house of God," [1] is always urgent. Certainly, the first essential is that affection and will should be roused; but, this done, the understanding, as the regulator of prayer, must be in good order, unless, indeed, we are to waste our time in the divine presence, or do something worse than waste it. As we grow older, brethren, the understanding should have more and more to do with the regulation of devotional impulse—of prayer. As the years fly by a man and the horizons of thought continually expand, the material and the scene of prayer is, or should be, always enlarging. As we pass, first one, and then another mile-stone on the road of life, we should listen for the echoes of that apostolic saying, "Brethren, be not children in understanding: but in understanding be men;"[2] for a man's religious life must keep pace with the growth of his knowledge and of his powers of reflection, or he will assuredly learn to think of his religion as a thing divorced from the practical interests of his life—as a mere reminiscence of his childhood. He will gradually drop, if he does not deliberately reject it. A man's prayers must prompt—must accompany—the most deliberate actions of his life. They must, if it may be, keep abreast—well abreast—of the entire range of his mental and moral effort. New subjects will be constantly crowding for recognition in prayer—new forms of occupation, new friendships, new materials for speculation, new difficulties, anxieties, and trials—new hopes, new fears, the varying fortunes of his family, the course of public events, the conduct of the rulers of the country, the failures or the triumphs of the Church, the departure of one after another of those whom he has known and loved to the other world, and the sense which each day that passes must deepen in his own soul, if he thinks at all, that his

[1] Eccles. v. 1.     [2] 1 Cor. xiv. 20.

own turn, too, must come ere long. All this is material for prayer—material which is constantly accumulating, and which the understanding must arrange, and sift, and digest, before bringing it into the presence of the All-holy and the Eternal. The understanding will, in practice, have more than enough to do without encroaching on the province of spirit. Its task will only worthily be achieved if that task is made a subject of forethought and deliberation in the hours which can be snatched from toil or from rest. At such a time as this there is material enough for prayer ready to the hand of every man who sincerely believes that prayer is a power. Not to mention the sufferings and the struggles of our Christian brethren in Eastern Europe, or the many subjects nearer home which have a claim upon our sympathies, let me remind you this afternoon that some millions of our fellow-subjects in India are threatened with nothing short of extermination by a famine much more terrible and devastating than any of which we have had experience since India has been ours. Already, we are told by the sanitary commissioner in Madras that a million and a half of people are under relief, and that half a million have already perished. Think for one moment what that means. There is no sufficient reason, alas, to question these dreadful facts; and it is certain that the evil is on a scale which the resources of the Indian government are quite unable to grapple with. Let us Christians pray for the sufferers, believing as we do that, distance notwithstanding, our prayers really can and will help them.

But let us do more. The Lord Mayor has opened a fund for their relief at the Mansion House, and he invites all Englishmen, but particularly the citizens of London, to contribute what they can possibly afford to an object which has every claim upon us as Englishmen and as Christians. Let us during the coming week do, each of us, what we can to further this generous effort, and let us remember that to pray sincerely with the understanding is also to attempt to do all that lies in a man's power towards furthering the object of his prayer himself.

# SERMON XIX.

## LIVING WATER.

### JOHN iv. 13–15.

*"Jesus answered and said unto her, Whosoever drinketh of this water shall thirst again: but whosoever drinketh of the water that I shall give him shall never thirst; but the water that I shall give him shall be in him a well of water springing up into everlasting life. The woman saith unto Him, Sir, give me this water, that I thirst not, neither come hither to draw."*

THERE is no scene in our Lord's whole earthly life in which it is easier to bring Him vividly before our eyes than the scene which gave occasion to these words. He was walking from Judea, along the great road through Samaria; and in the middle of the late autumn day, weary with His journey, He sat down (the original language expresses His attitude) resting on the edge, and so leaning over a well, at the mouth of the valley which led up to the ancient city of Shechem. The well is there now at this very hour, recognised beyond dispute by the most sceptical of travellers as the well of Jacob,—as the well of the conversation with her of Samaria. They tell us that it is just nine feet in diameter, just one hundred and five feet in depth, and that in the spring-time there is commonly about fifteen feet of water in it. Now this well had a history. It was a relic of the age of the patriarchs. It had been dug by Jacob partly to mark his possession of the spot, just as in southern regions of Palestine Abraham had dug, and Isaac had cleared and repaired, similar wells, partly as a sheer necessity for great cattle drivers, as were the first fathers of Israel, tending their flocks and herds under an Eastern sun. The Samaritans loved and revered this particular well, believing themselves, not very accurately, to be the children of Jacob and of Joseph. They were really converted heathens with Assyrian blood in their veins. They looked on this well as a connecting link with their presumptive ancestors. And as the disciples left their Master sitting on the well's brink, fatigued as He was, and wended their way up the narrow valley towards the distant city in which they were to buy provisions for their remaining journey, down that same valley there came a Samaritan woman, veiled and with a pitcher in her hand, to draw water, just as Rebekah, just as Rachel, just as Zipporah, had drawn it in the ages before her. She came, and the stranger asked her to give Him a little to drink; and she, marking the dialect or accent of His speech, and knowing how for more than four long centuries a fierce religious feud had separated the Jews from the Samaritans, expressed her surprise that He should claim at her hands a token of neighbourly—almost (for so the heathens deemed it) of religious—communion. Our Lord does not answer her question. He had come on earth not to argue but to teach. He answers not the enquiry which fell upon His human sense of hearing, but the deep unexpressed yearnings of the soul of the speaker, which though not a word was uttered He could read in all its hidden misery. "If thou knewest the gift of God, and Who it is saith to thee, Give me to drink, thou wouldst have asked of Him and he would have given thee the living water."[1] She knew of no living water save that

[1] John iv. 10.

which lay just ninety feet beneath them at the bottom of the ancient well. She could not understand how the Stranger, Who had nothing to draw with, could promise her the clear spring water out of that well; and if He was thinking of another well, and living water in it, purer and more refreshing than this, was He then, she thought, claiming to be greater than the patriarch of the race— "our father Jacob which gave us this well, and drank thereof himself, and his children, and his cattle."[1] Again Jesus says in answer, not directly to her spoken question but to the real questions of her inmost soul, " Whosoever drinketh of this water shall thirst again: but whosoever drinketh of the water that I shall give him shall never thirst; but the water that I shall give him shall be in him a well of water springing up into everlasting life." What the Speaker exactly meant the woman of Samaria can only have vaguely apprehended; but she felt at least that He was speaking of some water with properties far more exhilarating and precious than any of which she knew. She knew that she for many weary years had toiled down the road to that well of Jacob and back to the city, day after day, with a laggard step and with a heavy heart, and it seemed to her as if she might somehow be relieved from her thankless toil, from her aching sense of misery. "Sir," she said eagerly, "give me this water, that I thirst not, neither come hither to draw."

It will do us good, my brethren, if God gives us His blessing, to ask what was this water of which Jesus spake, and of which the poor woman desired thus earnestly to drink. We Christians, of course, look on our Lord's earlier words in the light of His later revelations; and we are not reading into them meanings which they will not bear, because we ascribe to Him, and to those whom He

[1] John iv. 12.

commissioned to speak for Him, a consistency of language which warrants us in interpreting one utterance by another,—the preceding by that which follows,—the scanty intimation by the explicit statement.

Observe, then, first of all, the nature of the gift of which Jesus speaks. Our Lord calls it "a well of water," and "living water." This expression had already an ascertained sense in the Hebrew Scriptures. It meant pure water ceaselessly rising from a spring, as opposed to still or stagnant water. Such was the water (it is the very same expression) which Isaac's servants found when they digged the old wells which the Philistines had stopped in the vale of Gerar. Such was the water (it is the same expression) over which, according to the Jewish ritual for the cleansing of the leper, one of the offered birds was to be killed in an earthen vessel. And although the exact expression does not occur, the idea of water running freshly from a spring, as a source of life and health, is prominent in such visions as those of Ezekiel,[1] who beheld an abundant stream pouring forth from beneath the temple gate of Jerusalem, and then flowing eastward,—or of Joel[2] who told how a fountain should come out of the House of the Lord, and should enter into the vale of Shittim,—or of Isaiah[3] seeing deeper still into the future, and explaining to the coming generations, "With joy shall ye draw water out of the wells of salvation." There is, indeed, much else to the same purpose in the Old Testament, and the banished Apostle, in his vision, gathers up its completed meaning when he tells us how the angel showed him "a pure river of water of life, clear as crystal, proceeding out of the throne of God and of the Lamb."[4]

Now if the question be asked, what it was that our

[1] Ezek. xlvii. 1–12.　　[2] Joel iii. 18.　　[3] Isai. xii. 3.　　[4] Rev. xxii. 1.

Lord precisely meant by the "living water," we have to consider that He, especially as His discourses are reported in the last gospel, speaks of Himself as the Life—the one Being that is, Who quickens, upholds, invigorates, movement and growth in the soul of man. As the Life, He is, He says, the Bread of humanity: as the Life He is also the Resurrection. As the Life, He claims to rescue men alike from moral and from physical death: all that are in the graves shall hear His voice. As the life, He bids all who would live indeed come to Him, cling to Him, feed on Him. Doubtless the figure of water is used in Holy Scripture as a physical likeness of the cleansing action of the Divine Spirit of God; but the Spirit of Christ is thus termed because it is His work to unite us to Christ, to graft us one by one into Christ's divine Humanity; and Christ Himself is termed by St. Paul a quickening spirit with reference to this, His capacity of becoming an inward Gift. Nor in the words "living water" does there seem to be any clear, or at least primary, reference either to Baptism, by which Christ's life is originally imparted, or to faith, by which it is received. It is the gift, and not the method of its bestowal, which is here in question; and Christ our Lord is His own Gift, as He is His own blessed Message—as He is His own Gospel. He has nothing higher to announce—He has nothing better to give us—than His adorable Self.

But as we dwell on the figure which our Lord employs, it suggests vividly to us the characteristics of His gift; for a well of living water is, in the first place always fresh. It does not stagnate like rain-water; it does not become brackish or foul. The new supplies which, minute by minute, burst upwards from the soil keep it pure and clear. So it is with Jesus Christ. History is a great store-house of buried memories, some of which are galvanised into a momentary life by our antiquarians, but which soon die away from the grasp of memory, since they belong to a past age and do not answer to our wants or correspond to our sympathies. But eighteen centuries ago One appeared Who spoke words which have the same incisive and trenchant force, the same exquisite and mysterious attraction, as if they were the novelties of yesterday. His several actions, His life as a whole speaks to this nineteenth century as it spoke to the first; provoking sharp hostility now as then, but then as now winning its sure way to empire over true hearts. He is, in short, ever fresh and young, and such as He is in history, such is He also within the sanctuary of the soul. In that vast treasure-house of the dead, the human soul, amid all that there is stagnant, amid all that belongs to the irrevocable past, amid all that bears upon it the marks of advancing change and corruption—amid the thoughts which pall, the memories which depress, the forms of feeling which once quickened within us the highest, the most subtle enjoyment, but which have long ceased to move, or which are roused into a moment of life only to create something like a positive repugnance—there is (I dare to say it) for Christians one thought which is ever fresh, one memory which is ever welcome and invigorating, one train of feeling which kindles within the soul into a burning tide of the keenest and the purest passion. It is the thought, the memory, the love of our Lord and Saviour. Just as literary men have said that, if they had to choose one book in the world which should furnish them, in the absence of all others, with high and sufficient interest and enjoyment, and that unfailingly, they would choose the Christian Bible, so within the soul the thought, the memory, of the One Perfect Being is the one warrant of a continuous refreshment, because He is far more than a thought or a memory,—because He is a living Presence—a well of water (that is His own figure). He lives within regenerate souls in His perpetual freshness. As He was guarranteed against seeing corruption in His earthly tomb, so, now that He has risen, is He much more proof against its ravages. The centuries pass; all else fades; but He renews His youth. Life waxes and wanes, but He smiles on its sunset not less refreshingly than on its spring-time. "Thou art the same, and Thy years shall not fail."[1] "With Thee is the well of life."[2]

A spring of water is also in continual motion, and herein also Christ is true to His metaphor. He is in history, He is in the soul of man, ever different, and yet the same. As the sky presents the same outline of clouds on no two days on which we carefully observe it, and yet is the same sky—as the sea, visit it as often as we will, never looks quite as it looked before, yet is the same sea—as the smallest jet of water, whose volume of weight never varies, yet presents us minute by minute with an infinite variety of forms—so is it in the world of spiritual experience with the presence of Christ. He is movement, and yet He is identity: He is to us what He was to our forefathers, and yet He is ever displaying to each successive generation new aspects of His power and His perfections—to those, at least, who hold a true communion with Him. He is at one and the same time, stability and progress, here preserving the unalterable lines of His one perfect revelation of Himself—there leading us on to new and enriched perceptions of its range and its significance. And as He is Himself movement, so He is the source of movement in the soul of man. He has set the human soul moving; He has kept it moving. He has quickened the very intelligence which would drive Him from His

[1] Ps. cii. 27: P. B. Version.    [2] Ps. xxxvi. 9: P. B. Version.

throne, for the truths which He has brought to us have moved us to the very depths of our being—moved human nature so profoundly that, whether man accepts those truths or not, man cannot rest as though he had not heard them. As it is said in the Gospel of Christ's last entry into Jerusalem, that when He had entered all the city was moved, so it is with His entrance, whether He be welcomed or not, into the soul. Faculties which had been dormant for years are stirred to meet Him, and He keeps them in motion because He is perpetually exhibiting new aspects of His power and His beauty. It is said, I know, sometimes of the Christian Creed, that it is the stagnation of active thought. Undoubtedly, in one sense, the Creed does arrest thought. It gives a fixed form to our ideas on subjects of the highest importance: it fixes them thus in the Name and with the authority of the all-wise God. We Christians certainly are not now discussing the divine attributes or the destiny of man, as if those were matters on which the light of certainty had never been thrown. But mark you, fixed thought is not the antagonist of active thought, any more than the wall or the rim of the well was hostile to the movement of the water springing up within it. Those who have had anything to do with education know how often a naturally stupid and dull person has been quickened into intelligence, at least on one set of subjects, by learning to take a practical interest in religion. The vast ideas which the Christian Creed contains, when once they are living realities to a soul, move it to its depths. God, eternity, the past with the account to be given of it, the future with its mighty hopes, with its awful fears, the love of Jesus in His Incarnation, in His Redemption—these things cannot become something more than mere words to any human being and leave the soul unmoved. And thus it is that a well of springing water fertilises. All around the green edge the verdure tells the story of its life-imparting power. And Christ is the great fertiliser of the soul of man. He has made the human mind capable of productions of genius, as we call them, which without him could not have been produced. Dante and Shakespeare are, in their different ways, distinctly His creations. He has fertilised affection. Family life, as we understand it in Europe, is Christ's work. His authority is reflected in the Christian father, His tenderness in the Christian mother, His lowly obedience in the Christian child. Above all He has fertilised will. He has made the human will capable of quite new measures of self-sacrifice—of heroism and self-sacrifice the most prosaic and the most unnoticed, as often as of heroism which meets the eye and which challenges the admiration of the world. Ah! if by any national infatuation in the years to come we should try to do without Him, we should soon discover, even in the things of this life, the magnitude of our mistake. When human thought has nothing upon which it can seriously fix itself beyond the province of sense,—when human affection is forbidden to spend itself on any form that is not earthly, palpable, material,—when the human will is invigorated by no motives that are drawn from a higher world—then this human life, depend upon it, will soon become barren and unfruitful: we shall gradually but surely exchange the civilisation of Europe for the civilisation of China or Japan. We are so accustomed to the sun that we take his light and warmth as a matter of course, and we do not rack our imaginations by thinking what the world's surface would really be without him. And yet be sure that the world would not be more forlorn, more lifeless to the eye of sense, than to a spiritual eye is the soul of a man or of a nation which has enjoyed and lost the presence of Christ.

Note, brethren, the scene or seat of this gift. "The water that I shall give him shall be *in him*." This is the claim—it is the triumph—of Jesus Christ. He does His work in the very seat and centre of man's being. Others, too, have done great works, have effected vast changes on the surface of human life. They have founded empires, impressing the will of a man or of a race upon millions of reluctant subjects; they have changed customs and laws and even languages; they have altered the whole outward character of the civilisation of a continent. Others, too, have penetrated deeper. They have founded empires not of force but of ideas; they have so wrought upon and fashioned the shape, the setting, of human thought, as to reign long after their death in the thought of millions who never heard their name. But Christ has done more even than this. He is more than the founder of a kingdom. He *is* that. He is more than the founder of a world-wide philosophy. He penetrates beneath the sphere of force, beneath the sphere of speculative thought, down to the very centre of the soul. A government may be hated while it is obeyed; a philosophy may be accepted while no personal allegiance or love is felt for its author. Christ reigns, where He reigns at all, not merely over men's conduct, not merely over their ideas, but in their hearts. He places Himself at the very centre of their souls, in that inmost sanctuary of the consciousness whence thought and feeling and resolve take their origin. There it is that He will raise His throne, and He is there not merely as a King but as a Friend,—not merely as a Force but as a Source of life. It is not an iron hand, the pressure of which the Christian feels; it is a sense of buoyancy, of invigorated power, of kindled affections, of enlarged and enlarging thoughts, as though the Christian's own personal being were superseded, and another higher and wiser than himself had taken possession, and were making him that which of and by himself he could not be. Yes, this gift is really within man. And hence Christians know, as they only know, the secret of man's dignity. The old heathen philosophies said much, and said it well, about the human soul. Men speculated about the nature of the soul, the origin of the soul, the connection that subsists between the body and the soul, the probabilities for and against the life of the soul after the death of the body; but they did not really proclaim the dignity of man as man. Much, indeed, was said of the dignity of particular individuals, classes, races of men. To be a Roman citizen, to have patrician blood in your veins, to govern a city or a province,—that was great according to the ideas of the ancient world. But nothing was said about the greatness of conquered races, the greatness of women, the greatness of slaves—of slaves who outnumbered the freemen of the empire, and who were bought and sold, and abused or made much of, simply as a form of personal property, having no rights of their own, no accorded permission to plead the common instincts of humanity, the common claims of justice. Of their dignity, I say, nothing was said, though they too were men with warm hearts, with keen intellects, with a sense of what they might be, with a sense of what they were, not less vivid than that of their masters. And Christ when He came did not do His blessed work at once. He would not provoke an uprising of the oppressed populations expressing their too natural and pent-up vengeance amid scenes of fire and of blood. He did not talk, as others since have talked, of the rights of man. He did more. He placed at the very centre of the human soul—alike of the soul of the slave and the soul of the master—the true sense of man's real dignity,—the instinct, the irrepressible instinct, of communion with the All-Holy, resulting in an abundant outburst of man's noblest life within; and then He left this gift to do its predestined work, as the centuries passed, surely but slowly. Deposited as it was in the unwieldy mass of human society, it has wrought from then till now. It has been heaving visibly, and with no trivial results, in our own days, beyond the Atlantic. It has yet work to do far and wide and deep, ere the work of proclaiming the secret of man's true greatness as man is really complete. That proclamation will be made in its integrity only when the preciousness of Christ's gift to the human soul is the creed of the human race.

Christ's gift is within, and, as this is the secret of the Christian's dignity, so it is the source of his spiritual independence. If Christians were dependent on the things of sense, the world might crush out—it might have crushed out long ago—the Christian life. I do not deny that the Christian life is largely ministered to by that which meets the eye and ear. After all, we are what God has made us: we are men and not angels. I do not deny that the language of the written Word, and the Grace of the Sacraments, can alone reach the soul through the organs of sense; so that if all the copies of the Bible could be destroyed, and the administration of the Sacraments really prevented as well as forbidden, the ordinary means of Grace would be cut off; but when it is driven to bay, and in the last resort, the soul falls back upon a certificated Presence which is independent of sense. The world in the first ages could proscribe the Christian worship; it could destroy the Christian Scriptures; but its legislation, its judgments, were just as powerless against the Presence of the divine Redeemer in the inmost sanctuary, as they would be against the clouds and the sunlight. It was this which made bonds, imprisonment, death, easy and welcome to our first fathers in the faith. They knew that they had not merely in Heaven, not merely in the collective Church, but within their breasts, each one of them, One Who would not desert them, One Who would be light to them when all else was darkness, One Who, when all outward aids were denied, was of Himself "a well of water springing up into everlasting life."

For the effect of this gift is not its least characteristic. "Springing up into everlasting life,"—or to render more exactly, springing up into that higher life of man which belongs to the future and endless age of his existence. This is the effect, the real effect, of Christ's gift of His invigorating presence to the soul. It does much besides. It makes human thought and feeling, as we have already seen, fresh and active and fertile; but its true object is to be found not in the present but in the future,—not in the life of this world but in the life of the next. The life of love directed towards love's one worthy Object begins here. It does not end here. It is the life of those blessed beings who inhabit the eternal world; and Christ's gift expands within the soul of His own to prepare them for that world. Without it man would not, could not be happy even in Heaven. Heaven would be hell itself to those in whom the life of the eternal world had not begun on earth,—to those whose whole thought and energy had been persistently centered upon the things of sense. To some who hear me it will occur to think that what has been urged is, as men speak, mystical,—language intelligible, no doubt, to minds of a particular cast, but not suited to the practical, matter of fact views of conduct and duty of simple people. You know nothing, then, my dear brother, of this well of water springing up to the eternal life; and yet it may be that, like the unnoticed sunshine, the unnoticed atmosphere, it is there within you. You know nothing, you say, of this inward gift. Then at least trust those who do. In the days of ancient Greece there were African travellers who penetrated so far as to find that at noonday their shadows actually turned towards the south. They returned and reported the fact to their countrymen, and it was treated by the leading historian of the time with entire incredulity. We know that those travellers had simply crossed the equator, and that their experience is shared by the passengers who crowd every mail packet that departs for the Cape of Good Hope. But the reports which Christians bring back from the world of spiritual experience are not less certain—they are not more apparently incredible—than the story of the Greek travellers. The well of water springing up to the eternal life only seems mystical until its blessed reality has been practically ascertained by faith, by obedience, by prayer,—until, like the Samaritan men, they have heard the inner Teacher for themselves, and know, not merely from outward report but from within, that "this is indeed the Christ, the Saviour of the world."[1] And to others, no doubt, it will occur to think, "This is all very well for men who have their way in life,—who take no thought for the morrow as the morrow is probably well provided for, —who occupy themselves with spiritual experiences because they have leisure and abundance at command; but what," you say, "of the very poor? what of the hardworking? what of the multitudes to whom life is a struggle for existence,—to whom each day is, like other days, a long mechanical plodding through monotonous work,—to whom each year is like other years, only that energy waxes fainter, and the margin between the struggler and the dark waters is narrower—those dark waters which are the

[1] John iv. 42.

only home to which despair can look forward? Ah!" you say, "this talk of an inner refreshment for the soul rouses indignation in presence of the appalling proportions of human bodily suffering: it is a maudlin substitute for the plain honest duties of active charity, of better education, of improved sanitary regulations, of relief administered to bodily want, to bodily pain." If it were so, brethren, you would be right in denouncing it. If it were so, you might well doubt whether, after all, Christ had blessed this world with His gospel. But as matters stand, look around you, and say whether, generally speaking and in the long run, the philanthropists and the educators are not also the Christians,—whether this inner spring of water does not fertilise this life, this outward life, as well as spring up into those moral and spiritual graces which prepare for the next. Surely—it is the language of common sense—surely, one duty (a spiritual duty) does not proscribe another (a social duty); and whether a man be poor or wealthy he equally does need the inner source of life; and if he enjoys it beyond any other gift that he can have from heaven or in earth, it enables him to bear his lot in this world well, manfully, thankfully: it enables him according to his means to bless his fellow-creatures. Indeed, it is the presence or the absence of this inward gift which constitutes the one abiding difference between man and man. The names and titles we bear, the property we inherit or have acquired, the reputation which follows us,—these things are just as little our real selves as the coat which we put on in the morning, which we take off at night. That which really belongs to us is within; it is part of that indestructible essence which is man's, each man's, inmost self,—which does not weaken with disease, which does not die with death, which lives on somehow, somewhere, necessarily, for ever. It is here that we have, or have not, that of which Christ spoke to the Samaritan woman,—that which will last when all else is passing,—that which will comfort and sustain when all else is proving itself to be of no avail.

To us, too—at least to some of us—it may be that Christ comes, as He came to her of Samaria, as a petitioner. He asks us to aid His poor, to support His church, to assist in the propagation of His gospel. He would place Himself, for the moment, under an obligation to us. "Give me," he says, "give me to drink." And yet it may be that if we knew, if we only knew as we might know, the gift of God, and Who it is that saith to us "Give me to drink," we should long ago have asked of Him and he would have given us, as He has given to millions of His faithful, the living water. It may be that while we are, as was said of a great jurist in a past generation, buttresses of the Church, we lack that which alone makes the Church worth supporting. Outward activity and benevolence are no good substitute for the life of the soul; and whether the soul shall really live is a question of prayer, of earnest, importunate prayer, addressed to Him Who has given us all that we have ever received in nature or in Grace, and Who only waits for our petitions in order to give us more abundantly. "Sir, give me that water, that I thirst not, neither come hither to draw." Prayer is a question of earnestness, and earnestness is only natural—it is only common sense—when men have taken the true measure of life and of death,—of the things which are seen and which are temporal, of the things which are not seen and which are eternal.

# SERMON XX.

## CHRISTIAN EDUCATION.

1 Cor. iii. 11.

"*Other foundation can no man lay than that is laid, which is Jesus Christ.*"

ST. PAUL uses a metaphor always intelligible and especially familiar to his first readers, who for the most part must have watched the city of Corinth rise from its ashes, when he speaks thus of the work of building up the Church of Christ. Here the Church is pictured as a public building inhabited by a divine Spirit, and constructed out of such materials as the convictions and hearts and souls of men. St. Paul is the prudent overseer of the works, who has taken particular care that the foundations of the building are sound and to be relied on. When they had been firmly laid, other hands might complete the building; and there were at Corinth some who wished to complete it according to their own plans, which differed considerably from those of the Apostle. Whatever these builders might do, St. Paul warns them at least to beware of tampering with the foundation itself which he had laid, since to do this would imperil the entire structure. "As a prudent master-builder," he says, "I have laid the foundation, and another buildeth thereon. But let every man take heed how he buildeth thereupon. For other foundation can no man lay than that is laid, which is Jesus Christ." As to the whole Catholic Church of Christ, it was already built on Jesus Christ as its historical foundation. It grew out of the fact of His appearance in the world and of His ascent to Heaven. He was the reason and the account of its existence, so that if He had not lived and died its existence, as St. Paul found it when he entered it at his conversion, would have been simply inexplicable. In this sense no man could lay a new foundation other than that which was already laid, which was Jesus Christ. It was impossible to undo history, and history was there to say that the young Apostolic Church was built on Jesus Christ, and on no one else. To insist upon this is not altogether superfluous, as a paradox which found favour with some of the earlier moods of German rationalism ran to the effect that St. Paul and not our Lord was the real founder of Christendom. How the writer of the indignant appeal, "Was Paul crucified for you?" and "Were ye baptised in the name of Paul?"[1] could ever have been seated to the satisfaction of the minds of any intelligent readers of his epistles on his Master's throne, might raise our wonder, if it were not that experience proves that of all credulity the easiest is that which is enjoined by unbelief, of all theories the wildest those which are put forward to discredit the creed of Christendom. If the Church is built upon the labours of apostles as her foundation, the apostles themselves rested on the chief Corner Stone, and indeed the paradox in question is now discarded well nigh everywhere. When St. Paul wrote it was pretty nearly half a century too late—it is nineteen centuries too late now—to speculate on a new foundation for the historical fabric of Christendom. The Corinthian teachers could no more touch that than we can. But there

[1] 1 Cor. i. 13.

is another sense in which a religious teacher may lay a new foundation. Admitting that Christ is the Founder of the Christian Church, he may deny that the Person of Christ is the fundamental fact in the Christian religion, the one Foundation upon which it is possible to build up the divine life in the Church and in the soul. The Corinthian teachers, no doubt, had the highest respect for Jesus Christ; but the essential thing in Christianity, as some of them at least understood and taught it, was a certain degree of observance of the old discarded Jewish law. That was their foundation, and Christ's Person, His teaching, His death, His resurrection, His intercession, His Sacraments, are part of the superstructure, highly ornamental, but something less than absolutely necessary. In St. Paul's eyes this dislocation was fatal not merely to the beauty and symmetry but to the very existence of the whole thing. "Other foundation," he said, earnestly, "can no man lay than that is laid, which is Jesus Christ."

The truth which is thus before us may be looked at either in its bearings on the form of the Christian Creed and life, or as imperiously governing the convictions and conduct of Christians in dealing with the various efforts at human improvement which are made in the world around us. Let us take these points in order.

I. The mistake of the Corinthian teachers, as regards its form, was only possible in the apostolic age, when as yet the real relations of the Church and the Synagogue were imperfectly defined; but in its spirit it is a mistake which under other forms may reappear, does reappear perpetually, and we do well to notice one or two samples of these other foundations against which it is prudent to guard.

It is, then, Jesus Christ, and not doctrines about Jesus Christ taken apart from His Person, on which the soul can really build. To say this is not to disparage the precious guidance of texts of Holy Scripture, or Creeds, or definitions of councils. Those apostolic words, those later and majestic definitions, which furnish in our day the favourite topic for so much shallow declamation, are, as well informed and believing churchmen know, when accepted by the undivided Church, the voice of that Eternal Spirit by Whom the whole body is governed as well as sanctified. They guard and sustain in Christian thought the divine Saviour's peerless honour; they forbid in tones of merciful severity false and degrading beliefs about Him; and yet He Himself, our living Lord, is the Foundation, and no immortal soul can possibly rest upon formulæ which do not uphold and regulate our estimate of His glory. We prize both Scripture and the Creeds for His sake, not Him for theirs, and to rest upon them as distinct from Him Whom they keep before us would be like building a wall upon a measuring rule, instead of upon the block of granite of which it has just given us the noble dimensions.

Still more true is it that it is Jesus Christ Himself, and not feelings about or towards Jesus Christ, upon which the soul's life can be built. Feelings are indeed great aids to devotion: they are often as we may trust, at least in part, special gifts of God: they are the play, no doubt, in many souls of His blessed Spirit upon our life and affections, raising them towards high and heavenly things. And yet what is so fugitive, so protean, so utterly unreliable as a feeling? It comes and it is gone; it is intense, and forthwith it ends; it promises much, and presently it yields us nothing but a sense of moral languor and exhaustion that succeeds it. Feeling! It will cry "Hosanna" to-day, and to-morrow, "Crucify." Feeling! It will pluck out its right eye for the apostle of its choice, and suddenly he is become its enemy because he tells it the truth. We look hard at it, and we see that when it was at its best much of it at least was physical; that in feeling nature had donned a religious guise, and was mimicking Grace. It may, perchance, here and there have made obedience easier for a moment; it may have seemed to this soul or to that to lend wings to charity; it may have roused us from time to time to efforts of which in our average moods we are incapable; but, speaking broadly, it is much too soft and unsubstantial a thing to be the foundation of a stern life of action and suffering. After all feeling in any case only points to Jesus Christ; its root is in ourselves, and we cannot supply the foundation-stone out of the exhausted quarries of unrenewed human nature. We must go out of ourselves if we would build on a foundation that will not give way.

Again, it is Jesus Christ Himself and not even His teaching or His work apart from His Person, which is the true foundation. His work indeed can only be appreciated in the light of His Person. His death is at best heroic self-devotion, if it be so much as that, unless His Person is superhuman. If Jesus is only Man, or if His Person be left out of view, there is in reason no more cause for reliance on His death than on the death of Socrates. His Sacraments are only picturesque unrealities unless He Who warrants them lives and is mighty. Apart from His Person they have no more validity than an armorial bearing or a rosette. And His teaching cannot be represented as a foundation of Christian life which may be substituted for His Person and enable us to dispense with it, for the simple reason that the persistent drift of that teaching is directly and indirectly to centre thought, love, adoration upon Himself, as though in Himself, as distinct from what He said and did, mankind was to find its true, its lasting strength and peace. Doubtless His words are beyond those of any other the stay of the soul—He spake as never man spake—but they are this not simply on account of their intrinsic merit, or rather of our power of doing justice to it, but because they are His words. His Person is the foundation; His teaching relatively to His Person is but part of the superstructure; and when, therefore, He reveals hell or proclaims the absolute authority of the Old Testament, serious Christians believe Him just as implicitly as when He pronounces the Beatitudes, simply because it is His voice that speaks. In this respect we of this day are in a different position from His disciples before the Resurrection. They learnt devotion to His Person through listening to His words; we who have received the faith are at least so far like the apostles after Pentecost,—we believe His words because we know Whose words they are. His Person is for us the fundamental fact which underlies, justifies, explains, sustains all that is built upon it.

In the same way it is Jesus Christ Himself, and not even His example, which is the foundation of the soul's life. It is impossible to separate His example from the consideration of His Person. The estimate we form of it must vary with our belief about Himself. Take that condescension of His to which St. Paul has so especial a devotion. If He is only the Son of Joseph and Mary, if for the first time He existed when He drew breath in the manger at Bethlehem, then His condescension is at least not greater than that of princes and philosophers who have from age to age bent the knee before Him, and who for His sake spent their lives in teaching the ignorant and in relieving the poor. If Christ be merely human much of what Christians believe to be His condescension is but an acceptance of His natural circumstances; but when St. Paul would reveal to the Philippians the secret of his own apostolic enthusiasm on the subject, he sets out by saying that He who bent Himself down to the life of a slave and to the death of a felon, had before existed in the form of God and did not make an illicit claim when He claimed a strictly equal share in the divine prerogatives with the Father. In the light of this truth His example is indeed a moral power so great that, as the mind dwells on it with patient reverence, it might well seem irresistible; but it is this because in order to be understood it must be referred to His Person,—because He who condescended so low was what He was, is what He is,—because, to appreciate it, His Person more than His acts, more than His example, must be distinctly before us. In modern times a great effort has been made to make an extract, so to describe it, of Christ's teaching and even of His example from the pages of the New Testament, leaving His Personality in the shade as if it did not affect the essence of the gospel. What Christ was or is, men say, cannot matter if we can possess ourselves of His teaching, if we can but profit by His example. In this sense Fichte says, that merely historical truth about Christ can only make a man wise, that it cannot make him happy. "If any man," says he, "is really united to God and is in God, it is a matter of indifference to him by what means he attained this," and it would be, he thinks, a very useless and perverse employment to be ever recalling to mind the means instead of living in the thing itself. "If Jesus," he continues, "could return to the world, it might be expected that He would be perfectly contented to find Christian teaching really in the minds of men, whether His own merit in the matter were acknowledged or slighted." In the same sense Strauss remarks, that "if it were Christ's purpose to make the world entirely free, it must have been His will to make it free from Himself, that God might be all in all." And if Christ is merely human, and the question of His Person therefore not a question of exceptional and surpassing importance, it is impossible to deny the justice of these remarks. A high-minded, disinterested man will be anxious, after doing his best for his fellow-creatures in his day and generation, whether he be a teacher or a philanthropist, to withdraw as far as possible from the notice and memory of man. In exact proportion to his moral elevation is his sincere anxiety to escape from a merely personal distinction, as from that which might too easily taint the disinterestedness and purity of his life and work. At the bottom of this feeling in us there lies the profound sense of our personal imperfection and nothingness before the great God, and our Lord sanctions it by making service not position the measure of greatness among His apostles,—by selecting the widow who gave the mite for especial honour,—by His counsel not to let the left hand know what the right hand doeth. We understand this like all other deep moral teaching, only so far as we endeavour to act upon it. If it can give us any real pleasure to see our name in subscription lists or in the newspapers, or to know that we are being talked about, if no sense of "deep remorseful fear," as the poet of the CHRISTIAN YEAR expresses it, on the score of what we know about ourselves turns such praise, such notice, into gall and penance, then we may be disposed to think and to speak of such a feeling as this as morbid,—then, but not otherwise. And if, therefore, Christ imposed His Person and not merely His maxims upon the thought and heart of the world, this departure from the ordinary instinct of high human goodness must have depended upon the fact that such a course was necessary. It implies that Christ's Person was in His own deliberate estimate of more importance to mankind than His own teaching or His philanthropic activity, and that apart from His Person neither His actions nor His words can be justly appreciated. To say that it only implies that He was sinless is to forget that the negative absence of sin does not destroy the consciousness of imperfection, which a creature must feel in all moments of spiritual sincerity before the sanctity of God. Something else is meant by the moral fact which is here before us, the startling spectacle which we have here of holiness putting itself deliberately forward to court the homage of human minds and human hearts throughout all time. All is surely and sufficiently explained if only we believe with the great Apostle that Jesus Christ is over all, God blessed for ever. To make Christ the foundation of the soul's life would be to interpose a creature between its deepest sanctities and its Maker, unless Christ Himself be God. A purely human Christ might be the architect, he might be even the scaffolding of the spiritual temple; he could not be its one foundation. It is the divine Christ of St. Paul Who is that one Foundation, Whose words have absolute authority, Whose example carries a weight that defies criticism, Whose redemptive work saves us, if we will, to the uttermost from our strongest enemies sin and death, Whose grace and power are not a thing of antiquarian interest, but a living and a perpetual fact to-day in the Sacraments of His Church, Who is the solid Foundation of our life and of our hope. It is His living Person in Which Christians are rooted, upon Which they are built up, certain that from Him they can draw all needful nourishment, certain that upon Him they can rest with an unwavering trust.

II. If we pass to the bearings of the Apostle's doctrine upon the efforts at human improvement around us, it is obvious to remark that to nothing can it apply with more urgency and directness than to what we will term deliberately the sacred work of education. Education is the most important department of the self-maintaining activity of the Church of Christ. By education the Church takes possession of her place and share in the coming age; by it she hands on to the minds and hearts and hands of another generation the treasure of faith and love and duty, which came to her nineteen centuries ago, and of which, to the end of time, she is the sole trustee in the interests of humanity. If she had nothing better in her keeping than a mere human speculation, as men speak, about God, there would be undoubtedly a certain degree of immodesty and violence in this uninterrupted effort to cramp and mould the otherwise free thoughts and aspirations of a coming time within the narrow formulæ of the past; but to possess a revelation from Heaven is to be already in advance of the highest efforts of human religious genius, and to communicate that revelation is the very first duty which its guardians owe to human ignorance and to human suffering. "He made a covenant with Jacob, and gave Israel a law, which He commanded our fathers to teach their children; that their posterity might know it, and the children which were yet unborn; to the intent that when they came up, they might show their children the same; that they might put their trust in God; and not to forget the works of God, but to keep His commandments."[1] Education, then, is necessary not merely to the well-being but to the very existence of the Church. Could she cease to educate she would cease to live, she would die out from being among men by a process of inevitable exhaustion. And if the Church of Christ is to educate to any purpose, Jesus Christ must be just as much the Foundation of her teaching in the school as of her teaching from the pulpit. He must be the one Foundation on which she builds, whether it be the fabric of intellectual truth or the fabric of moral and spiritual character.

[1] Ps. lxxviii. 5–8: P. B. Version.

Now what this practically means we shall best decide by briefly contrasting it with one or two doctrines about education which, more or less distinctly, are emerging now-a-days somewhat prominently into view. There is the theory which would identify education with the communication of useful knowledge, as it is termed, that is to say, of knowledge of such subjects as enable a boy or a girl to make his or her way in life without entering on the great question about man's origin and destiny. This idea of education is put forward from many motives which need not now be analysed. Suffice it to remark that it is in no sense based upon the one Foundation whereon alone Christians can consent to build. It ignores Jesus Christ altogether and of set purpose, and in doing this it inflicts upon education itself the gravest injury. For, first of all, it abandons the true idea of education, as the art of making the very most of the whole man that can be made of him,—the art of training, exercising, unfolding, perfecting of all his faculties, moral, spiritual, even bodily, as well as intellectual. It substitutes for this grand and comprehensive conception the narrow, petty aim of communicating certain sorts of knowledge, useful under certain narrow and transient circumstances, to his mind. By the very phrase "useful knowledge" it begs at the outset an enormous question as to what knowledge is really useful or most useful to man,—a question which, as I submit, can only be answered when it is decided whether man does or does not exist in an eternity where his happiness depends upon his conduct in time. Thus even its intellectual aim is a very narrow and poor one. It keeps its pupil's eye off all the higher horizons of human thought and interest, because in resting on them it would be obliged either definitely to accept or explicitly to reject the Christian Creed. It merely supplies matter for conjecture on the subject of deepest interest to a human being: it offers nothing in the way of guidance or solution. And as to morals, if it is tolerably consistent, it abstains from all interference except so far as the law of the land or the law of conventional standards may oblige it, and allows a boy to take care of himself. Christians can have no objection to giving the very best instruction that can be given in this so-termed useful knowledge, but they cannot admit that it is an adequate substitute for the knowledge and love of the perfect moral Being Jesus Christ to teach a boy algebra, or history, or the languages, or the art of reasoning. Nor can the heart and will be safely left to parents and clergymen while the whole real training of the intellect is made over to the secular schoolmaster. The secular schoolmaster is too likely in the long run to be in England what he generally is in France, and secular educationalists who are strongly opposed to teaching a definite Christian Creed do not always object, at least violently, to a systematic depreciation of all Christianity whatever when the opportunity occurs. But even if the secular educator be a silent Christian, silent under the constraint of the system which he administers, the effect upon his pupil's mind must be disastrous if the tree of partial knowledge is planted in that pupil's mind by other hands than those which plant the tree of life. The silence of the master to whom the boy is conscious that he owes the full expansion of his mental powers more than avails to counterbalance the mother's voice, who is, no doubt, so good, but of course not really educated; and when this divergence between intellect and heart is complete in the soul it is not difficult to predict the consequences. I need not anticipate them.

Then there are those who would take a larger view of the scope of education: their formula is "developed nature." Give all that you mean by nature free unrestricted play. Natural thought, natural feeling, natural impulse—these are the saplings which education should water and foster. Let them grow at will: do not prune, do not divert what you will only spoil. If they should expand into a very jungle, what matters it? The great thing is to avoid mannerism and artificialities. Let a boy think and feel as he likes; let him do what he likes (with due respect to good manners and the policeman); and let education confine itself to augmenting his stock of mental and physical power, instead of attempting to give him a direction. This theory, in forms very variously modified, has many apologists among us at the present day, but it may be doubted whether any of them are so consistent or so eloquent in its advocacy as was the celebrated son of the Genevese watchmaker in the last century. As the apostle of natural freedom, of unconventionality, of doing what you like because you like it, Rousseau is unrivalled. According to Rousseau it was not merely the still subsisting feudalism, the still dominant Church, the old society with its tyrannies and corruptions, that was fatal to the well-being and happiness of the people; the very arts and sciences themselves were culprits. Man is really happy, he maintained, only in a state of pure nature. Civilisation brings with it only moral decline and the worst evils of corrupt society. With Rousseau this was no mere passionate rhapsody; it was a serious conviction. He would prove it historically by pointing to the nations of antiquity. In Egypt, Greece, Rome, the moral qualities of patriotism and courage declined as the arts of civilisation advanced. Spartan morals were at once purer and ruder than those of Athens. He would prove it psychologically by tracing to each branch of knowledge some attendant form of moral decay. Astronomy has been the source of superstition: eloquence, of ambition; geometry, of avarice; ethics, of self-complacency! Without the sciences, he thought, man would never have been the prey of paradox; without the arts he would never have been enervated by luxury. Rousseau feels that it is never possible to recede far enough from the eighteenth century civilisation of France. He taxes his original and fervid eloquence to describe a so-termed state of nature, in which man lives without education, just as he came presumably from the hands of nature; in which innocence, simplicity, personal freedom, equal rights, are seen in their perfection—an ideal state which once, he tells us was real, and to which society, he urges, must return if it would be saved from the miseries and vices which thicken around the steps of advancing civilisation. Rousseau was consistently enthusiastic in his praise of the Hottentots and other savages. They had, at least, escaped all the mischiefs that come with culture. They were an anachronistic relic of primitive man. Rousseau's "Emile" was naturally condemned by the Archbishop of Paris; his theory of society was attacked by the polished and withering sarcasms of Voltaire; but for all that Rousseau was in harmony with much that belonged to his age, and in turn he influenced it to an extent which it is difficult for an Englishman at the distance of a century even to understand. But between Rousseau on the one hand and Jesus Christ on the other there is this vital difference: it is not that Rousseau would give man freedom, while Jesus Christ would enslave him; it is that Rousseau ignores the real facts of human nature, while Jesus Christ insists upon recognising them. Rousseau maintains broadly that man is born good; the Gospel, that he is born with a taint upon him of inherited corruption. Rousseau will have it that all the evil which a man learns comes to him from without; our Lord declares[1] that out

[1] Matt. xv. 19.

of the heart proceed evil thoughts, adulteries, fornications, envyings, revilings, murders, and such like; just as the Old Testament had proclaimed that the heart was in its centre and essence " deceitful above all things, and desperately wicked,"[1] and that man was shapen in iniquity and conceived in sin.[2] Here, I say, there is simple contradiction as to a fact of the very gravest importance; and whether we analyse a single human soul, a single child's character, or whether we look at the opinion which society has notoriously and instinctively formed about its component units by the precautions which it takes in elaborating government and in enacting law, we cannot doubt which of the two doctrines is in harmony with experience. Rousseau had scarcely sunk into his grave when his dreams of the perfectibility of human nature were rudely answered by the atrocities of the revolutionary Reign of Terror, perpetrated as many of them were while the idealists of theophilanthropy were still chanting the praises of a theory which contributed at least as much as any political agency to deluge France with blood. It is enough for a Christian that such a theory lays another foundation "than that is laid, which is Jesus Christ."[3] Jesus Christ came among us in His love and in His power because nature had already been tried and found wanting. It was, when He found it, already crushed to the very earth by a depressing sense of weakness; it was already responsible for centuries of crime. How could the fabric of solid truth be reared upon a very quicksand of inconclusive guesses? How could the edifice of virtue be supported by a morass of moral rottenness and vice? Jesus Christ came to be the solid unyielding Foundation of man's new life precisely because nature was thus incompetent and demoralised, and it is only when He Who is the real Foundation has invigor-

---

[1] Jer. xvii. 9.     [2] Ps. li. 5.     [3] 1 Cor. iii. 11.

ated it by His regenerating touch, that nature, renewed and purified, can furnish stones for the building which is based ever on its Restorer.

But a third form of opinion encounters us. "Grant," it says, "that education cannot be narrowed down to the idea of communicating useful knowledge, and that, practically, it was very unwise to leave human nature to develop itself; but cannot the intellectual training be sufficiently supplemented by the moral idea of duty,— that which has to be done whether by the head or by the hands—duty, that for the sake of which something, sometimes anything, must be suffered? This looks like a moral idea, sufficiently fertile, sufficiently strong, to serve as a good working basis for education and life. So it seemed to the professional moralists of the old heathen world—the Stoics: so it is in the judgment of the practical unspeculative Englishman. "England expects every man to do his duty," is a saying which, apart from its associations with a magnificent moment in our history, is exactly suited to strike a chord in the heart of a people like ourselves, too impatient of theories and eager for some visible fruits of moral convictions. Among no other people in Europe has the idea of duty, in its abstract unanalysed form, exercised such sway and empire as has been the case in England during the last hundred and fifty years; nor can we wonder if, at the present day, it appears to furnish many a teacher with that moral leverage which he wants in order to do his work. Teaching a child to do his duty, —that, at any rate, may pass for a sensible working fundamental rule in education—a formula that will cut short a great deal of useless discussion—a sort of practical receipt which keeps clear on the one hand of Utopian dreams about the perfection of child-nature, and on the other does not enter even by a single word upon the thorny questions which are said to lie inside the frontier of theology. Nor is it my business, or my inclination, to throw scorn upon a principle which, rightly understood, lies close to the heart of every Christian; but if the idea of duty is to be put forward as a good practical substitute for definite religious belief, then the question in reason must be asked, What is duty? That which we each of us have to do, is the answer. But why have we to do what we have to do? Here religion would reply—Because God tells us. But since this would at once raise the grave question of what we know about God, and the abstract idea of duty is to be kept quite clear of theology, the answer must run thus— Because our circumstances obviously prescribe it. But then, why are we bound to recognise, or still more to obey any such dictation on the part of what are called our circumstances? Why, for instance, may we not steal, if we want to steal and find that we can steal with impunity? Here two schools of moralists, each of them conscientiously dispensing with God, come forward to give an answer. "You must not steal," says the Utilitarian moralist, "because, taking a wide view of the interest of human society, it is obviously a bad thing for those interests that you should steal, even if it should not turn out that dishonesty is a bad policy for yourselves." "You must not steal," insists with better reason the Intuitionalist, "because there is within you an original principle of right and wrong, which, whether you will or no, must condemn your doing so." "To measure duty by utility," sharply observes the Intuitionalist, "is profoundly immoral: such a rule may sanction some of the very worst actions of which our nature is capable." "To measure duty by the moral sentiment," dryly remarks the Utilitarian, "is unspeakably foolish. It is, in reality, to appeal to the ever varying taste of the age,—to a transcendental faculty, the existence of which cannot be scientifically proved." The idea of duty, it must be admitted is here in a fair way to evaporate altogether. But it will probably be urged that a child who knows when he is whipped and when he gets a prize will not wander into a controversy between the Intuitionalists and the Benthamites. True, but then you wish by the idea of duty to give a child that which will lead him to do right under all circumstances; and I say that an abstract principle like duty, apart from God, is not strong enough to do this. A child must rest upon the concrete, upon the personal. A child's common sense tells him that duty implies a law to be obeyed, and that a law implies a law-giver. Who is the law-giver whose enactments are to be obeyed always and at all costs? You name God: you cannot for the life of you help it. But then the question arises, If God the Holy and the Mighty has given a law in conscience or elsewhere, as man have you kept it? and, if man has not kept it, is God indifferent to the neglect? Is He powerless to notice it? Is He unable to reconcile the justice of His government with the presumable yearnings of His compassion? Thus we reach the one Foundation through the very questions which the idea of duty cannot but raise. "What the moral law could not do, in that it was weak through the flesh, God sending His own Son in the likeness of sinful flesh, and for sin, condemned sin in the flesh: that the righteousness of the law might be fulfilled in us, who walk not after the flesh, but after the spirit."[1]

But here a last desperate effort is made to lay a new foundation,—anything to escape from doctrinal theology. It is admitted that something less abstract, less cold than the idea of duty is wanted in an education with aspirations towards a higher world, and some sort of sanction from on

[1] Rom. viii. 3, 4.

high must be provided for; but this, it is argued, can be done very well without committing yourself to a definite creed. Extract only the pure spirit, the genuine essence of religion, from the dregs of the dogmatic ages and systems, and then place that extract at the service of humanity. "All that a boy wants"—I am quoting words that have been lately used—"is a vague and general notion of religious duty." Now I make bold to assert that advice of this sort is not so much the product of serious thought as of embarrassing circumstances. In the person who gives it there is on the one hand, a clear practical perception of the moral fruitfulness and force of religion as a power in human life; on the other there is disbelief, secret or avowed, in those soul-constraining truths which alone evoke and sustain religious life in the soul. But what God has joined together man cannot put asunder, and it is just as impossible to have religion without some sort of theology as to enjoy the sunlight without the sun. Religious vitality is strongest where the objects of faith are most clearly represented to the soul, just as the light and heat of the sun are stronger in a clear sky than when the sun is partially or wholly overclouded. A religious feeling directed towards the vague and the indefinite is not a thing to influence grown-up men at all seriously; to children it is simply unintelligible. This is not owing to the undeveloped condition of the childish intellect, it is that herein children represent the broad common sense of mankind, unsophisticated by theories arising out of the conflict between unbelief on the one hand and man's deepest practical interests on the other. Just see how this theory of vague religious earnestness works in practice. It does not like the Creeds or the doctrinal statements of the Prayer Book, but it still reads the New Testament, and it directs especial attention to the moral beauty of Christ's human character.

An intelligent boy meets with the words, "When the Son of Man shall come in His glory, and all the holy angels with Him, then shall He sit upon the throne of His glory."[1] His master, if he is an educated man, knows that no serious critical reasons can be alleged either for denying that Jesus Christ Himself spoke those very words, or that by the Son of Man He meant Himself. The boy asks, if he thinks at all, whether this is a serious prediction of what is one day going to take place, and perhaps his master goes so far as to say that it is only an allegory. "But supposing it to be an allegory," asks a sharp boy, "what is it which is allegorised?" One thing most assuredly among others, it must be replied, namely, that Jesus Christ, at some time or other, in some way or other, is to be the Judge of all human beings. If the allegory does not mean this it means nothing—it is altogether misleading. But if it does mean this, how does such a statement by Jesus Christ about Himself fit in with the character of a good man? The boy has heard of many good men, and he knows some, but he never heard of any one who talked about himself in this way, and he asks with perfect reason, "What right had Jesus Christ thus to speak?" We know the true, the only answer to that question, but that answer cannot be given without dealing a vital, a crushing blow to the theory of vague religious feeling. That theory is in truth just as little at home in the New Testament as it is at home in the Creeds, and the questions which are naturally asked by a thoughtful child demonstrate its utter impotence just as well as a clear philosophical analysis.

The new educational foundation, then, which it is so often proposed to lay in our time will not suffice for the work. Useful knowledge alone will not do, because it

[1] Matt. xxv. 31.

leaves two-thirds of human nature altogether untouched. It says nothing to the heart and conscience; it says almost nothing to the will; whereas true education deals with man as a whole. "Nature developed" will not do, because what is wanted is something higher and purer than nature, something altogether distinct from it. Duty as an abstract idea will not do, because duty, if detached from the idea of God, is strangled in a conflict between opposing moral theories, and is besides too abstract and too artificial an idea to content the heart, that is the expansive and motive power in man. Religion in the vague sense of the term without a creed will not do, because religion, practically speaking, cannot exist apart from its object. To be religious in any sense you must know God; to be religious in the Christian sense you must know Jesus Christ, God and Man. If I do not mention dogmatic deism as another thing that will not do, it is because it scarcely claims to be an educational basis at all. Objections to Christianity in our day are as a rule objections to any serious theism. Other foundation can no Christian consent to lay than that is laid, which is Jesus Christ. As the Truth, He consecrates and welcomes all efforts to acquire any solid truth in all departments of real human knowledge: as the perfect Man, He ennobles, reinvigorates humanity with more than its ancient strength, redeems it if we will from its degradation and its shame: as the real and living Legislator of the world, He gives the idea of duty point and strength and life. Duty with Christians is but the passionate and practical sense of loyalty to the Redeemer. As fairer than the children of men in His condescension and His glory, as the Redeemer of the soul from sin and death, He enables religious feeling to be a permanent and practical force in the soul. The soul believes, acts, suffers, hopes, perseveres, as it exclaims, "Who shall separate us from the love of Christ?"[1]

The future of education in this country is a question infinitely more important than any one of the very anxious questions which are under discussion at this present moment. Nothing, I believe, would cut out by the very roots the Christian faith of the English people so effectually as a system of compulsory secular education. The influence of parents and pastors would be no match whatever for the secular educator, for reasons at which I have glanced. Two powerful currents are running in this fatal direction. There are those who ask for a real national system of education with a view to making it secular; there are others who consent more or less unwillingly to the prospect of a secular system in their passionate desire that there shall be an education which may be really national. Nothing that could fall from a Christian pulpit could have weight with the first of these classes; but to Christians who lend their name or influence to the latter demand, however indirectly, I would ask as earnestly as I can, Which is really most for the good and happiness of man, a uniform system of instruction in knowledge which is only serviceable in this world, or a less uniform effort to base the thought and life of the coming generations at any rate in some sense, to some degree, upon the one Foundation Jesus Christ our Lord? It seems to me that Roman Catholics and Christian Dissenters must so far agree with members of the English Church, that our deepest differences are insignificant in presence of a dreary materialism which utterly ignores the other world; and that, until we can once more worship around the same altars, no union can be more certainly blessed by God or more beneficial in the highest sense to man than a union among all who name the pre-

[1] Rom. viii. 35.

cious Name of Jesus Christ, with the purpose of resisting to the very uttermost all attempts at imposing a system of compulsory secular education on the people of this country. And certainly within a narrower sphere the present duty of us Churchmen is clear enough. While we have time let us do what we can to strengthen and extend our present Christian system; to make the secular teaching which it administers by all means more thorough and the religious teaching more definite, more constraining, more attractive, more affectionate, more capable of leaving upon the souls of children ineffaceable impressions. Would that all who take part in the sacred work of teaching in Christian schools could rise to understand the great dignity, the extreme responsibilities of their blessed task; would that the thousands who, in this metropolis, lavish their gold on baubles with which within a short fifty years at most they will have to part forever, would do something more worthy of Christ our Lord for making our parochial education really Christian, really adequate, or rather less inadequate than it is, to the wants of our vast populations.

The Forty-first Annual Report of the schools of this parish states that it is with the utmost difficulty that the treasurer is able to procure the funds necessary for carrying out a work of such vital importance to society and to the Church, and that but for the munificence of one generous nobleman the balance-sheet of this year must have exhibited a very serious deficit. Permit me to say, these things ought not to be so. The schools for which I am pleading have an importance which is not merely parochial. The parish to which they belong invests them with a large share of public interest, and from their success or their failure will be argued that of the system of which by reason of their position and importance, they are such conspicuous representatives. Give freely to them this afternoon in the name and for the love of Jesus Christ. As you believe that He is the one Foundation of our real and highest life here and hereafter, of our soundest knowledge and our most precious hopes—as you would bear your part in bequeathing to the generations who will walk these streets when we lie in our graves, when we are waiting for the Judgment, that truth about God, about man, about Himself, which the Eternal Christ lived and died to teach us—do not be found wanting on an occasion which so deeply concerns His interest and His honour, the wellbeing of your fellow creatures, and your Christian consistency.

www.ingramcontent.com/pod-product-compliance
Lightning Source LLC
Chambersburg PA
CBHW020234240426

**43672CB00006B/522**